Triumphs
of the
Spirit
in
Children's Literature

Triumphs of the Spirit in Children's Literature

Edited by
FRANCELIA BUTLER
and RICHARD ROTERT

With a foreword by
Marcia Brown
and an introduction by
Madeleine L'Engle

Library Professional Publications
1986

Printed in the United States of America
∞
The paper used in this publication meets the minimum requirements
of American National Standard for Information Sciences—Permanence
of Paper for Printed Library Materials, ANSI Z39. 48-1984.

Marcia Brown, excerpted from *Lotus Seeds*. Copyright © 1986 Marcia Brown.
Reprinted with the permission of Charles Scribner's Sons.

Reprinted by permission of Schocken Books Inc. from
Hannah Senesh: Her Life and Diary by Hannah Senesh, trans. Marta Cohn
Copyright © 1966 by Hakubbutz Hameuchad Publishing House.
English edition Copyright © 1971 Nigel Marsh Ltd.

Set in Bembo by Coghill Composition Co., Richmond, Virginia
Designed by Jill Breitbarth

Library of Congress Cataloging-in-Publication Data
Triumphs of the spirit in children's literature.
Includes bibliographies and indexes.
1. Children's literature—History and criticism.
I. Butler, Francelia, 1913–   . II. Rotert,
Richard, 1948–   .
PN1009.A1T76   1986   809′.89282   86-20143
ISBN 0-208-02110-8 (alk. paper)
ISBN 0-208-02111-6 (pbk.: alk. paper)

For
Charlene and Clifford Wright
R.R.

Contents

I. Prevailing against Personal Odds

II. Surviving Social Upheaval

III. Myth and Fantasy and Some Real Life, Too

IV. Foreign Writers and Literatures

V. Religious/Philosophical Approaches

VI. Historical Approaches

*Foreword**

MARCIA BROWN

"It is hard to say just what effect the books we read in childhood have on our later life, but we all know they do have an effect—in images that will not be erased, in people as real as those we know, in conversations heard as echoes. . . .

"A young child shares with the primitive an extraordinary power to identify himself with people, animals, and things of this world, and this power makes him extremely accessible to the magic power of symbol. . . . The heritage of childhood is the sense of life bequeathed to it by the folk wisdom of the ages. To tell in pictures, to tell in words, to tell in dance—however we may choose— it is a privilege to pass these truths on to children who have a right to the fullest expression we can give them. Neither so self-conscious as a parable nor so contrived as an allegory, fairy tales are revelations of sober everyday fact. They are the abiding dreams and realities of the human soul.

"Myths and legends tell a child who he is in the family of man. In a book with ancient mythic origins, some of the poetic depth of the story should be implied in the illustrations. The child, looking and reading, will understand and recall tomorrow more than he can tell you today. . . . Myths tell us who we are. They warn us of the monsters that lurk within us, as well as the shadows of our world.

"[The child] grows—and looks—and listens—and chooses—and blends with the crowd that presses onto his ever-widening stage. He grows—and the characters he counts closest are fewer, are apt to be his own age. The older ones recede into the background; their words and calls echo across ever-widening spaces. . . . The stage shrinks—the lights pick out only a few characters; eventually in the dark is left one, having a dialogue with one. . . . The once-child arises, staggered from this dialogue, to step into the drama of his adult life. The arena of his mature struggle will be one of feeling and spirit as well as thought, and the choices he will make will sound the keynote of that dialogue as he seeks his fathers, his heroes, his gods, within himself.

*Composed from extracts from her book *Lotus Seeds: Children, Pictures, and Books* (New York: Scribner's, 1986). Used by permission.

"Even a young child responds to a heroism less obvious than that of knights and warriors—a heroism that is inner rather than outer. . . . A young person's heroism may consist in pushing himself beyond the limits set for him by his society, his class, his race. For land, race, class mean nothing so much as being human. . . . Youth sometimes fears commitments, gifts of the self, which if betrayed, damage whole areas of the psyche. And yet something tells them and us that what was feared, that final gift of one's spirit, the total risk of oneself, is a key that will unlock life to them, will reveal the hero within. . . . A child can measure himself against the heroes in the stories of Hans Christian Andersen and find, many years later, that they are still with him. These stories, which often synthesize several folktales with simpler plots into one, are ageless. The stakes of their heroism are high; the moral choices are serious; the conflicts and the rueful humor that makes the conflicts bearable are those of life. . . . Today a staunch soldier, through circumstances not of his own making, goes through terrible trials but remains steadfast in his devotion to his ideal. . . . Using the images of the tales of terror and horror told to him as a child, the poet distilled the stories that enabled faith in life to put evil in its place. . . .

"So much of living swings between the extremes of dark and light. The most honest books we can give our children do not tarnish the dazzle by obliterating the gloom. Banish pain, hurt, controversy, from a child's books and you damage the child's capacity to empathize and endure and cope with them. . . . Each time we offer a child gadgetry and tricks in his books instead of spirit, we show our mistrust of him and deprive him of his chance for self-identification. . . . Young people can easily betray themselves. More easily are they betrayed by people who ask too little of them. . . .

"Those who work with children should be encouraged to hand on to them their personal involvement with the world. A child needs the stimulus of books that are focused on individuality in personality and character if he is to find his own. Some of the most precious exposure we can give the young is to personality—all kinds—[and] often the most precious [is] the most obsessed. . . .

"A child is individual; a book is individual. Each child should be served according to its needs. . . . Of all the forces that shape a child . . . perhaps books are more important than we know."

Preface

Attempts to define "spirit" have been numerous, elaborate, and largely unsuccessful. The manifestations of "spirit" have ranged from heathen animism to theistic divinity. Traditional philosophies remain inconclusive as to the essential nature of this personal emotive force, this essence of self-in-action which inclines one to succeed, sometimes to overcome extraordinarily difficult odds. Even more basically, spirit defines one's unique humanity, and projects one's identity. However, failure of explanation and exact definition have not deterred us from documenting this phenomenon. We recognize spirit by its influence rather than by its appearance. Though we can neither see nor touch this transcendent quality, we are assured of its existence by the trail of accomplishments—of triumphs—left in its wake.

Triumphs of the human spirit over adversaries of many kinds are found in books for children. Often these triumphs are those of the children in the stories as they meet with ugliness, abuse, fear, temptation, or death itself. Many of the encounters of the human spirit with forces bent on its destruction are imbedded in folklore; some take place against a backdrop of common misery and pain, such as the Holocaust or the Great Depression. For some, encounters that provide the opportunity for triumph or disaster take place in a critical moment of time; for others, such as members of a social or economic minority, the spirit must gird itself to triumph again and again over the small cruelties of prejudice as well as larger assaults. But whatever the setting, whatever the frequency, the human spirit ultimately must face each challenge by itself, and each of them one by one.

The twenty-five essays we have edited for this volume were written originally and especially for it. We greatly admire and appreciate the authors of these pieces for their diverse and interesting approaches to the theme. They have shown that the human spirit has many different facets and as many different ways of triumphing. When the authors were invited to contribute to this volume they were simply given the theme and asked to reflect upon it, and write according to their interests and experience.

As for the theme, we wish to acknowledge our indebtedness to our editor, Virginia H. Mathews of Library Professional Publications, who suggested it and the title that expresses it. Very special thanks are due also to Madeleine L'Engle who, since she shares our belief in and gratitude for the undeniable reality and unquenchable resilience of the human spirit, was pleased to write a highly personal and touching introduction. Our thanks go also to children's book illustrator Marcia Brown, unique in being the only three-time winner of the Caldecott Medal for a year's most distinguished picture book for children, who permitted us to weave excerpts from her book about children's literature into a foreword so that she could be part of our enterprise.

A book—any book—and this book especially—is in itself a triumph: a triumph of collaboration among many people in far-flung places; a triumph of technology, of organization, and of timing. It is a celebration of the spirit of many more books for children than could possibly have been cited, books which help young readers to understand that despair and apathy and materialism and cowardice and fear need not be the whole story of their lives.

FRANCELIA BUTLER
RICHARD ROTERT

Introduction:
The Triumph of the Human Spirit

MADELEINE L'ENGLE

We grow through the things that stretch us, that hurt us. There isn't any other way. And yet we live in a society that teaches us to avoid pain at all costs. If it hurts, take a pill. Pursue pleasure, immediate gratification. Don't take risks; you might fail. Don't go out into the unknown; you might hurt yourself.

What are we doing to our children with this defeatist attitude? We're frightening them, making them believe that we human beings will kill each other off, and that they will be dead before they ever grow up. We may be making them believe, too, that pain or adversity will kill them. Twenty-five or more years ago, my own children, living in a small New England village, were taught at school to climb under their desks with their hands over their heads to protect themselves in case of nuclear warfare. We are not offering them a much more substantial hope twenty-five years later.

We project for them a kind of death instead of life with all its joys and terrors, its laughter and tears. Now it is time for us to let the children teach *us*.

My children taught me. When they were little, in the world's fifties, we were always in a state of international crisis. War between the United States and the USSR seemed imminent. We tried not to let the children see how anxious we were as we listened to the news. But they knew. And it came out at bedtime in their prayers.

One night my little boy, maybe four years old, paused in his long list of "God blesses" and said, commandingly, "And God: remember to be the Lord." And another night, "And God, please make people remember about do unto others as you would they do to you. Please make them do these words. Make them think. Make them think and not destroy this world."

Our eldest daughter suggested that if the children of the world could get together and talk, they would know how to make peace. And, I thought, she was likely right. To maintain peace in a household full of children and animals and grown-ups is a lesson in maintaining peace among nations.

During that same decade of the fifties we experienced a good deal of personal tragedy. Four of our closest friends died, and because we live in a small community our friends and neighbors were there with help and support. And the children of the village were not left out of what was going on. We talked about it with them. Whenever anything happened that was beyond the ordinary daily joys and sufferings, I would take my children and go to the top of neighboring Mohawk Mountain to watch the stars come out, and to talk about whatever it was that was hurting us, and try to make some kind of creative sense out of it. We didn't try to pretend that bad things had not happened; conversely, we didn't project visions of bad things that had not yet happened. My children helped me to understand the need to live where we are, in the immediate moment.

I think I will always need children to teach me, and to awaken in my adult self the hidden child. If I lose the child within, I lose the ability to become mature. I do not refer to the childishness which retards development, but to the child-self which is willing to take risks, which rejoices in beauty, which is willing to love, and is therefore vulnerable.

As my children taught me, so do my grandchildren. I remember particularly one summer when one of my granddaughters was hit by a truck while walking home from swimming. She was so broken to pieces that it is miraculous indeed that she is now a bright and beautiful teenager. That long summer, shortly after her ninth birthday, she spent in a city hospital with a fractured skull, the smaller local hospital having no facilities for possible grave neurological problems. By the time, ten days after the accident, that she returned to full consciousness, she could not be moved because both her femurs had been broken and she was in traction. Her ribs had been crushed, her jaw broken in two places. She was in a great deal of pain, but could be given no pain killers because of the skull fracture.

When she returned to consciousness, the first thing she said was, "I love you," and the second, "Read to me." And so we read, and read, and read, and while we were reading her brain was focused on the story center, not the pain center. We read till we were hoarse.

I tell about this incident in my book, *Walking on Water,* and that

"Jacques Lusseyran in *And There Was Light* tells us that for the child what happens is from God, and is Good. A child will never feel self-pity unless some adult is stupid enough to suggest it.

And he reminds us that courage, which we grown-ups make so much of, is for the child the most natural thing in the world.

I saw the truth of these words as I watched this little girl during that long summer, when she never once said, "Why did this happen to me?" or questioned the rightness or wrongness of her pain in any way. Not once did she whine; she screamed with pain: if anyone bumped the ropes which held her legs in traction, it caused her excruciating pain; but she didn't whine.

And I saw the triumph of the human spirit as this child's spirit soared while her broken body slowly healed.

When at last she was out of traction she was put in a body cast from armpits to toes, and when that was finally removed she walked on crutches. I remember watching her heave herself up the three steep flights of stairs she had to climb when she came home from school. It was not a cause for complaint or a demand for attention. It was simply something which had to be done.

She was healed by doctors and nurses, but also by the stories she heard that summer. Children in literature are glorious examples of the triumph of the human spirit, but they triumph in literature because they triumph in life. The children in the books we read to my granddaughter affirmed her own response to what had happened to her, and encouraged her own natural courage. Literature and life nourish each other.

What are we doing to our children? Let us give them the very best, so that they will be stretched creatively and spiritually, and there will be hope for us all.

Contributors

GILLIAN ADAMS teaches English at the University of Texas, Austin.

JANICE M. ALBERGHENE teaches children's literature at Bowling Green State University in Ohio.

CELIA CATLETT ANDERSON teaches English at Eastern Connecticut State University in Willimantic, Connecticut.

MARCIA BROWN is author or reteller and illustrator of many picture books including *Stone Soup*, an early favorite, and *Cinderella, Once a Mouse*, and *Shadow*—the last three winners of the Caldecott Medal, of which she is the only three-time winner.

FRANCELIA BUTLER, a founder of the Children's Literature division of the Modern Language Association and its journal, teaches English at the University of Connecticut and is the author of an autobiographical novel on child abuse and many other books. She directed the first National Endowment for the Humanities institutes on children's literature.

STEPHEN CANHAM teaches English at the University of Hawaii, Manoa.

JOHN CECH is editor of *American Writers for Children 1900–1960* for the *Dictionary of Literary Biography*. He teaches children's literature at the University of Florida, Gainesville.

JESSE CRISLER teaches English at Brigham Young University, Hawaii.

GERALDINE DELUCA, coeditor of *The Lion and the Unicorn*, teaches English at Brooklyn College.

LIA HADZOPOULOU-CARAVIA is a Greek specialist in children's literature.

JIM HASKINS is the author of over 50 books for children and adults, including *The Cotton Club*, which inspired the movie of the same title. He is professor of English at the University of Florida, Gainesville.

MARGARET R. HIGONNET has held a number of grants for research in France, and is now professor of English at the University of Connecticut.

GLORIA JAMESON teaches children's literature at California Polytechnic State University, San Luis Obispo, and is a specialist in English as a second language.

GUO JIAN is a member of the faculty of Beijing Normal University in China and is the author of over a dozen books on American, British, and French literature and criticism.

ANNE DEVEREAUX JORDAN is a founder of the Children's Literature Association and the managing editor of *Fantasy and Science Fiction*.

ELIZABETH LENNOX KEYSER teaches at the University of California at Santa Barbara.

MADELEINE L'ENGLE is the author of a number of distinguished works of fiction, among them *A Swiftly Tilting Planet, A Ring of Endless Light, The Young Unicorns,* and the Newbery Award-winning *A Wrinkle in Time.*

JAY LIVERNOIS, a scholar in comparative literature, is currently teaching at the University of Rouen, France.

GARETH B. MATTHEWS is the author of *Philosophy and the Young Child* and *Dialogues with Children.* Currently at the Institute for Advanced Study, Princeton, he teaches philosophy at the University of Massachusetts and writes a regular column on children's stories for the journal *Thinking.*

The REVEREND HOWARD A. MAYER teaches English at the University of Hartford. He holds a degree in theology in addition to his doctorate in English.

LEONARD R. MENDELSOHN teaches children's literature at Concordia University, Montreal.

BARBARA ROSEN is the Editor of *Children's Literature* and teaches English at the University of Connecticut.

RICHARD ROTERT is a scholar in comparative literature. He is coeditor of *Reflections on Literature for Children* and *The Wide World All Around.*

MARY SHANER teaches English at the University of Massachusetts, Boston. She and her husband, poet Rick Shaner, are the authors of a survey of twentieth-century children's literature published as volume 8 of *Masterworks.*

M. SARAH SMEDMAN O.S.B. teaches English at the University of North Carolina, Charlotte.

JOHN DANIEL STAHL teaches children's literature at Virginia Polytechnic and State University, Blacksburg.

DEANNA ZITTERKOPF teaches English at Kansas Newman College, Wichita.

I.

Prevailing against Personal Odds

1.

The Triumph of the Spirit in Cynthia Voigt's "Homecoming," "Dicey's Song," and "A Solitary Blue"

GLORIA JAMESON

Dicey Tillerman, her younger brothers, sister, and her grandmother, are the central characters of two important books for children by Cynthia Voigt. Jeff Greene and his father are the focus of a third, which brings Dicey and Jeff together as teenagers in a small community in eastern Maryland. Voigt's characters become authentic, compelling individuals as their stories unfold. Their spirits triumph in different ways as Dicey, Jeff, and those close to them struggle to survive, to accept others and themselves, and to find a place of safety. In each book a sense of place is significant in the development of characters and plot. The author uses home as a focus in *Homecoming,* as a frame in *Dicey's Song,* and as an evolving reflection of the protagonist in *A Solitary Blue.*[1] Her use of these archetypical Odyssean, Promethean, and Oedipal patterns adds the power of myth to her stories.[2] They are also linked and strengthened by archetypical motifs: the barren isolation of urban existence; the restoration of life in contact with the ocean, rivers, or water; the power of music to reach out, support, and heal; the importance of individual choices that reflect concern for others. Lines Dicey reads on a gravestone, "Home is the sailor, home from the sea/And the hunter home from the hill," are recalled in significant places in the first two books.[3] The great blue heron that fishes alone becomes a symbol for Jeff, his "sign from the gods" of a safe haven, and the third book's title (106).

The author's literary skill in weaving modern realism in archetypical patterns makes an impact on the reader. The power of the story remains in the memory when the book is put down, and her characters continue to speak to the imagination. The excellence of the three books has been recognized in the nomination of *Homecoming* (her first book, submitted as an unsolicited manuscript) for the American Book Award in 1982, the Newbery Medal for *Dicey's Song* in 1983, and the selection of *A Solitary*

Blue as a Newbery Honor Book in 1984. Voigt comments on her
"Newberry Medal Acceptance,"

> The field of children's literature is controlled by two factors
> which operate in its favor, making it somehow more possible to
> achieve excellence. The first of these is money, . . . an adequate
> but not seductive financial base insures that the main motive of
> all concerned . . . can be overall quality of the field, . . . the limit
> works for excellence. The second is the audience. It is in the
> nature of children to be creatures in process. Perhaps because
> they are so aware of that, it is in the nature of children also to
> know what we have foolishly forgotten, or improperly subordi-
> nated—that the possible is a viable and functioning part of the
> real. This insight of theirs marks the field of children's literature,
> encouraging excellence.[4]

Homecoming, with a safe home the goal of a tale of physical adventure
in the Odyssean pattern, opens as Dicey, James, Maybeth, and Sammy
leave their primitive cabin at the end of Cape Cod. Momma has nurtured
them there in love and song and poverty. Unskilled, and struggling
alone to support her children, her spirit fails when she loses her job as a
supermarket check-out. She attempts to drive them to the one relative
who has kept in touch, Aunt Cilla, in Bridgeport, but at the first stop she
wanders away and does not return. Stranded, the children must continue
their journey alone.

Thirteen-year-old Dicey has carried much of the responsibility for the
younger children since their birth. She is a fighter, resourceful, fiercely
loyal to her family, and determined to keep them together. Her past
contacts with authorities make her sure they will be separated in foster
homes if she asks for help. She tries to keep the four of them invisible to
the adult world by blending into their surroundings and producing
appropriate stories whenever they are questioned. They do not have
enough money for bus fare from Peewauket to Bridgeport, so Dicey
takes the map and they begin their long walk down Route 1. Like a
modern Odysseus she struggles to help the younger children—each
carefully individualized—walk through the heavy traffic of the towns and
suburban sprawl, endure exhaustion, and keep going forward. She
manages to secure the necessary food for them to survive, and finds a
pleasant island where they rest and recover in a state park on the ocean.
Restored, they resume their journey and reach Old Lyme. Dicey can find
no way to walk on; they are out of money and food. Discouraged, she

crouches down to watch the river that bars their way—and gets the idea of carrying grocery bags at a supermarket to earn money. Later, they eat on the river bluff and look at the river. Dicey sings one of Momma's sad songs, "The water is wide, I cannot get o'er . . . Give me a boat that will carry two, and two shall row . . ." and realizes they can use one of the many boats tied to the docks. Late that night they row across in a dinghy, secure it where it can be found, and walk until they find a graveyard with trees (85). Before leaving the next morning they look at the stones and statues. On one of them Dicey sees the haunting verse "Home is the sailor, home from the sea/And the hunter home from the hill," and thinks about its meaning.

They finally reach Aunt Cilla's Bridgeport address, but it is not the big white home she wrote about. It is one of a long row of small, asphalt shingled houses near the center of town, and Dicey and James realize she had lied about being rich. Their experience in the city is barren. Aunt Cilla is dead. Her daughter Eunice takes them in, and her priest and others attempt to be kind. Dicey senses the children are drifting apart as a family, becoming less themselves. She knows they are in danger of being separated. She works and saves money, planning to go to Maryland to see the grandmother they have learned about. James discovers this and insists that they all go together. Dicey writes their cousin a note, and their Odyssey resumes as they quietly leave the city on a bus. They feel they have escaped from prison, though they know they should be grateful to Cousin Eunice. Dicey thinks of the inscription: Home is the sailor, home is the hunter. . . . "Home free—Dicey would settle for a place to stay. Stay free. Cousin Eunice's house . . . was expensive. The price was always remembering to be grateful. And there was danger" (171–72).

The Chesapeake Bay, a river, and circus friends are significant in this stage of their journey. Dicey and James manage a story that earns the children a sail from Annapolis to the eastern shore. On the water Dicey feels part of the boat; her thoughts lose themselves and wander.

A boat could be a home. The perfect home that could move around, a home that didn't close you in or tie you down: and a sailor would always be at home if he was on the sea. . . . Or maybe each boat was a kind of family. Then what kind of a boat would the Tillermans be?

Everybody who was born was cast onto the sea. . . . And the boats—they just went along as best they could, trying to find a harbor. . . . Dicey didn't feel like finding a harbor. She knew she needed one, and they needed one, but she would rather just sail along. . . . Couldn't you live your whole life without going into harbor? The land would get you in the end. "Home is the sailor." But until then, you could keep free. . . . Dicey smiled to herself. The ocean at Provincetown had always sung at her too. As long as I'm near the water, she thought, that'll be enough, even if I'm on land. (202–3)

Dicey is allowed to sail the boat, and she lets it tell her where it wants to go, her body tuned to the pull of the tiller.

> Boat, waves, water and wind: through the wood she felt them working for her. She was not directing, but accompanying them, turning them to her use. She didn't work against them, but with them, and she made the boat do that too. It wasn't power she felt, guiding the tiller, but purpose. She could not stop smiling. (205)

The children are not welcomed by their grandmother. She tells them they cannot stay, but offers a place for the night. Dicey matches wit and determination with the strong, angry woman she resembles, and supported by James, Maybeth, and Sammy earns a day at a time by seeing work that needs to be done and undertaking it. Weeds grow from the road, through the pine wood to the house, and on to the marsh and dock on the bay, everywhere except in the large vegetable garden. The house and barn need repairs. The children sing as they work together, and in the evenings. Their grandmother watches and listens. The children feel she cares for them even though they cannot stay. Two weeks later she takes them to town in her boat, to register for school temporarily. Afterwards they wait on the dock to go back to the farm. Dicey jumps in to hold the boat and sees James studying his grandmother as if he were hungry in a way food could never fill (316). She challenges her grandmother's refusal, and Gram's pride cracks. In touch with the water Dicey has again found a resolution and a way forward. The Tillermans have completed their Odyssean journey. They have won their safe harbor; they have reached the home where they are free to become themselves.

Prometheus, the creator-champion of humankind in the classical world, supported men and women in their development of their best traits in the long climb from savagery to civilization. His gift of fire spearheaded the establishment of families and homes, then the extension of order to larger and larger groups as the basic needs of food, shelter, and clothing were satisfied. Lucy Waddey refers to children's books that are neither Odyssean nor Oedipal but begin with the protagonist as an exile who must create a home, becoming fond of what is created and defined by it as the creation proceeds.[5] There are wide variations in this pattern. In *Dicey's Song* Dicey, James, Maybeth, Sammy, and Gram do not physically wrest their home from nature, but they do transform both the house and the farm as they live together—and in so doing are themselves transformed. In the preface to this story, which uses home as the secure frame that enables their creative individuality to develop, Dicey stands in the old barn in a patch of moonlight on the evening of the day Gram registered them for school. Earlier she had discovered a sailboat in the old barn, and Gram had said she could have it.

> What a day, Dicey thought. What a summer, for that matter.
> . . . You never knew where a road would end, you just knew
> that roads ended. Not like water, which always kept moving.
> . . . Dicey's road, and James's, Maybeth's, Sammy's, had ended
> here . . . rolled up against Gram's house. . . . They were going to
> live here, on the rundown farm, with Gram—Dicey's heart
> danced again. . . . Home . . . a home with plenty of room in the
> shabby farmhouse, room inside, room outside, and the kind of
> room within Gram too—Dicey had seen Gram and how she
> listened when Maybeth sang, how she talked with James, how
> her eyes smiled at the things Sammy said and did—the kind of
> room that was what they really needed. One of the lessons the
> long summer had taught Dicey was how to figure out what they
> really needed. . . . Home for Dicey, too, with the Bay . . . just
> out of sight, with this grandmother whose character had sharp
> corners and unexpected turns, with the sailboat waiting here in
> the barn. . . . This happiness blew through her like wind,
> buoyed her up like water. (from the preface to *Dicey's Song*)

On the farm the children put down roots, reach up, and reach out. But as Dicey says, "And they lived happily ever after," never applies to the Tillermans (1). When the younger children take more responsibility, make friends, struggle to work through their own problems, Dicey sees the changes of the summer becoming permanent. She experiences emotions she doesn't recognize and feels edgy, reluctant to grow up. "She was used to seeing trouble and doing something about it. . . . What Dicey was used to, she realized, was things being simple, like a song. You sang the words and the melody straight through. That was the way she had brought her family to Crisfield, singing straight through" (17).

Gram shares with Dicey what she has learned from her mistakes, saying you must continue to reach out, hold on to, and support those you love. Dicey tries to do this. They help James, Maybeth, and Danny face their individual problems; Dicey also looks beyond her family to accept others. Underneath the children's struggle with adjustment and growth in this secure home, like a silently flowing river, is their sadness over Momma lost to them, catatonic and incurable, according to the doctors, in the state hospital in Boston. When she thought of all this Dicey realized "The trouble with holding on was Dicey only had two hands. She felt like she was always off balance, trying to hold on to everyone" (106).

Shortly after the children help Gram prepare their first Thanksgiving dinner, shared by the music teacher, Mr. Lingerie, Dicey talks with her new friend Minna about everyone's flaws. You accept family members regardless of these, they agree, then Dicey adds, "But with other people, not family, you choose. . . . What do you think? Do you think we choose by what's important to us? Like whether someone's brave or not. . . . And music" (165–66). Courage and a love of music are traits of those she is drawn toward. When Dicey reaches home the Boston doctor has phoned that Momma is dying. Mr. Lingerie drives Gram and Dicey to the local airport and stays with the younger children.

Boston is bitterly cold. Gram and Dicey take turns sitting by Momma (Liza), holding her hand and telling her all that has happened since they last saw her. She makes no response. Gram sends Dicey to choose Christmas presents for the children and return to the motel, staying through the night by Liza, who dies in the early morning. There is no restoring ocean for Dicey, but the bleak cold and confusion of the city are touched by a different spirit. The warmth of the nurse who has cared for Liza and made the arrangements for them, and the slow, gentle kindness of the woodcarver in the shop where she chooses something special for James, Maybeth, and Sammy, ease Dicey's pain. She is able to answer the woodcarver's quiet questions and tell him a little about her mother and the family in Maryland. The woodcarver puts down his pad and says slowly,

"I'm sorry the world is the way it is and always has been. It's not easy, is it? . . ."

"I tell myself," he said, "that it's like the wood. Sometimes, things just have to happen, it just has to be the way it turns out. Are you old enough to have something you tell yourself?"

That surprised Dicey. She swallowed, remembered, and nodded her head. "I saw a tombstone, once. It had—Home is the hunter, home from the hill, and the sailor home from the sea."

He studied her face for a long time, and then didn't say any more. (188)

Later Dicey takes Gram to the shop to select a box for Momma's ashes. They choose one with a band of black walnut like a ribbon. He asks to give it to them.

> "Yesterday, I thought to give her something," he said to Gram. "I don't know why—yes, I do know why, but I couldn't put words to it. But not out of pity. I would like to give this box to you. I'm honored, you see. You do see that, don't you? But I don't know if you would take it as a gift."
> Gram stared at the hands around the box. Then she said, "Yes, I'll take it," in a low voice." I'll take the gift and I'll thank you for it," she said more briskly. Dicey could almost hear the creaking of Gram's fingers as she let go of her pride. (194)

The children and Gram bury Momma's ashes beneath the old paper mulberry tree. The wires that held the four trunks together were clearly visible now, running like a fence between the branches. Gram had told Dicey the tree would spread out and split, broken apart by its weight, if the wire weren't there—the first day Dicey came to the farm. "That tree is like families," Gram had said, and Dicey, looking up now at its branches, wondered what, in that case, the wire was like" (206).

Later Gram brings the old photo albums from the attic for the first time. They study the pictures, and she begins to tell their stories. Dicey's eyes drop from the pictures to her hands; she thinks of herself as a boat dropping anchor to let the storm blow itself out. "And then she smiled to herself, because she had a suspicion that the confusion wasn't a storm that would blow itself out, it was going to be a permanent condition. Well, she guessed she could get used to it. She guessed she might even get to like it. She might as well try to like it, she thought, since it wasn't going to go away (210–11)."

Dicey has accepted the changes and testing of growing up. The frame of a loving home has nurtured the Tillermans and given them the freedom to become themselves. The children's presence has enabled Gram to grow also. She can let go of the pain of the past, reach out, and hold on again, this time with more wisdom.

Oedipus provides the classical example of the individual who uses his intelligence, who by reasoning seeks to explore the mysteries of life and solve its problems. A story with this underlying pattern will focus on interior rather than exterior action, although both may be significant. It is the struggle of mind and spirit that occupy the protagonist; the resulting physical actions reflect his stages of understanding and the choices he makes. Jeff Greene's major struggle is within his mind and spirit, and Voigt sensitively traces this in *A Solitary Blue*.

The reader sees Jeff first through the crowded yet empty tract house in Baltimore, then through the beautiful, ghost-filled rooms of his great-grandmother's house in old town Charleston, and finally through the home he and his father make from a cabin in the marsh near Crisfield. The story begins when Jeff is seven. His mother, Melody, writes notes to him and his father and then leaves them—to help people everywhere and the damaged world. Jeff understands she is happy only when she is doing something about the sick world because she has explained this to him, but not why she has to go away from them in order to help. He hardly knows the quiet Professor, as he always thinks of his father, except that the Professor doesn't like crying and emotions. Jeff fits into the Professor's schedule and meets his requirements, hides all emotion, and tries to become invisible at home and at school, to cause no one trouble. If he loses his father, he reasons, he will have nobody. He succeeds so well he no longer sees himself as a person. Not bothering his father when he has a relapse of flu leads to severe pneumonia. Melody is contacted about a doctor, and later his father tells Jeff she wants him to spend the summer with her at her grandmother's house in Charleston.

Melody is warm and loving the first two days in Charleston. After that she seldom sees Jeff. She starts to teach him to play her guitar, but doesn't have time. He learns the songs she sings and often sits holding the guitar, placing his hands where she placed hers, happy in remembering. Gambo, his great-grandmother, welcomes him as the last of her line, telling him stories of the family. "The slow days passed. Jeff passed through them, a Boudrault in his own country. Their general history was his own history, too, the story of his own family was part of the history. His ancestors, all the Boudrault men, had stepped in their long boots where he stepped now or riding tall horses" (43). Melody's beauty and warmth, Gambo's welcome, the discovery of his roots, heal the wound that drained Jeff's spirit. On the return trip to Baltimore Jeff feels he is going from one self to another, from "the last in a long line of Boudrault men . . . to Jeff Greene, self-sufficient and reticent, no trouble at all, occupying his corner of the world. But he knew now how it felt to be loved, to be happy" (45).

Jeff lives his Baltimore self, reads history books about the South and Charleston, and writes regularly to his mother, who never answers. He buys a guitar and teaches himself to play, participates even less in classes, and is overwhelmed when at Christmas his father gives him a Martin guitar—one of the old ones. Jeff says "thank you" and rushes to his room so he won't embarrass the Professor with his emotion. Later he wonders if his father really understood, as he'd said Jeff could return it for a new one if he'd rather. "What if Jeff had gotten the greatest present anyone could have given him and the Professor thought he didn't like it. But he'd said thank you. Melody would have understood, he thought impatiently. But what if the Professor didn't" (58). He goes down the hall and knocks on the Professor's door, to be sure he isn't hurt. The Professor *had* misunderstood. Jeff struggles to keep the tears from his eyes when he tries to explain how wonderful the old Martins are, and hears the humor in his father's voice when he thanks Jeff for taking the trouble to make it clear. For the first time they can laugh together and relax.

A second visit to Charleston almost destroys Jeff. Gambo has had a stroke and is no longer interested in him. Melody is away for weeks at a time with Max, the man in her life, and angry if Jeff makes any protest. Jeff feels unwanted in the house and spends his days exploring the town and the sea island to the south. When Melody returns to repack her things for another trip, just before Jeff is to leave, he realizes she lies constantly to everyone. Jeff's anger explodes. He's never fought with anyone, and at first it feels oddly good—but Melody knows how to completely shatter his spirit and skillfully does this. At dinner she pretends nothing has happened, putting on an act to show Gambo how much she loves Jeff and he loves her. Broken and bruised Jeff tries not to look at her. The next morning he rows to the sea island, explores, collects shells, and spends the night on the beach watching the stars and listening to the wind and the water. He walks the beach until noon before going back.

> He felt—washed clean, healed. He felt if he could just live here he would be all right. He felt as if he had never been alive before. He felt at ease with himself and as if he had come home to a place where he could be himself, without hiding anything, without pretending even to himself. He felt, thinking his way back up the beach, as if his brain had just woken up from some long sleep, and it wanted to run along beside the waves, to see how far and how fast it could go. (90)

As Jeff splashes the oars into the water to row away, a great blue heron squawks, rises from the marsh croaking its displeasure, swoops over

Jeff's head and lands again on the far side of the ruined dock. "Just leave me alone, the heron seemed to be saying" (91). Jeff sinks his rowboat and returns to Baltimore. He feels whole only in the safety of the tower room in his imagination, where he protects the vivid memory of his healing on the island. Living in his safe tower room soon absorbs all Jeff's time and energy. In January his father, scared, finally confronts him. Jeff and the Professor are able to communicate, and Jeff understands for the first time how deeply his father cares for him. "It wasn't easy for the Professor to think about how to say to Jeff what he wanted to say. Not like it was easy for Jeff to see. But the Professor was doing it, trying as hard as he could, making himself. Because Jeff mattered to him, and Jeff saw that now, too, and saw that he could count on that. He could feel himself relaxing" (101).

The Professor has published a book that is selling well. There is enough money now to buy a new house. They search in wider and wider circles around Baltimore on weekends and holidays until they drive with an agent to a cabin in the marsh near Crisfield. Jeff explores the creek bank by the bay, startling a blue heron. When he reports this his father remembers and says, "You take that as a sign from the gods?" and Jeff nods (106). Both like the three high acres, his father commenting that it's like an island. They buy the cabin acreage and remodel to fit their needs, with a wide bay view, a dock, and a skiff with an outboard for Jeff. The Professor calls it "the property," and arranges his schedule to spend only two nights each week in Baltimore. Jeff calls it a "safe place" to himself, and takes the Professor exploring in the boat when they move there the end of July. Their new home reflects their growing ability to accept themselves and be open to one another.

The October Jeff is in tenth grade he has the last period free and often spends it playing his guitar outside. Working on a song he'd heard on a record, "When first unto this country, a stranger I came, and I courted a fair maid and Nancy was her name," he sees a kid with somewhere to go come out as soon as the bell rings.

> The kid wasn't anyone he knew, a narrow head with ragged, dark hair, cut-offs, T-shirt, and long, skinny legs. What held his eyes, as he sat playing his guitar . . . was the lift of the kid's chin. That chin raised—not high, not angry. Brave maybe. Purposeful. He looked at the kid's face. Even features and a straight nose, eyes dark and the mouth large. . . . The kid turned in Jeff's direction, as if the music were some kind of string winding around the long legs. . . .

"I never heard that song," she said. She didn't want to say that, she didn't want to be drawn to him, but she couldn't do anything to stop herself. She couldn't stop herself from coming over or from asking, even though she wanted to. (136–37)

Jeff recites the words, introduces himself, and asks her name; then Dicey rides off on her bike. In the year that follows he is often part of the Tillerman family, and in the summer he runs a crab trotline with James and Sammy, supplying the local restaurants and giving the boys a needed income.

Melody brings pain into Jeff's life several times in these years, but each time he is better able to handle it and protect his father. He sails with Dicey after she has repaired the sailboat, and eventually asks her to come and meet the Professor. She hesitates, but says,

"Gram would tell me to do it. She likes you."
"Really?" That did surprise him.
"Really. She says you've got staying power and a gentle spirit. She says you're a rare bird."
Jeff didn't bother to hide his pleasure. "Wow," he said. Then, "She could be wrong." He felt . . . as if he'd just gotten a letter, out of the blue, from somebody wise enough to know the truth, from everybody, or at least everybody who mattered.
"Hello," the letter said. "Hello, Jeff Greene, I've been watching you and I like you and I want to know you better. This is just to say I'm glad you're alive in the world." The list of signatures, he thought, would include his own. (184–85)

Jeff has overcome his inner fears. He has learned to step aside and look at his feelings, to examine and evaluate his actions. Like his mother he is aware of the inner feelings of others, and the motives behind their behavior. Unlike her, Jeff uses his knowledge to support and free others. Like his father Jeff uses his intelligence. He makes himself stand aside and look at a situation honestly; he evaluates and learns from his experience. When he is wounded deeply he withdraws and needs time to recover, but he learns, and can change, though he finds he keeps on loving. In many ways Jeff's interior and exterior life now reflects its home on the marsh: quiet, secure, and open to the world.

Perhaps, as David Rees suggests, our craving for myth comes from the loss, long ago, of our tribal singers and poets.[6] In his essay on Katherine Paterson, after she had received the 1981 Newbery Award for

Jacob Have I Loved, he calls her novel the most deserving the committee had seen in a long while, an advance over all she had previously written "in background detail, imagery, characterization, above all in the sureness of tone of voice and sheer writing ability."[7] Paterson's story of the struggle of the older sister with her twin is undergirded by the archetypical struggle of two brothers—Cain and Abel, Isaac and Ismael, and the more complex story of Jacob and Esau.[8] It draws strength from its familiar pattern as well as its literary qualities, as do the three books of Cynthia Voigt. It is interesting that all four are placed in rural, little-known eastern Maryland, and that their authors' vivid setting detail makes a major contribution.

Voigt's protagonists live with modern reality but reflect mythic themes. The Odyssean, Promethean, and Oedipal patterns of the books speak to our subconscious with strong voices. Her insights and very human characters remain in the reader's imagination. The cleansing and renewal of life in contact with the ocean strikes another deep chord, as do Stevenson's lines in "Requiem." We all long to be healed, to have a home, to go home, to be secure in our home. We want this in the here and now, and in the hereafter. We know we need times of solitude if we are to understand ourselves and live richly. We long to triumph in the spirit so that our lives have meaning. Stories that enable us to do this vicariously speak to our inner nature. They will continue to be read, and they will be remembered.

Notes

1. *Homecoming* (New York: Ballantine, 1981); *Dicey's Song* (New York: Ballantine, 1982); *A Solitary Blue* (New York: Atheneum, 1983).

2. Lucy Waddey, "Home in Children's Fiction: Three Patterns," *Children's Literature Association Quarterly* 8 (1983), 13.

3. Robert Louis Stevenson, "Requiem," in *Selected Poetry and Prose of Robert Louis Stevenson,* ed. Bradford A. Booth (Boston: Houghton Mifflin, 1968), 500.

4. Cynthia Voigt, "Newbery Medal Acceptance," *The Horn Book Magazine* (August 1983), 410.

5. Waddey, "Home in Children's Fiction," 14–15.

6. David Rees, *The Marble in the Water* (Boston: The Horn Book, 1980), 87.

7. David Rees, *Painted Desert, Green Shade* (Boston: The Horn Book, 1984), 90.

8. Helen M. Luke, *The Inner Story* (New York: Crossroad, 1982), 98–112.

2.

Of Good Courage

ANNE DEVEREAUX JORDAN

Courage is generally associated with grand and glorious deeds that ring throughout history, and literature for children has repeatedly reflected this association. There are numerous fiction and nonfiction books that show the individual rising above the crowd to change the course of events through personal heroism. Ingrid and Edgar Parin d'Aulaire's picture book, *Abraham Lincoln,* for example, shows the young Lincoln's humble upbringing and then pictures him facing and conquering the tempest of the Civil War: "He had done what he should do. He had held together the great nation brought forth upon this continent by his forefathers."[1]

Yet few people face the challenge of saving their country. People *are* courageous, however, and they demonstrate their courage daily without recognition. For courage is the awareness that one fears, yet going ahead despite that fear; it is conquering fear through control of oneself. The events that arise from conquering one's fears are often ignored by the annals of world history. However they are inscribed in the individual's memory and enshrined in his or her own personal history. These are the events that shape the individual, that build character. Children's litera-ture often commemorates courage of this sort.

For the very young child some of the most fearsome things inhabit the mind. Adults often forget that, for a child, the things conjured by the imagination seem as real as reality itself. The young child lives in a world peopled by other human beings but also by monsters who feed upon the bedtime darkness. They face the possibility of Mommy and Daddy disappearing forever, and/or the horrible idea of losing their love. The child exhibits great courage in facing and conquering these very real fears; the heroism thus exhibited is worthy of a medal for bravery.

One basis of fear is a feeling of not being in control, particularly of the thing one fears. Mercer Mayer's picture book, *There's a Nightmare in My Closet,* recognizes the courage necessary for children to exert control and conquer their fear that there is something in the bedroom closet that will "get them." At the start of this delightful book, the little boy pictured tells of his fear: "There used to be a nightmare in my closet. Before going to sleep, I always closed the closet door. I was even afraid to turn around and look."[2] At first the small boy is dressed only in sleepers but as the story progresses he dons an army helmet and arms himself with a popgun. Although some critics object to this outward manifestation of violence, the little boy is doing real battle with his own, very real fears and must be properly equipped. Mercer Mayer softens the story and alleviates much of the stress associated with the encounter by whimsically rendering the "nightmare" as a silly, childish being who, it turns out, cries when attacked.

It is at this point in the story that control shifts. At the start, the child's imagination—the nightmare—was in control; when the nightmare is confronted and shows weakness, the child assumes control and sees that when fear is faced it often is not the "monstrous" thing it was thought to be. The little boy then comforts the weeping nightmare and tucks it into bed; he has conquered his fear and is not a cruel victor. *There's a Nightmare in My Closet* teaches both children and adults an important lesson. When fear is faced, it can be conquered, or, although that fear may still exist, action can be taken. In this instance, and with great courage, the child has taken control of his world.

This need for control is seen throughout children's picture books. In *Peter's Chair* (1967) by Ezra Jack Keats, Peter is unhappy and fearful because all his baby furniture is being painted pink and given to his new baby sister. He has no control over the disposal of his things. Is he being replaced in his parents' affections by this small interloper, he wonders? Taking his baby chair with him, Peter runs away to sit in front of his house, but then finds he can no longer fit into the chair. Faced by this evidence and with the reassurances of his parents, Peter is able to summon up the courage to overcome his fears and accept his new sister into the family. He is now in control and it is he who controls the disposal of his things; it is he who paints his chair pink for his sister.

There are many picture books that utilize this idea. Beatrix Potter's *Tale of Peter Rabbit* (1903), Evaline Ness's *Sam, Bangs, and Moonshine* (1966), and even *Outside Over There* (1981) by Maurice Sendak show characters coping with uncertainty, change, and fear. They portray characters summoning up great courage to exert control over their feelings in order to conquer their fears, initiate change—or subdue monsters.

In books for older children the theme of courage is continued with two important differences. Often this theme of courage is a central one rather than a secondary one as it is in many picture books, and frequently the thing feared is very real rather than imaginary. However the characters, as in picture books, usually manage to summon up their courage through the process of realization, confrontation, and control.

Interestingly, a majority of the Newbery Award-winning books utilize courage as a central theme. Paula Fox's *The Slave Dancer,* the 1974 winner, is a good example. Paula Fox tells the story of thirteen-year-old Jesse Bollier who, in 1840, is kidnapped and taken to sea on a slave ship. His job is to play his fife so the slaves can "dance" and keep their bodies strong and profitable. Jesse fears he will never escape. Although he is able to overcome his fears, escape, and survive the horrors of the slave ship, the experience has a lasting effect on him:

> I was unable to listen to music. . . . For at the first note of a tune or of a song, I would see once again as though they'd never ceased their dancing in my mind, black men and women and children lifting their tormented limbs in time to a reedy martial air, the dust rising from their joyless thumping, the sound of the fife finally drowned beneath the clanging of their chains.[3]

Jesse is frightened by the fact that he has little control over his own life and is horrified that the slaves have *no* control over their lives. That this has a life-long effect on him is not surprising; what is surprising is that Paula Fox chooses to show this. Many books dealing with individual courage stop when the obstacle or fear presented is overcome, ignoring the fact that the experience shapes a person's life thereafter.

It is this concern for the past, present, and future character that marks the Newbery Award-winning books dealing with courage. Among others, Armstrong Sperry's *Call It Courage* (1940), *Rifles for Watie* (1957) by Harold Keith, Elizabeth George Speare's *The Witch of Blackbird Pond* (1958), Scott O'Dell's *Island of the Blue Dolphin* (1960), and Jean Craighead George's *Julie of the Wolves* (1972) all deal with characters who recognize their fears and have their lives irreparably shaped by the actions their courage has engendered. Their actions, however, have no great public or historical ramifications. These books portray young people changing only the course of their personal history. Necessity and circumstance have dictated courage rather than a call to glory or a desire for heroism.

Necessity and circumstance also dictate courage in books of a more transient nature. The preteen and teen romance novels deal with the courage of personal decision. Questions such as "Should I have a sexual relationship?" can conjure up as much fear for the adolescent as night-mares did for the preschooler, and attempting to find answers to such questions requires just as much courage as facing the imaginary monster. While these situations are all too frequently played out following a heavy-handed, melodramatic formula, there are junior novels that honestly and realistically do try to demonstrate the personal courage necessary to seek answers. One of the earliest junior novels to do so was Maureen Daly's *Seventeenth Summer* (1942).

Seventeenth Summer is the story of a girl's first love, a standard plot in junior novels for girls. Unlike other junior novels, however, the story is told quietly and poignantly without a tinge of melodrama, and the main characters, Angie and Jack, do not "live happily ever after." At the end of the novel, Angie says good-bye to Jack and goes away to college. Throughout the story Angie demonstrates reserves of quiet courage, resourcefulness, and moral stamina. She experiments with her first beer with hesitancy—an adventure that, considering the drug experiments and jaded sophistication of today's youth, now seems a little naive—and decides she doesn't like it and says so. To *not* go along with the crowd, to control her experiences, takes courage for Angie, a courage that often goes unrecognized.

More current are the books of Judy Blume and Paul Zindel, to name but two authors. Judy Blume follows in the tradition of Maureen Daly and does not adhere strictly to the dictates of the formulaic romance novel. She attempts to deal with issues. Her heroines face more complex problems than any Angie would have in the 1940s, but do so with similar courage. In *It's Not the End of the World* (1972), for example, Karen is undergoing many of the problems typical of adolescence, but it is the failed domesticity of her parents that concerns her the most. Karen learns to cope with her parents' situation but only by drawing on her own strength and courage. She is forced to acknowledge her own fears about the situation and is courageous enough to admit that she cannot run other people's lives for them.

Paul Zindel is more hard-hitting and humorous than Judy Blume but equally popular with adolescents. In *My Darling, My Hamburger* (1969) he confronts directly the issues of teenage pregnancy and abortion. Liz must decide whether or not to have an abortion when she learns she is pregnant. Zindel plays out all sides of the issue and grippingly projects the very real fear Liz feels. She is juxtaposed with her admiring girl friend, who is tentatively exploring the world of boys and dates. The contrast between the two girls makes an effective comment on the complex world of today's adolescent and points up the courage that is necessary to live in such a world and to face the consequences of one's actions in the midst of shifting values and other constant change.

What these books, and those mentioned previously, are dealing with is the archetypal theme of metamorphosis, one of the most pervasive themes in literature. Even the slightest change can be accompanied by fear, for each change, each decision made, introduces new unknowns into one's world. To overcome this fear, to act, takes great courage. Change is not simple or isolated; rather it mutates and often distorts the relationship between oneself and the world, or even the universe. When faced with the elemental, the courage needed to confront an imaginary monster, to escape from a slave ship, or even to take a sip of beer, is admirable. Seizing control of one's life, initiating change by doing something as simple as painting a chair, is, for a child, actively seizing and shaping the world, perhaps even the universe; nothing will ever be the same again. Such courage is not to be taken lightly or slighted in the annals of heroism.

Notes

1. (New York: Doubleday, 1939), np.
2. (New York: Dial, 1968), np.
3. (Scarsdale, N.Y.: Bradbury, 1973), 176.

Additional Reading

Primary

Martha Alexander, *Nobody Asked Me if I Wanted a Baby Sister,* illust. by the author (New York: Dial, 1971).

Marcia Brown, *Once a Mouse,* illust. by the author (New York: Scribner's, 1961).

Russell Hoban, *A Baby Sister for Frances,* illust. by Lillian Hoban (New York: Harper, 1964).

H. A. Rey and Margaret Rey, *Curious George Goes to the Hospital,* illust. by H. A. Rey (Boston: Houghton Mifflin, 1965).

Charlotte Zolotow, *William's Doll,* illust. by William Pene Du Bois (New York: Harper, 1972).

Intermediate

Carol Ryrie Brink, *Caddie Woodlawn* (New York: Macmillan, 1935).

Elizabeth B. De Trevino, *I, Juan De Pareja* (New York: Farrar, 1965).

Felice Holman, *Professor Diggins' Dragons,* illust. by Ib Ohlsson (New York: Macmillan, 1966).

Robert Lawson, *They Were Strong and Good,* illust. by the author (New York: Viking, 1940).

Scott O'Dell, *The Black Peril,* illust. by Milton Johnson (Boston: Houghton Mifflin, 1967).

Maia Wojciechowska, *Shadow of a Bull,* illust. by Alvin Smith (New York: Atheneum, 1964).

Advanced

Willa Cather, *My Antonia* (Boston: Houghton Mifflin, 1947).

Nat Hentoff, *I'm Really Dragged but Nothing Gets Me Down* (New York: Simon and Schuster, 1962).

John Knowles, *A Separate Peace* (New York: Macmillan, 1960).

Isac Bashevis Singer, *The Fearsome Inn* (New York: Scribner's, 1967).

John Steinbeck, *The Grapes of Wrath* (New York: Viking, 1939).

3.

Farley Mowat
in the Wilderness

RICHARD ROTERT

The naturalist John Burroughs noted in *The Light Of Day* that "children readily, even eagerly, believe almost any impossible thing you may tell them about nature. As yet they have no insight into the course of nature, or of the law of cause and effect, no fund of experience to serve as a touchstone to the false or impossible."[1] His observation may be considered as applicable to technologically advanced civilizations as to the children about whom he wrote. The uninformed mind is inherently exploitable; and even in our contemporary society there exists a fascination with still inexplicable, universally observed natural phenomena.

The wilderness projects considerable symbolic power because of its kinship to these vaguely understood emotive forces. Any significant association with them, through involvement with the natural world, has led to the metaphysical fallout pervasive in mythology and mysticism, as well as in children's literature.

As abandoned infants, Zoroaster, Siegfried, and others were suckled by wilderness creatures of divine impulse and became heroes for their supernal affiliation. Numerous prophets became prophets only after an introspective, often dangerous wilderness trek had imbued them with special qualities, transforming them into conduits between the masses and their particular authority. A Medina-bound member of the Quraysh tribe became the messenger of Allah during a desert hegira; a wandering Galilean returned from forty days of solitude to be proclaimed Son of God; and a peregrine ascetic earned unity with the Oneness of Nirvana. In fact, the symbolic "wilderness retreat" is still sanctioned by religious and other groups and eagerly experienced by those who are trying to free themselves of everyday concerns to think creatively.

Extraordinary accomplishments have been attributed to renowned woodsmen as well. But even Messieurs Boone and Crockett might well have traded in their buckskins if required to perform the feats of mythic

"Dani'l" and "Davey." This willingness to accept such hyperbolic asser-
tions characterizes our reverential, though nescient regard for that prime-
val realm, whose "eternal" quality we would have as our own.

But mortal existence remains our enigmatic and most elemental
success. It is a spiritual triumph serving as the basis from which all others
derive. Once infused with this magical phenomenon, maintaining it
becomes the real trick. Still reserved for the fittest, survival has redefined
the attributes of its beneficiaries to revere the cognitive as well as physical
qualities. The fight to live is won by knowledge as well as knuckles, by
brain as well as brawn. Intelligently circumventing a potential disaster
occasions elation, self-confidence, and a prolonged life. It is this confidence which animates the accomplished characters in Farley Mowat's
books, which are anthologies of survival techniques disguised as wilderness adventure stories.

As author and naturalist, Farley Mowat documents human and phenomenological natures without the perspective altering prejudices of the
romantic or the clinician. His observations reveal his boyhood interest in
biology and extensive travels in the arctic, two occupations which
involved him directly with the environment. Mowat maintains in his
twenty-five books that communion with the environment is humanity's
primary, if not ultimate, apotheosis. He is skeptical of modern influences, both tangible and theological, neither of which is required for
spiritual experience. Actually, they have interposed themselves between
man and his previous wilderness experience, thus setting man apart from
and at odds with the natural world and, consequently, with his own
nature as well. These impositions insidiously have become the terms by
which man now defines himself, heedless of prior ties to the natural
world which, for Mowat, is man's genuine source of sustenance and
inspiration.

When stranded at sea in a raging hurricane or blinded by a whiteout at
the top of the world, Mowat's characters rely on knowledge of natural
phenomena to secure their survival. Neither heroes nor prophets, they
understandably look to the land for solutions to their terrestrial problems
rather than appealing to metaphysical systems. For, in Mowat's understanding, the tundra, prairie, and open sea are more than just backdrops
for the visitation of man-made furies that destroy the calm. These
wilderness settings also proffer salvation to those would-be victims who,
by their resourcefulness, are able to fashion alternatives to catastrophe.
They prevail by aligning their native intelligence with the forces at large
rather than by physically struggling against them. The resultant comple-
mentary relationship reveals the best of both man and his natural

environment. "Particularly do I like natural things," Mowat has said, "and this includes people who live natural lives. . . . These are the kind of people I have always chosen to write about—people who are attuned to the natural world and who feel competent and at home with natural existence."[2] Demonstrating a familiarity with nature once common to all mankind, and now represented by his admired Eskimos and Indians, Mowat's survivors seem anachronistic, especially in this era of vanishing human competence in the wild.

Lost In The Barrens is an adventure story which rivals *The Boy Scout Handbook* (originally written by another renowned naturalist, Ernest Thompson Seton) in techniques which make life in the wild not only possible, but unexpectedly comfortable. The young orphan Jamie Macnair leaves the metropolis of Toronto for the north Canadian home of his uncle. Embracing the uncustomarily harsh and envigorating lifestyle, Jamie soon gains a companion in Awasin, a young Cree Indian boy who is to be Jamie's tutor to the ways of the wilderness. Braving the subarctic environment and their supposed enemy, the Eskimo, the pair join a starving Chipeweyan hunting party headed for the Barrenlands. A broken promise, an unresisted temptation and a boat-shattering mishap strand the partners in unknown, hostile territory. In the ensuing months of hardship, as Jamie and Awasin overcome each travail and threat to life, Mowat treats the reader to a trove of wilderness lore and logic.

Initially, Jamie is representative of "civilized" men whose primary needs are furnished by society and who, separated from nature, orient themselves by concrete curbs rather than compass points and game trails. He is of the city, that closed system of anthropocentric rationality whose principles are inconsequential when dealing with the laws of the wilderness. Though a capable individual, Jamie lacks "insight into the course of nature," and ironically would fail for want of the knowledge once common to his ancestors.

When injured and undone by the apparent futility of his predicament, Jamie prematurely resigns himself to destruction. He is unable to fashion an acceptable "re-solution" to the dilemma, and wallows in despair.

> "What'll we do?" he asked anxiously.
> "I think maybe my leg's broken. . . ."
> He gave way to a mood of self-pity.
> "You'd better leave me and walk back
> yourself," he said. . . . I got us into this.
> It's my fault. You'd better leave me here"[3]

Jamie's fear, the precipitate of his ignorance, is the precondition of his failure.

But these same circumstances warrant a different, more informed conclusion from his talented companion who has retained his ancestral acumen: "As Awasin looked critically over the collection he felt almost confident. There was enough equipment here for any real woodsman to make a living for several weeks at least (62)." It is characteristic of Mowat's works to demonstrate fate as sealed not by external or celestial forces, but rather by one's resourcefulness. Calm decision-making under pressure is allied to personal proficiency, and truly our every outcome lies "not within our stars, but within ourselves."

Because of his familiarity with nature, Awasin repeatedly avoids impending crises. Moose-hide laces avert starvation when used to snare ground squirrels. Dried moss and shards of wood become a functioning fire board. Knowledge of caribou migration targets the more significant animals, the trailing males, for their abundant fat renderable for oil lamps, superior nutritional value, and durable hides. And an observation of air convection inspires an ingenious plan for an in-ground air trough which transforms a potential tomb into a comfortable hut.

> That night they slept comfortably on beds of moss in their new home. When they dozed off they were as proud as if they had built a castle.
>
> They had reason to be proud. Good sense and hard work had conquered the last of their major problems. Now, barring some unforeseen misfortune, they were almost certain to survive the winter in the dreaded Barrenlands (153).

Misfortunes occur, of course, but the boys prevail and experience euphoric interludes as their confidence increases with their developing talents. And their elation is at a high when they finally encounter the reputedly savage Eskimos who in reality prove hospitable and gracious. From this direct interaction with phenomenological realities, Jamie and Awasin establish self-reliance, a spiritual high, which liberates them from mischievous fate and fallacy, reaffirming man's station as a part of this world, and not apart from it.

Straying from man's natural element, as expressed in ancestral wisdom, also threatens the Eskimo, Katalak, in "The White Canoe," a short story from a collection entitled *The Snow Walker*. Enticed by the foreign culture encountered at trading settlements, Katalak forsakes his heritage and disregards the admonishings of Kakut, his father.

"Men become blind when they travel over new snow on a day when there is haze over the sun, and that happens because they deny the powers that lie in the wind and the snow and the sky and the sun. That is one kind of darkness. There is another. It comes when men deny or forget what their fathers' fathers knew. We must pity you, Katalak, for you are blind."[4]

Abandoning the camps of his people, Katalak withdraws to the "wooden igloos" of the white men. For many years he studies their ways and thoughts, languishing in a cultural conflict. He had deserted the natural world for the promise of another as prescribed by man's laws, which transgress those of nature. Eventually he realizes that his perceptions have been confounded by his desertion rather than clarified, and that his previous freedom had been traded for emotional servitude.

During Katalak's absence, Kakut dies and is buried with all his possessions, according to custom, hidden far from camp beneath his white canoe. From its wilderness seclusion the canoe, symbolic of Eskimo heritage, appears apparition-like during a flood to rescue all from certain disaster, and to inspire Katalak's resolution of his personal crisis.

> Then it was as if I became two persons. I was a man of my people, but standing beside me was another self. . . . One of my beings was calm, feeling no fear, and this was one who had come back to his own place. The other was panic-stricken, mouthing the prayers he had been taught by the priest.
>
> I was two beings who struggled against each other; and it was the man of the people who won. . . . I thought of Kakut, and inside myself I asked him to take me back.
>
> These are true things I am speaking; and it is a true thing that when I lifted my eyes to look westward toward the place where my father lay, I saw his canoe. (180-81)

Katalak overcame this self-imposed distancing from his own people by acknowledging previously understood, temporarily denied truths much as Jamie overcame a culturally-imposed distancing from the phenomenological world. Each reverted to the integrity of natural order as represented by peoples of "primitive" societies to "re-order" his well being within the framework of natural principles.

Mowat's wilderness characters elude a form of "cultural irreversibility," as described by Robert Ardrey in *The Hunting Hypothesis*, by clearing a man's evolutionary backtrail of cultural obstacles which frustrate inquiry into fundamental principles. Ardrey suggests that dependence upon a cultural adaptation, say the hand-held hatchet, heralds the physical loss of a biological adaptation which provides the same function, in this case the elongated canine tooth once common to humanoids. Once in motion, this process disallows a return to the previous state, thus reinforcing dependence upon the new. On a broader scale, Mowat shows that man has broken from the natural world by creating his own supportive environment and beliefs. These cultural modifications deny man's return to the instinctual realm, and even recognition of that original existence in the wilderness. Consequently a gulf exists between contemporary societies and the knowledge and talents made obsolete by their creation. Farley Mowat spans that cultural Rubicon with his writing, whereby the reader regains some understanding of that primal land, and of those travelers, ourselves, who crossed it, and of our capacity for spiritual triumphs in this existential world.

Notes

1. (Boston and New York: Houghton Mifflin, 1900), 57.
2. Daniel L. Kirkpatrick, ed., *Twentieth Century Children's Writers,* 2nd ed. (New York: St. Martin's, 1983), 565.
3. (Boston and Toronto: Little, Brown, 1956), 60–61.
4. (Boston and Toronto: Little, Brown, 1975), 169.

4.

Bravery and Philosophy in the Adventures of Frog and Toad

GARETH B. MATTHEWS

Frog and Toad are reading a book. We can see from the picture that it is a book of fairy tales.[1] "The people in this book are brave," Toad says to his friend; "they fight dragons and giants, and they are never afraid."

A question occurs to Frog. "I wonder if we are brave," he asks.

If I wonder how much I weigh, I can go to a scale and weigh myself. Of course, there may be problems. I may fail to realize that I must take off my coat and my shoes to get a good reading. Then the scale might not have been properly set. More subtly, I might be weighing myself just after I have eaten a huge meal. Less subtly, the scale may be broken.

Still, finding out how much you weigh is not, or not usually, an overwhelming problem. Much more difficult is finding out whether you are good-looking. Mother and Father say, "Yes," your friends, if you dare ask them, say, "You've got to be kidding!" Are your parents more, or less, trustworthy than your friends? Perhaps your parents are more likely than your friends to accentuate the positive. For that reason they might be less trustworthy. But maybe your friends are more inclined to be in competition with you than your parents; so, in that way, they are less trustworthy. Doubtless you have seen your face in the mirror too long to be a good judge for yourself. But maybe others have not seen it long enough; they don't know whether it is a good face to wake up to every morning.

What about bravery? Is finding out whether you are brave more like finding out how much you weigh, or more like finding out whether you are good-looking?

In the story, "Dragons and Giants," Frog and Toad try looking in a mirror. "We look brave," says Frog. "Yes," answers Toad, "but are we?"

At this point readers of the story smile. If you read the story to small children, they will smile, too. How stupid it is to look in a mirror to see if one is brave!

Yet it is not entirely stupid. We do have pictures that are meant to portray bravery—David selecting a pebble for his sling, with Goliath towering nearby, or soldiers raising the flag in the Battle of Iwo Jima. Could my face be the calm face of David, taking the measure of Goliath, or the grimaced face of a soldier, struggling to raise the flag at Iwo Jima? Or are those futile questions? Is it always only the context that shows bravery, never the face itself?

Even if I am convinced I can look brave, all by myself, Toad's question should stop me cold. Am I *really* brave? How would the actor in the movies, or on TV, manage in the face of danger, real danger? How can we know? Can we know?

We don't know what David said after his encounter with Goliath, but we do know that many a soldier who gets decorated for bravery feels guilty or cynical about being singled out in this way. "I was scared the whole time," a soldier may protest, perhaps from an appealing modesty, perhaps from an anguished suspicion that bravery is an invention of generals and politicians, useful only in the myths that gain recruits for the army and the fire department.

In the manner of myth and saga, Frog and Toad decide to test whether they are brave. They climb a mountain. "That should tell us if we are brave," says Frog, confidently.

At the mouth of a dark cave they encounter a snake. "Hello lunch," says the snake, as he opens his wide mouth. Frog and Toad jump away. Toad is shaking as he cries, "I am not afraid!"

They climb higher. They meet more dangers archetypical for their species. They encounter an avalanche that threatens to flatten them. They identify the shadow of a hawk. Each time they confront danger they take evasive action. As they do so they scream, frantically, "We are not afraid!"

Having ascended the mountain of danger successfully, Frog and Toad now run back down, "very fast." They go past the place where they encountered the avalanche. They go past the place where they met the snake. They run all the way to Toad's house.

Toad jumps into bed and pulls the covers over his head. Frog jumps into the cupboard and closes the door. "I'm glad to have a brave friend like you," says Toad. "And I'm happy to know a brave person like you," responds Frog. Toad stays in the bed, and Frog in the cupboard, for a very long time. They stay there "just feeling very brave together."

Every story in Arnold Lobel's remarkable collection, *Frog and Toad Together,* exemplifies a trait I have called "philosophical whimsy."[2] The humor of philosophical whimsy makes a conceptual point. It prods us readers to reflect on some philosophically interesting issue. In "Dragons and Giants" the humor begins when Frog and Toad look in a mirror to see if they are brave. As I have already indicated, looking in a mirror to see if one is brave, while not totally stupid, is hardly an effective way to make the determination. We all realize this. Even very young children realize this. But what should Frog and Toad have done instead? It isn't that they should have gotten out the yardstick, or the stopwatch, or the thermometer, instead of looking in a mirror. As we soon realize, if we think about it, there is no simple procedure for determining whether one is brave.

The procedure Frog and Toad employ, such as it is, is mythically woven into the fabric of our culture. If children of today learn little or nothing of the trials of Hercules, they learn instead of the exploits of modern superheroes. Anyone with literary sophistication who sees "Star Trek" or checks out the latest dolls in the toy store can make the connection.

How serviceable are these myths of our culture? When Frog and Toad tremble and scream, "We are not afraid," we readers smile. But, again, the joke is serious. Do knocking knees count against the claim to be brave? Does an honest avowal settle things, the way an honest avowal of a headache, or of nausea, settles things? If not, what would settle things? Would standing fast in the face of danger?

When the snake emerges from the dark cave and intones, "Hello lunch," Frog and Toad jump away. Would bravery have required them to stand fast? Perhaps standing fast in the face of imminent demise, for no good reason other than to find out whether you are brave, would be foolhardy. But when does standing fast in the face of danger show bravery and when does it show foolhardiness?

One way in which children's stories can be philosophical is by presenting us readers with a thought-experiment that goads us into reflection. The thought-experiment may invite us (1) to explore a concept or (2) to test a principle or (3) to consider whether or not some attitude is well placed. Natalie Babbitt's beautifully sensitive story, *Tuck Everlasting,*[3] presents a thought-experiment that invites us to consider whether our attitudes toward our own mortality are well placed. William Steig's engrossing tale, *The Real Thief,*[4] presents a thought-experiment that, among other things, invites us to test the principle that honesty is the best policy.

"Dragons and Giants" invites us to explore the concept of bravery. Bravery is as difficult to be perfectly clear about as it is hard to ignore or devalue. It has puzzled and intrigued philosophers from Plato down to the present day. Aristotle's complicated and subtle analysis in his *Nicomachean Ethics* is as interesting an account of what bravery consists in as any we have. But it is hard to understand and there are certainly reasons to be dissatisfied with it.

When I use "Dragons and Giants" as a basis for discussing the concept of bravery—whether with third-graders or with college students—I usually find that the group divides naturally into two camps. Those in one camp are so impressed with the core idea that bravery is standing fast in the face of danger that they are willing to count as brave an Evel Knievel who will jump his motorcycle across the Grand Canyon. Those in the other camp seem to realize, implicitly anyway, that bravery, being a virtue, is a characteristic of an ideal person. An ideal person, they reason, wouldn't do something stupidly dangerous. For those in the second group, foolhardiness clearly trumps bravery. For those in the first group it isn't so clear; for them stupidity, unless it clouds one's awareness of the danger, is no direct threat to bravery. I suspect the natural way in which my discussion groups divide up on the relation between bravery and foolhardiness reveals an important ambivalence concerning bravery in the culture.

In any case, children are admonished from a very young age to be brave. Maybe the threat they face is the shot they are to receive in the doctor's office. "Be brave," we say, "it will be over in a minute." Feeling the need to put on more pressure, we may add, "I was so proud of you last time, the way you didn't cry."

But what is it to be brave? Clearly it is something more than not crying in the doctor's office, or when one starts to bleed, or when one loses Mummy in the crowd. But what more? And why?

Children, because they are just finding out what demands the world will be laying on them and what opportunities they will have for gaining its rewards, are wonderful conversation partners in the exploration of a concept like bravery. Blessed is the adult, whether parent or teacher, who invites, recognizes and values the fresh insights that a young child can bring to the consideration of what bravery really is, and why it is important. And blessed is the child who is invited to follow up those natural chuckles over Frog's and Toad's exploits with some of the ruminations that this delightful story so appropriately provokes.

Children are sometimes remarkably brave. But whether or not they are brave, they are, from my experience, even more remarkably open to discussing and reflecting on what bravery requires. A wonderful thing about Arnold Lobel's "Dragons and Giants" is that it provides the material for making that discussion as natural as playing a game, and at least as rewarding.

Notes

1. Arnold Lobel, *Frog and Toad Together* (New York: Harper and Row, 1971).
2. Gareth B. Matthews, *Philosophy and the Young Child* (Cambridge, Mass.: Harvard University Press, 1980).
3. (New York: Farrar, Straus and Giroux, 1973).
4. (New York: Farrar, Straus and Giroux, 1975).

5.

The Imaginative Uses of Secrecy in Children's Literature

JOHN DANIEL STAHL

Secrecy in children's literature is an enlightening conspiracy between adult author and child reader. In the process of creating, discovering, and keeping secrets, the child reader finds ways to grow as an individual and as a social being. To the adult author, the writing of stories about secrets and secrecy offers the dual pleasure of recapturing childhood states of mind and of commenting on the limitations of childhood. Children's literature that deals with secrecy therefore frequently reveals a dual perspective: the naive but authentic internal perspective of childhood, and the experienced though also limited external perspective of adulthood, sometimes indulgent or ironic, frequently affectionate or nostalgic.

The idea of secrecy appeals to adults occasionally, not only to children. What then are the distinctive functions of secrecy for the young reader? It is clear that secrecy and mystery have for young readers the sort of universal appeal that can be exploited by formula fiction. Witness the many books of the Hardy Boys and the Nancy Drew series, as well as many of the books on the mystery shelves of the juvenile department of our libraries. But secrecy is not the province only of cheap mysteries, just as romantic love is not the subject matter only of shallow romances. Secrecy, like initiation or death, is a theme capable of being treated banally or brilliantly. It has the special quality of paradoxically symbolizing not only the author's relation to the reader (reading is an act of entering into a shared consciousness with the writer—a shared "secret"), but also the adult author's relation to the child as character and as reader. The author of a children's book reenacts the mysterious truth that one consciousness can contain another. The child's secret becomes the adult's stated truth.

Secrecy is often the child's method of declaring and developing his or her individuality and independence. Louise Fitzhugh's treatment of a child's secrecy is particularly trenchant in part because her narrative perspective is free of condescension. The narrator in *Harriet the Spy*[1] approximates Harriet's point of view, as Virginia L. Wolf has pointed out.[2] Harriet's "spying" is really curiosity masked in secrecy; Harriet wants to find out without being found out. Her explorations of various people's lives serve the function of helping her to grow in awareness of the options of adult identity, of what directions she can take in the process of becoming. Secrecy, especially the privacy of her notebooks, is important to her because she needs the opportunity of judging without shaping her responses to the expectations of others, adults and peers. Her notebooks allow her to assess potential adult role models and to criticize cowardice, stupidity, and other faults in her classmates and friends. Fitzhugh emphasizes this function of secrecy by satiric portrayals of adult foibles.

As long as Harriet's thoughts remain secret, she can be honest. The loss of the protection of secrecy leads to a compromise of her integrity. She must pretend to be sorry for what she wrote in order to win back her friends. Though the repudiation of the honesty of her confidences to herself is a necessary compromise for the sake of social growth, through her notebooks Harriet is able to develop her skills as a writer and to explore her perceptions and emotions through her secret dialogue with herself. Many readers of *Harriet the Spy* report starting a journal like Harriet's after reading the book as children, which suggests that the secrecy of Harriet's writing offers children a form of self-realization to emulate.

"Secret" can be synonymous with knowledge. When Harriet is spying on the bed-loving Mrs. Plumber, she overhears the following conversation:

> "Well," Mrs. Plumber was saying decisively into the telephone, *"I have discovered the secret of life."*
> Wow, thought Harriet.
> "My dear, it's very simple, you just *take* to your *bed*. You just refuse to leave it for *anything* or *anybody*."
> Some secret, thought Harriet; that's the dumbest thing I ever heard of. (44–45)

Harriet is disappointed. She recognizes that this adult's knowledge is clearly affectation or stupidity or both. On the other hand, Mata Hari is a model Harriet is eager to imitate, even when it means learning the—to her—odious skill of dancing. Mata Hari's secret identity and activities guarantee the integrity of her character for Harriet. By testing adults' various kinds of knowledge against her own judgment, Harriet approaches, very imperfectly, to be sure, the Dostoevskian command to love everything and perceive the divine mystery in things.

Through secrecy, children may seek a knowledge of their own which is sometimes forbidden or in danger of being abused by adults. In Frances Hodgson Burnett's *The Secret Garden*,[3] the garden is a place of privacy which needs to be hidden from adults. The garden is directly connected to the awakening of Mary's imagination, and with the development of her own personality:

> The Secret Garden was what Mary called it when she was thinking of it. She liked the name, and she liked still more the feeling that when its beautiful old walls shut her in no one knew where she was. It seemed almost like being shut out of the world in some fairy place. The few books she had read and liked had been fairy-story books, and she had read of secret gardens in some of the stories. Sometimes people went to sleep in them for a hundred years, which she had thought must be rather stupid. She had no intention of going to sleep, and, in fact, she was becoming wider awake every day she passed at Misselthwaite. (80)

In the garden Mary discovers for herself purposeful activity and fulfillment. "If no one found out about the secret garden, she should enjoy herself always," the narrator says, from Mary's perspective (94). The garden is imaginatively transformed into a magical realm, a place where Colin eventually grows toward healing. Identification with Mary and Colin's pleasure in preserving and enjoying their secret paradise can be a cathartic experience for readers of the book, because the garden is synonymous not only with growth in nature and of personality but with liberation from adult restraints and inner bonds of self-pity and defeat. Burnett achieves a complex rapport with the reader partly because she shows us Mary and Colin truthfully as they appear from an external perspective ("she was a disagreeable child") and sympathetically from within.[4]

Often secrecy in a children's story is not created by the children who are the main characters. In many mystery stories the secret lies in the outside world and presents itself as a puzzle to be solved. Both the inner secrecy (the child's creation) and the outer secrecy (a mystery in the larger world which calls for the child's discovery or quest for discovery) represent ways of ordering experience into meaningful patterns. To give an example of what is here meant by outer secrecy, in the story *The Horse Without a Head* by Paul Berna,[5] a band of children lose their beloved three-wheeled metal horse to mysterious and threatening thieves who apparently place an extremely high value on the battered old toy. The question which the story's events pose and around which the book is structured is, why do the thieves want a seemingly worthless rattle-trap tricycle? The adults are not overly concerned about it all, until it turns out that the horse contains (literally) a key which leads to the solution of an adult mystery. The presence of something unexplained, the effort to find clues about the explanation, and finally the discovery of the desired answer: this sequence in a story is appealing because it is in fact the pattern of such a large part of growing up. Moreover, in recapitulating and symbolizing processes of learning and of the formation of purpose-ful, goal-oriented activity, the unriddling of mysteries offers a variation of the "principle of hope" (Ernst Bloch's phrase). Like the punishment of evildoers or the successful performance of a trial task in the folktale, the pursuit, discovery, or protection of secrets of literary stories for older children have hermeneutic potential.

Often children who are concerned with secrets will form clubs or gangs at the same time. Private secrets represent the development of an individual identity; shared secrets often denote a shared identity. In *Huckleberry Finn,*[6] Tom Sawyer organizes a band of boys, to be called Tom Sawyer's Gang, which requires an oath and one's name written in blood for admission.

> Everybody was willing. So Tom got out a sheet of paper that he had wrote the oath on and read it. It swore every boy to stick to the band, and never tell any of the secrets; and if anybody done anything to any boy in the band, whichever boy was ordered to kill that person and his family must do it, and he mustn't eat and mustn't sleep till he had killed them and hacked a cross in their breasts, which was the sign of the band. And nobody that didn't belong to the band could use that mark, and if he did he must be sued; and if he done it again he must be killed. And if anybody that belonged to the band told the secrets, he must have his throat cut, and then have his carcass burnt up and the ashes scattered all around, and his name blotted off the list with blood and never mentioned again by the gang, but have a curse put on it and be forgot, for ever. (9)[7]

Mark Twain has captured with comic accuracy the intense seriousness of children's preoccupation with cementing social ties of their own creation, in fantastic mimicry of romanticized adult models. But the very straightforwardness of Huck's—and Twain's—reporting of these activities itself signals an adult amusement at childish innocence, and invites knowing hilarity without deflating naive identity. The contradiction of thinking of themselves as robbers and murderers (i.e., outlaws) and yet wishing to have recourse to suing in a court of law if their sign is used improperly, of forming an antisociety society, may or may not be evident to any particular child reader.

The gang is the juvenile replica of adult society, on a smaller scale. Often the gang requires that its activities be clandestine because it seeks to elude adult supervision. Erich Kästner's classic German children's novel *Emil and the Detectives*[8] furnishes an example. Kästner recreates the state of mind of the child who cannot confide certain difficulties to any adult. When Emil wakes up in a train and finds that the money which was pinned inside his coat pocket has been stolen, he is terrified, because he feels he cannot call the police to aid him even though the loss of the money is a very serious matter. Emil has a guilty conscience because he defaced a monument in the park, and expects to be accused and jailed if caught. This is what he thinks:

> Now, to top it all, he had to get mixed up with the police, and naturally Officer Jeschke could keep silent no longer but would have to admit officially, "I don't know why, but that schoolboy, Emil Tischbein of Neustadt, doesn't quite please me. First he daubs up noble monuments. And then he allows himself to be robbed of a hundred and forty marks. Perhaps they weren't stolen at all?
>
> "A boy who daubs up monuments will tell lies. I have had experience with that. Probably he has buried the money in the woods or has swallowed it and plans to go to America with it. There's no sense trying to capture the thief, not the slightest. The boy Tischbein himself is the thief. Please, Mr. Chief of Police, arrest him."
>
> Horrible! He could not even confide in the police! (80–81)

But he can confide in other children. In the metropolis of Berlin, he meets a gang of boys and girls who, once initiated into the difficulties of the situation, organize into a spy ring which eventually tracks down and delivers the thief to justice. All of this happens without adult assistance, and on the sly, of course. The book is the adventurous history of Emil's voyage away from home, alone, into independence from the adult world through the assistance of his peers. The reader's imaginative participation in fictional gangs such as Emil's can be a form of vicarious socialization. The secrecy and self-sufficiency of clandestine children's groups in stories is a form of empowerment of the younger generation. Kästner recognizes and, like Twain, affectionately mocks the tendency of children to mimic adult behavior, for instance in nicknames such as "Professor" and in Emil's cousin Pony Hütchen's ironic formality.

The gang and the secret code are not, of course, desired by all children. In Nina Bawden's *The White Horse Gang*,[9] despite the title, the gang is a loose organization with plenty of internal conflict. Bawden presents the variety of attitudes children at different stages of social development have toward secret organizations. The gang is begun at Rose's suggestion, and neither Sam nor Abe (her friends) are enthusiastic.

> They both looked at Sam. "All right," he said. "We'll call it the White Horse Gang. And we got to have a secret sign."
>
> Giggling, Rose placed her left forefinger against the side of her nose. Sam suggested that they should use the other hand at the same time, and pull at the lobe of the right ear, but Abe said they didn't want to make it too obvious.
>
> "And we'll sign our names backwards," Rose said. She looked blissfully happy, so happy that neither boy could bring himself to protest that this was a childish device. They practised with a pencil stub on an old bus ticket Sam had in his pocket. Esor and Mas and Eba. "That's lovely," Rose sighed. " 'Course, we ought really to sign in *blood.*"
>
> "Blood's for kids," Sam said. He had once got a septic finger from pricking and extracting blood for this purpose. "What we want more is a *reason.*" (72–73)

In its portrayal of the conflicts that separate and distress the members of the White Horse Gang, Nina Bawden's book is more psychologically realistic than Erich Kästner's smooth-working, effective Robin-Hood-style gang; Kästner's book is in this respect closer to fantasy. But whether in realistic or in mythic guise, the fantasy is of a kind very appealing to children; it has a great deal of resonance in children's experiences. The secret club or gang appeals to dream-wishes for group identity, and represents an early recognition of the truth that there is strength in numbers. The secret organization provides readers with fantasy versions of substitute families and of social roles among one's peers which are not determined or monitored by adults.

Secrecy is a means for fictional characters to create a meaningful sense of self, frequently in productive, not necessarily hostile, opposition to grown-ups or rivals. One value of such themes lies in children's being encouraged to imagine similar sources of self-awareness in their own lives. In Astrid Lindgren's *Bill Bergson Lives Dangerously*[10] some of the appeals of secret signs, secret languages, and secret organizations are made more explicit than in many books for children, surely one of the reasons for the popularity of Lindgren's work. The book opens with the war of the Red Roses against the White Roses, and it becomes clear that the war and the mystery surrounding it, especially the secrecy about the totemic object called the Great Mumbo, are ways of introducing purpose and entertainment into random, dull experience: "Bill grinned contentedly. The War of the Roses, which with short interruptions had been raging for several years, was nothing one voluntarily denied oneself. It provided excitement and gave real purpose to the summer vacation, which otherwise might have been rather monotonous (10–11)."

The Whites (with whom the story is primarily concerned) have a secret language, which involves doubling each consonant and placing an "o" in between. The Whites can flaunt their identity with their secret language: "There was no surer way of annoying the Reds. Long and in vain they had tried to decipher this remarkable jargon which the Whites spoke with the greatest facility, chattering at such insane speed that to the uninitiated it sounded like perfect babel (33)." When the Reds capture and interrogate Anders, the leader of the Whites, he does not reveal any secrets under "torture."

Lindgren's narrative perspective does not disguise adult awareness of children's maintenance of secrets. In fact, it acknowledges secrecy as the child's way of creating self-identity; but the open, indulgent attitude of the adult narrator defuses potential conflicts between generations. Eva-Lotta, a member of the Whites, meets her mother in the market place. When asked where she is going, Eva-Lotta says, " 'That I must not tell. . . . I'm on a secret mission. Terribly secret mission!' " (75). Despite Eva-Lotta's refusal to tell, the exchange between mother and daughter is affectionate and amusing:

> Mrs. Lisander smiled at Eva-Lotta.
> "I love you," she said.
> Eva-Lotta nodded approvingly at this indisputable statement

and continued on her way across the square, leaving a trail of cherry stones behind her. (75–76)

Her mother's acceptance of Eva-Lotta's right to have secrets is a liberating, loving attitude. That the secret mission represents the development of an independent personality is suggested by Mrs. Lisander's concerned thoughts about her daughter: "How thin the girl looked, how small and defenceless somehow! It wasn't very long since that youngster had been eating biscuit porridge, and now she was tearing about on 'secret errands'—was that all right, or ought she to take better care of her? (76)."

But Eva-Lotta's experiences are narrated also from a perspective that implies the child's need and ability to face danger on her own. For a while, a secret box, containing mysterious documents, is the object of an entertaining struggle between the Reds and the Whites. But secrecy only comes into full play in a dangerous situation when Eva-Lotta is alone with a murderer in an abandoned house. The murderer has every reason to kill her: she holds the key to knowledge of his guilt. When Anders and Bill arrive in this frightening situation, she communicates with them through secret signs: with the danger sign, then with a song in secret code that tells the boys that the man is a murderer. The boys respond with another secret sign (pinching the lobes of their ears) which means that they have picked up the information. Here, quite explicitly, children have to protect themselves from harm from the adult world through the code they have created. Secrecy is necessary for self-preservation, just as in *Nobody's Family Is Going to Change* the "Children's Army" has to conceal its existence from adults in order to function effectively as a children's rights advocacy organization.

Lindgren, like many other of the best of children's authors, is able to convey the comic incongruities of childhood experiences without diminishing their significance. In the final chapter of *Bill Bergson Lives Dangerously,* after the murderer has been captured, the Whites teach the Reds their secret language. Bill explains why: " 'We can't have it on our consciences, letting the Reds walk about in such dreadful ignorance. They'll be absolutely done for if they ever get mixed up with a murderer' " (209). Though that statement may strike an adult reader as comic, murder is not minimized in the book. Eva-Lotta's reaction to finding the body of the murderer's victim is a state of shock that realistically lasts several days. Despite the implausibilities of the plot, the theme of secrecy is treated with a seriousness that does justice to its importance as a means of achieving identity and as a defense against the danger of harm by powerful adversaries.

Secrecy in children's literature, in a variety of forms, emphasizes the ambivalent consciousness of the adult author writing for children. The adult, having once been a child, has access to memories of childhood in the form of internalized experience—the alter ego that always remains a child within us. But the adult writer also has a mature and sophisticated consciousness that analyzes the child's experience and the child's placement in many contexts of family, society, psychological and moral development, inheritance, and environment. The triumph of the spirit in children's literature that reflects children's preoccupation with secrecy lies in skilled authors' ability to combine the dual perspectives of childhood and adulthood in an instructive tension. At the root of this illuminating tension lies respect for the development of the child's personal and social identity. Sympathetically conceived works of fiction invite imaginative participation in the experiences of fictional characters who create and discover secrets. Like fairy tales, stories about secrets and secrecy have imaginative connections with children's psychological and social development which go beyond the literary qualities of particular stories. But the artistry of works such as those discussed here connects the private world of the child's imagination with the reality of experience and with the realm of all great literature.

Notes

1. Louise Fitzhugh, *Harriet the Spy* (New York: Harper and Row, 1964).
2. "The novel does not attempt to portray reality fully or journalistically. It is rooted in Harriet's experience, and that is a limited experience. If, then, characters seem like caricatures or types, this is justified. We can only experience them when and as Harriet does. The merits of this limited point of view result from the distortion it causes." Virginia Wolf, "Harriet the Spy: Milestone, Masterpiece?" in *Children's Literature* 4 (1975), 123. See also Wolf's article, "The Root and Measure of Realism," in *Wilson Library Bulletin* 44 (1969).
3. (Philadelphia and New York: J. B. Lippincott, 1911).
4. In a symbolic and disappointing way, the garden eventually opens up to include not only virtually every character previously outside it but also the gender and class values of elite Victorian society. See Elizabeth Lennox Keyser, " 'Quite Contrary': Frances Hodgson Burnett's *The Secret Garden*," in *Children's Literature* 11 (1983). As U. C. Knoepflmacher's discussion of Burnett's "Behind the White Brick" suggests, secrecy in Victorian children's stories can exist in a subversive association with aggressions sublimated into dreams ("Little Girls without Their Curls: Female Aggression in Victorian Children's Literature," in *Children's Literature* 11 [1983], 26.).

5. (New York: Pantheon, 1958).

6. Mark Twain, *The Adventures of Huckleberry Finn* (London: J. M. Dent and Sons, 1955).

7. In a discussion of children's oaths, Iona and Peter Opie write, "it should be emphasized that the asseverations in the following pages (mostly collected from ten- and eleven-year-olds) are not treated lightly by those who use them. An imprecation such as 'May I drop down dead if I tell a lie' is liable to be accorded the respect of its literal meaning, and distinct uneasiness may follow its utterance, even when the child concerned is fairly certain that he has not departed from the truth" (*The Lore and Language of Schoolchildren* [Oxford: Clarendon Press, 1959], 121).

8. Trans. May Massee (New York: Doubleday, 1929).

9. (Philadelphia and New York: J. B. Lippincott, 1966).

10. (New York: Viking, 1954).

6.

Secrets and Healing Magic in "The Secret Garden"

GILLIAN ADAMS

> The maintenance of secrets acts like a psychic poison, which alienates their possessor from the community. In small doses, this poison may actually be a priceless remedy, an essential preliminary to the differentiation of the individual.
>
> *Carl Jung*

Opinions differ on why Frances Hodgson Burnett's *The Secret Garden* is such a powerful and compelling work of children's fiction, particularly for its female readers. One critic, for example, finds the key in the special "contrariness" of Mary; another recognizes the garden as "the symbolic center of the book" but thinks that it is about "the completion of a process of mourning"; a third concentrates on the relationship of the garden to the georgic pastoral tradition and its central trope, rebirth through the cooperation of man and nature.[1] On the other hand, the title of the book calls attention to secrets as well as to the garden, and the revelation of the secrets hidden in the labyrinthine house as well as in the gardens of Misselthwaite Manor are what is generally best remembered.[2] For the child protagonists, Mary and Colin, the discovery of that which is secret both depends on and results in progressive spiritual development: first, development of the ability to "like" others and oneself, to think positively; second, development of the ability to use the imagination to further the healing process of positive thinking; and finally, development of the ability to realize that positive, imaginative thinking is part of something greater, the "magic" of God's creative power as it manifests itself in man and nature.

The importance of having a secret and of being able to keep it, particularly from adults, has been recognized as an important element in the process of a child's discovery of himself as a separate individual.[3] The fact that the child can have a secret that his parents do not know and cannot find out, unless he permits them to, places a boundary between himself and them over which he has total control in theory, if not in practice. The presence of that boundary confirms the child as an individual being, and the sense of control over something uniquely his own increases his self-esteem. Moreover, the possession of a secret, particularly an important one, gives children and adults the power over their superiors and their peers that comes from special knowledge, a power which can be exercised by granting access to the secret to a privileged few. Paradoxically, although the act of granting access may result in a feeling of power, once the secret is known there is a resultant loss of power which must be compensated for by another gain. In addition, a secret is a two-edged sword, and Burnett makes clear the distinction between good and bad, or sick and healthy, secrets as well as between good and bad childhood power.

At the beginning of the story, Mary is a victim of the wrong kind of secret and exercises the wrong kind of power as a result. Mary herself had been kept a secret by her mother who directed the native nurse (in India) to "keep her out of sight as much as possible" with the result that the servants "always obeyed her and gave her her own way in everything" lest she disturb the adults; in consequence, Mary is "as tyrannical and selfish a little pig as ever lived"(2).[4] Thus Mary is corrupted by the power granted to her in order that she may remain a secret, as in a similar fashion later in the story Colin, also a secret, although by his own choice, is corrupted by his power over the servants. In the case of both children, being a secret and the misuse of power are connected with negation in the form of ill-health and death; in India, Mary who "had always been ill in one way or another" (1) is the only survivor of the cholera epidemic, and Colin's illness, which he believes to be fatal, dominates the second half of the book.

Mary is initially a healthier child than Colin, however; not only is she able to survive cholera, but she has another source of power Colin does not possess, a love for gardening. For Mary a garden is not only something which is her own, but it provides her the opportunity, even when her gardens are make-believe, for productive labor ("something to do" as she puts it), which will prove an eventual source of self-esteem.[5] The importance to her of her garden is indicated by her angry, rude reaction to Basil, the son of the English clergyman who puts her up temporarily, when he offers a polite suggestion for its betterment. His response, to taunt her with the nursery rhyme "Mistress Mary Quite Contrary," provides her with a nickname that signals her distinguishing characteristic for the first part of the book, contrariness.[6] Mary's increasing sense of isolation exacerbates her contrariness; when Mrs. Medlock, the housekeeper at her new home, Misselthwaite Manor, informs Mary that she should not expect to see her uncle Mr. Craven and that she will have to look after and play by herself, in short, that she is to remain as isolated and as "secret" as she was in India, she "perhaps never felt quite so contrary in all her life" (29).

Mary's contrariness has its source not only in her isolation, a situation created by adults, but in her negative judgments of others and of herself, the result of that situation. The situation starts to change when she encounters the young housemaid Martha on the morning after her arrival at the Manor. Martha, unlike Mary's Indian servants, is not "obsequious" or "servile," and talks to Mary as an equal, leaving Mary to wonder at her "freedom of manner" and thus providing Mary with her first positive model of a young person of health, strength, and independence. Martha's account of her family, particularly her brother Dickon and her mother Mrs. Sowerby, interests Mary in something outside herself for the first time in her life, as does Martha's further revelation of the existence of a secret garden, kept secret by Mary's uncle and his wife during her lifetime, and now even more secret since she was killed there by a falling tree branch (62).

The next twelve chapters recount the gradual change in Mary from a contrary, negative thought pattern to a more positive one. The change is initiated by Mary's discovery of the unhappy self hidden within her, her own secret, a necessary prerequisite for starting to think positively about others.[7] The means for Mary's self-discovery are first provided by the irascible old gardener Ben Weatherstaff's friend the robin. Deserted by his companions, the robin's isolation helps Mary to discover that the loneliness generated by her own isolation is "one of the things that made her feel sour and cross" (50). In addition, Ben identifies Mary with himself, allowing her to see herself for the first time as others see her. The discomfort she feels at Ben's negative remarks about her leads Mary to wonder if she is really as "nasty–tempered" as he says, and, contrary to his judgment of her, she talks gently to the robin in a way totally new to her; as Ben remarks, "as nice an' human as if tha was a real child instead of a sharp old woman" (52).

That Mary's discovery of her secret, that she is lonely and has a nasty temper, causes a change of heart is indicated by her subsequent frequent use of the word "like" in reference to Martha, Ben, the robin, and Dickon. She still lacks self-esteem, however; in response to Martha's query about Dickon, Mary says, "He wouldn't like me . . . no one does" and to the crucial question, "How does thou like thysel'?" she answers,

"Not at all—really, . . . but I never thought of that before" (78). In spite of her negative vision of herself, liking others is enough to grant her access to the second secret, the hidden garden. Her compliment to the robin, "You are prettier than anything else in the world," is her first compliment to anyone, and is followed by his indirect revelation of the key and the door it opens (32).

At this point in the text, Burnett connects Mary's change of attitude with the growth of her imagination:

> Living as it were, all by herself in a house with a hundred mysteriously closed rooms and having nothing whatever to do to amuse herself, had set her inactive brain to working and was actually awakening her imagination. There is no doubt that the fresh, strong, pure air from the moor had a great deal to do with it. . . . In this place she was beginning to care and to want to do new things. Already she felt less "contrary," though she did not know why." (85–86)

Yet Mary's imagination has been as much awakened by Martha's stories about her family and about the secret garden as by the secret rooms, her idleness, and the effect of bracing air. In any case, there is a connection between "caring," "doing," and the imagination: if a positive future can be imagined, there is reason to care for those people and things that are a part of it and a reason to work toward it. Thus when Mary enters the garden, her imagination transforms the leafless stems, wintry brown grass, and dead-looking bushes into "the sweetest, most mysterious-looking place any one could imagine," "different from any other place she had ever seen in her life," and she is able to foresee its future life and health (97).[8] Mary at last has something to do; noticing some bulbs, she frees them from weeds and is "actually happy" in her "new kingdom" (102), "becoming more pleased with her work every hour instead of tiring of it" (112). Thus Mary's awakened imagination not only confirms a source of power she once enjoyed in India, gardening, but allows her to more richly enjoy her new source of power, the possession of a secret all her own. Mary thinks in terms of keeping her secret in isolation however; "if no one found out about the garden, she should enjoy herself always" (118).

Although Mary is now able to "like," and has a secret kingdom of her own in which to work, to imagine a future, and to be happy, she must become less isolated, less of a secret, before she is ready to use her caring and her imagination to heal others. Martha's brother Dickon provides the means for ending her isolation by becoming her first child friend. Attracted to him by Martha's account of his animal taming, Mary has long imagined what he would be like; once she meets him, the attraction grows. She finds, however, that she must let him into the garden if she wants to continue her association with him, even though doing so makes her feel "contrary," "obstinate," "imperious," "Indian," "hot," and "sorrowful" (127). It is not only Mary's new ability to like that makes it possible for her to share her secret with Dickon; it is the nature of Dickon himself, clearly a Pan-figure, "an un-self-conscious nature child."[9] "I don't like havin' to hide things" he says (200), but he does have secrets of a sort: he must constantly keep secret from other boys the location of the lairs and nests of the wild animals he has tamed. Dickon is too healthy to need to have secrets of his own, but only keeps secrets in order to protect others, perhaps because he has been granted permission by his mother, with whom he has an ideal relationship, to have "all th' secrets tha likes" (201). Unlike Mary, who thinks that "nothing belongs" to her and needs a secret kingdom of her own to give her power through nature, Dickon has enough power over nature to have gained the allegiance of a small natural kingdom.

Thus Mary can share her secret with Dickon because she recognizes that he deserves the trust of vulnerable creatures like herself, as she later says, "because birds trusted him." (237). Mary has identified herself with the robin, who has acted as the initial intermediary between her and Dickon. Yet Dickon does not see Mary as the male robin, but as the more vulnerable nesting, presumably female, missel thrush (139), whose nest must be kept a secret and protected.[10] Dickon's protective stance toward Mary as thrush occurs after she has revealed to him her second, personal secret, that of her contrariness, a secret at which Dickon laughs, saying, "there doesn't seem to be no need for no one to be contrary when there's flowers and such like, an' such lots o' friendly wild things runnin' about" (137). Once Mary recognizes that Dickon does not view her "contrariness" as a serious handicap but sees her positively, as a bird he wishes to protect, she dares to ask him if he likes her, "a question she had never dreamed of asking any one before" (137) and is assured that both he and the robin do. She is further rewarded for sharing her secret by being confirmed in her personal freedom (Mrs. Sowerby has already advised that a governess be postponed) and in her possession of "a bit of earth" by an ill and distracted Mr. Craven (149).

Mary is now no longer isolated or mentally or physically unhealthy (as remarks about her increasing good looks indicate). She can think positively about five other people, and she thinks positively enough about herself to take the risk of asking someone whether they like her. She has acquired a healthier power than the despotic power she once had in India, the power conferred by productive labor and by the possession of her own secret kingdom. She has discovered that granting access to her kingdom has its compensations, in fact enriches her, and she now is ready not only to share her secret again, but to use her awakened imagination as a means for healing people even sicker in mind and body than herself.

The process of exploration and discovery is another source of power and autonomy for children. Although Mary wants to find the secret garden, her discovery of the key and the door it unlocks takes place not because she searched for them, but because the robin "showed the way." On the other hand, the secrets of the house, "even stranger" than those of the garden, are revealed as the result of boldness generated by her "rebellious mood" at her enforced isolation (155). Her forbidden explorations of the secrets of the hundred rooms provide examples of the dynamic between the excitement of discovery and the growth of the imagination as she plays with the elephants in the cabinet and talks to the portrait of the little girl so like herself. Her most important discovery, and the one on which she will most exercise her power and her imagination, is that of her invalid cousin Colin Craven. Burnett makes clear how alike the two children are, with one essential difference: even in the midst of death, it had never occurred to Mary that she would not live, while Colin, although there is no specific threat, thinks that he is going to die: "he was too much like herself. He too had had nothing to think about. . . . He thought that the whole world belonged to him. How peculiar he was and how coolly he spoke of not living" (163). When Mary informs Colin of the existence of a secret garden, he is as attracted as she had been by the idea, and Mary triggers the revelation of his unhappy self, his self as symbolized by the portrait of the dead mother he looks so much like. Colin keeps the portrait secret because he hates his mother for dying, believing that if she had lived he would not be always ill and his father would have not hated to look at him. Not only does he hold his mother responsible for his condition, but he needs the kind of power over her he can get by withholding her from others and keeping her a secret, as he says, because "she is mine and I don't want every one to see her" (160). The same need for power motivates Colin to keep Mary a secret, although to do so is not necessary, since Mrs. Medlock will follow his orders in regard to having Mary come and visit.

Subsequently, Mary begins to heal Colin in much the same way she has been healed. Mary's effectiveness as a healer is based on her ability to use both truth and fiction and the power generated paradoxically both by her contrariness and by her growing "liking" for Colin. Her willingness to tell Colin the truth and to convince him of it puts her in sharp contrast to the medical professionals, particularly Colin's personal doctor and cousin who has clearly, probably unconsciously, exacerbated Colin's problems by encouraging his hypochondria. In her most powerful scene Mary, summoned by the nurse to deal with Colin's hysterics, fiercely takes charge of the frightened adults and uses a combination of bad temper and gentleness to convince Colin that he is not deformed. A description of what the garden might be becomes her ultimate weapon, a kind of incantation, through which Mary tames Colin as if he were one of Dickon's animals. The indication of the change in him is his use of the word "please" to Martha the next morning, a word no one has heard from him before.

Mary mixes truth and fiction to further heal Colin, "catching his fancy" (247) as hers had initially been caught by Martha's mention of the garden and stories about Dickon. Mary manipulates Colin's imagination, which, unlike hers, was already awake and stimulated by the books he reads, by fashioning stories based on her experiences in India and with Dickon and his animals, the robin, and the garden. She even imagines Colin to be like a young Indian rajah and confers the title upon him (and the power behind it) to such an extent that he comes habitually to use the formula "you have my permission to go" (260). Mary uses her stories to do three things: to relax Colin sufficiently to put him to sleep without "bromides"; to make him laugh; and, most importantly, to turn Colin's imagination away from himself, the past, and his largely imaginary illnesses, and toward others, the future, and good health. Mary is able to help Colin because, although she has as many negative thoughts about Colin as she does positive ones, she is still more capable than any of the adults of seeing him in a potentially positive light and imagining a future for him. Once Colin has started to think positively and to move away from the despotic, hysterical little hypochondriac he once was, he is able to tell Mary that he likes her and wants to meet Dickon and his animals. As was true in Mary's case, Colin's declaration of a liking for others wins him access to the garden; at his declaration Mary is struck by the realization that he can be trusted and reveals that she has found it.

Now that the secret garden has become less secret, the new secret is the physical healing of Colin, which, like the garden, is to be kept from the adults (with the eventual exception of Mrs. Sowerby) as long as possible. Thus a secret which centered on a place, the garden, has been enlarged by a secret which centers on a process, healing, and the boundary of the secrets is no longer drawn around one or two individuals, but is drawn between the children and some adults; it has become, in short, a conspiracy. Hand in hand with this enlargement of the boundaries of the secret, is that of the process of healing; Mary is no longer the sole healing agent, but is helped by the garden, the spring, and Dickon and his animals.

The shift from Mary as healing agent is accompanied by a shift from Mary's mental processes to Colin's.[11] The new focus is signaled by Burnett's comment in chapter 20 about Colin's imagining of spring: "shut in and morbid as his life had been, Colin had more imagination than she [Mary] had and at least he had spent a good deal of time looking at wonderful books and pictures" (261–62). Colin's imagination now has become so powerful that once it is turned from the imagination of death to the imagination of life, it moves to an extreme position; by the end of the chapter, as he is wheeled into the garden he cries "I shall get well! I shall get well!" (267). As the story progresses, however, imagination becomes incorporated into the area of magic, a term that begins to occur with increasing frequency. Martha has remarked, the morning after Mary has quieted Colin's tantrum with her fictions, that Mary "must have bewitched him!" "Do you mean Magic?" inquires Mary. She adds that she has heard about magic in India but cannot make it (177). Yet her stories and incantations do cast a magic spell on Colin, in spite of her denial and in spite of the fact that she never says that she wants to make any attempt at healing. Her descriptions of the garden, as well as her manipulation of Colin's great desire to see it, are the basis of her magic power.

While the servants think the magic that changes Colin happens through Mary, Mary thinks that Dickon is somehow responsible, given the power he has over wild things. For example, Mary thinks it is Dickon's magic which sends the robin to distract Colin just as he is going to ask about the tree which killed his mother: she "quite believed that Dickon worked . . . good Magic on everything near him and that was why people liked him so much and wild creatures knew he was their friend. She wondered, indeed, if it were not possible that his gift had brought the robin just as the right moment when Colin asked that dangerous question" (274). Dickon, on the other hand, believes that the spirit of Colin's mother is at work since Dickon's mother has told him that "maybe she's about Misselthwaite many a time lookin' after Mester Colin, same as all mothers do when they're took out o' th' world"(273–

74).[12] Whether the magic stems from Mary, Dickon, or Colin's mother, it is caring about the welfare of others that provides the impetus for its use.

Another source of magic is nature. When Colin asks Dickon if he is, in fact, making magic, he hands the process for making it over to Colin. By doing so Dickon unites the magic in nature with the magic in a human, in this case Colin who now has sufficient self-esteem to like himself, and identified also with nature: "Tha's doin' Magic thysel; . . . It's the same Magic as made these 'ere work out o' the' earth" (284). Burnett describes the magic in the garden at great length, and equates it with the growing plants and flowers and the movements of the small animals and insects there. Taking his hint from Dickon, Colin also amalgamates the two sources of magic, the natural and the human. "The Magic in the garden has made me stand up and know I am going to live to be a man" (300) and "her Magic helped me—and so did Dickon's"(301). Colin sees magic as what is positive and life-giving in man and nature and realizes that he must incorporate it into his thinking and then use the power of his thought to effect his own cure.

> I am going to make the scientific experiment of trying to get some and put it in myself and make it push and draw me and make me strong. Every morning and evening and as often in the daytime as I can remember I am going to say, "Magic is in me! Magic is making me well! . . . If you keep calling it to come to you and help you, it will get to be part of you and it will stay and do things."(301)

Burnett makes clear that Colin's experiment works for him; after he first walks around the garden saying "The Magic is in me," she comments: "It seemed very certain that something was upholding and uplifting him"(307). That something turns out to be more than the force generated by liking and being liked by others and himself, and more than the force of nature. When Colin declares, "I'm *well*—I'm *well* . . . and I shall never stop making Magic"(342), he feels the need for performing some final act of confirmation: "I feel as if I want to shout out something . . . thankful, joyful."(342). The singing of the Doxology, at Ben's dry suggestion, by all the children connects the Magic with its ultimate source, God, as Colin recognizes: "Perhaps it (the Doxology) means just what I mean when I want to shout out that I am thankful to the Magic. . . . Perhaps they are both the same thing"(344). Mrs. Sowerby makes a similar connection, naming the magic the "Big Good Thing" and the

"Joy Maker" which makes "worlds by th' million—worlds like us" (350).

Now that Colin is healed by the magic and on his way toward fulfilling his resolution to become as physically strong as Dickon (301), he and Mary still must resolve their conflicts with adults. Encounters with those able to "like" have enabled them to break out of their isolation and to cease feeling like secrets themselves while possessing secrets of their own which give them a sense of power and self-esteem. As a result of those secrets, however, there are still barriers between them and the rest of the adult world with the exception of Martha, Mrs. Sowerby, and Ben Weatherstaff. Just as the realm of magic has been enlarged to include the highest authority, the Supreme Being, the realm of humanity must be enlarged to include those in authority, particularly parents. Mrs. Sowerby enters the garden for the first time during the singing of the Doxology, "looking rather like a softly colored illustration in one of Colin's books," (345), and thus endowed with the special glamour with which the imagination invests those long hoped for. Mrs. Sowerby provides the means for both Mary and Colin to resolve the relationship with their (dead) mothers. She has already taken over many of the functions of motherhood, overseeing from afar the work in the garden, giving advice, and providing healthy meals; and her transactions with her own children, based on her positive vision of them, provides a model of the ideal parent-child relationship.[13] It takes little to show plain Mary that she can become like her mother in one respect by possessing her mother's best feature, her loveliness. Mrs. Sowerby, seeing Mary as positively as she sees her own children, assures her that she will be as beautiful as her mother: "I'll warrant tha'rt like thy mother too. . . . Tha'lt be like a blush rose when tha grows up, my little lass, bless thee"(348).

It is Colin who most needs to resolve his feelings of conflict with both his parents. Colin looks like his mother, not like his father, whom he has never wanted to resemble because he is a hunchback; one of the causes of Colin's morbid fancies is that he is at the age at which his father's deformity became evident. Colin has already taken the first step toward his mother when he permanently draws the curtain back from her portrait because he likes to see her laughing: "She looked right down at me as if she were laughing because she was glad I was standing there"(337). The change in his attitude toward the portrait is indicative of his more positive attitude toward himself; his resemblance to his mother has led him to equate himself with her, particularly as a replacement for her in the heart of his father. When Mary remarks that he is so like her portrait that he might be her ghost, he replies, "If I were her ghost—my father would be fond of me. . . . I used to hate it because he was not fond of me. If he grew fond of me I think I should tell him about the Magic. It might make him more cheerful"(338). Colin here begins to see himself as the next link in the chain of healing—that he has the potential to heal his father, sick in mind as well as body, as Mary healed him, and by similar means. Since Mr. Craven's mental illness was caused by the death of his wife, Colin thinks that he can be the means of his father's return to health.

By providing Colin with a surrogate, Mrs. Sowerby separates Colin from his mother so that he can become his masculine self. The meeting between the two is like that between a mother and son who have been separated a long time. To Colin's remark, "You are just what I . . . wanted. I wish you were my mother," she responds, embracing him, "Thy own mother's here in this 'ere very garden, I do believe. She couldna' keep out of it. Thy father mun come back to thee—he mun" (352). Mrs. Sowerby does, in fact, summon the absent father home, a father whose healing has already been started by "Magic" in Switzerland. His healing is completed by the sight of Colin, as the son he has always wanted, running out of the garden, the winner in a race against Mary.[14] The book ends with the union of father and son and the triumphal procession of the two masters of Misselthwaite across the lawn toward the only remaining adults not yet privy to the secrets, the servants. The end of secrecy, then coincides with the final healing of the father by his son.

Burnett's belief in the power of positive thinking, which pervades the novel, becomes explicit at the end of it: "One of the new things that people began to find out in the last century was that thoughts—just mere thoughts—are as powerful as electric batteries—as good for one as sunlight is, or as bad for one as poison"(354). Unfortunately, Burnett's eagerness to get her final message across sometimes leads her into over-didacticism as "imagination" is replaced by "Magic and Science" and she slips from showing to telling. Nevertheless in this work, written at the end of a long career, she has successfully portrayed the triumph of spiritual power, whether it manifests itself as thinking positively about others, as the workings of the creative imagination, or as "Magic," natural, human, and divine. Just as Mary, and later Colin, in their movement from isolation, secrecy, and a dormant or misplaced imagination to community, openness, and a productive imagination are healed and heal in turn, so Burnett, by recounting that movement in her fiction, heals the myriad children and adults who have found comfort in it. In

The Secret Garden then, Burnett achieves her goal in life: during her final illness she told her son, "With the best that was in me I have tried to write more happiness into the world."[15]

Notes

1. Elizabeth Lennox Keyser, " 'Quite Contrary': Frances Hodgson Burnett's *The Secret Garden,*" *Children's Literature* 11 (1983):1–13; Madelon S. Gohlke, "Rereading *The Secret Garden,*" *College English* 41 (April 1980):894–902; Phyllis Bixler Koppes, "Tradition and the Individual Talent of Frances Hodgson Burnett: A Generic Analysis of *Little Lord Fauntleroy, A Little Princess,* and *The Secret Garden,*" *Children's Literature* 7 (1978):191–207. In her discussion of *The Secret Garden* in *Frances Hodgson Burnett* (Boston: Twayne, 1984), 94–102, Phyllis Bixler points out how Burnett transforms many of the symbolic motifs found in nineteenth-century literature written by women into "images of female celebration"; such motifs must also have a powerful psychological effect on female readers.

2. The unanimity of the responses to questions about the book in an informal survey I took of about thirty readers, ranging from adolescents to adults in their seventies, is remarkable. "It was like a secret place all my own where I could get away" is typical. I could locate only one male reader, but the response was the same.

3. See, for example, Earl Koile, *Your Secret Self* (Waco, Texas: Calibre Books, 1978), particularly chapter 9, and Sissela Bok, *Secrets: On the Ethics of Concealment and Revelation* (New York: Pantheon, 1983), particularly Chapter 3.

4. All page references in the text will be to Frances Hodgson Burnett, *The Secret Garden* (New York: Frederick A. Stokes, 1911).

5. Gardening appears to be the only productive manual labor, aside from needlework and nursing, permitted the women of the English upper classes before the Second World War. For the importance of gardens and gardening to Burnett, both as a child and adult, as a stimulus for the imagination, see her account of her childhood, *The One I Knew the Best of All: A Memory of the Mind of a Child* (New York: Scribner's, 1893), chapters 3 and 14; her son Vivian Burnett's biography, *The Romantick Lady (Frances Hodgson Burnett): The Life Story of an Imagination* (New York: Scribner's, 1927), particularly chapter 25; and the standard biography, Ann Thwaite's *Waiting for the Party: The Life of Frances Hodgson Burnett 1849–1924* (New York: Scribner's, 1974). For a discussion of work and nature, see Bixler, 98.

6. In fact the first title of the *Secret Garden* was *Mistress Mary,* and Burnett was still using that title when it was accepted in 1910 for serialization by *The American Magazine* (Thwaite, 222). For an analysis of Mary's contrariness, see Keyser.

7. Bixler, 97.

8. In her autobiography, Burnett tells how as a child her imagination

transformed an enclosed garden, long shut up and abandoned, in a similar way (*The One I Knew the Best of All,* 254–260).

9. See Koppes, 199, for an analysis of Dickon as a Pan figure.

10. For a discussion of birds in women's literature that is pertinent to this passage, see Ellen Moers, *Literary Women: The Great Writers* (New York: Anchor, 1977), 372–382. Mary's growing intimacy with Dickon parallels her movement from male or neutral to female identifications and behavior patterns. For Mary's "female nurturant power" and the garden as womb, see Bixler, 100–101. The identification of the missel thrush with Mary is echoed by the name of the Craven house, Misselthwaite.

11. In the final seven chapters of the book, Colin is the dominant character. Mary is silent in the final chapter; the last words in the book are "Master Colin." Critics and ordinary readers think this an unsatisfactory situation; child readers, as adults, remember little of the end of the book. Keyser finds that only the section of the book in which Mary predominates meets her adult criteria (13), and that the consequence of Colin becoming a man is that "Mary will have to become a woman—quiet, passive, subordinate, and self-effacing. . . . Mary cannot escape the role that civilization has assigned her." Keyser connects "Burnett's ambivalence toward Mary and her indulgence of Colin" with conflicts in Burnett's own life (9–12). Other reasons for the lack of reader involvement in the end of the book may be the loss of excitement when secrets no longer remain to be discovered, and the author's growing didacticism (see below).

12. Burnett was interested in Spiritualism, Theosophy, and Christian Science and believed that the dead were present for the living. In a letter to an old friend she says, "They have not gone away from you—those who loved you every hour of their lives. They are close to you—they are a guard around you—they are talking to you—listening to you—taking care of you as you took care of them. When a helpful and uplifting thought enters your mind, one of them has put it there." (Vivian Burnett, 378).

13. The source of Martha and Dickon's strength and the gnomic wisdom that they pass on to Mary, Mrs. Sowerby is the mother of twelve children who is "put to it" to get porridge for them on the sixteen shillings a week that her husband, mentioned only once in the book (38), provides. Her poverty does not prevent her from being the only adult in the book who is portrayed positively.

14. In order for Colin to conclusively abandon his "feminine" role as an incapacitated male and confirm his masculinity, he must beat the stronger female in a physical contest. Keyser sees Colin as a surrogate for Burnett's son Lionel, who died of consumption in 1866, and "his recovery a wish-fulfilling revision of what actually happened" (11). Like Colin's, Lionel's father, Dr. Swan Burnett, actually was a cripple. Elaine Showalter in *A Literature of Their Own: British Women Novelists from Bronte to Lessing* (Princeton: Princeton University Press, 1977) notes that "it is a commonplace in feminine fiction for the sensitive man to be represented as maimed" (127). Colin is much more interesting as an invalid than when he is healthy and either exercising or preaching.

15. Vivian Burnett, 410.

7.

Diary of a Dream:
Triumph of the Creative
Spirit of Elizabeth Yates

JANICE M. ALBERGHENE

Certain phrases bring to mind immediate associations. For example, consider the following sequence of words: "the triumph of the spirit." Among other things, the phrase suggests achievement in the face of adversity. But what of achievement in the face of luxury, in the face of every possible advantage that a warm, loving, wealthy, and intelligent family can provide? Whence comes motivation for one who apparently lacks nothing? Such was the context in which the spirit of young Elizabeth Yates triumphed. She was the recipient of "great gifts—security, discipline, and their [her parents'] love," yet as demonstrated by the autobiography *My Diary, My World*, privilege can be a formidable foe indeed.[1]

My Diary, My World compresses into one volume Yates's selection from her diary entries and notebooks from 1917 (when she was twelve) until 1925. Adult readers tempted to extrapolate from the values which inform *Amos Fortune, Free Man* (the fictionalized biography which won Yates the Newbery Medal in 1951) might expect to find the following in Yates's record of her own youth: high ideals, a keen awareness of social injustice, belief in nonviolent resolution of conflict, the tenacity to hold fast to a dream and see it through to its realization, and affirmation of the human ties that link the individual to every other person in the world.

Extrapolating from a book's values to its author's character can be risky business (awful people do sometimes create works of truth and beauty), but in this case the extrapolation yields more than a passing similarity. Even Yates's comment on her own reading of *Amos Fortune, Free Man* indicates an important trait shared by author and character alike:

"... Amos lived by a dream within him though she [his wife Violet] did not know the dream. Always she thought of him as

climbing some mountain in his mind. . . ." Putting the book
down, I thought how true that is of everyone who sets out to
achieve an objective; especially of those who are their own
taskmasters, as writers are.[2]

A significant difference, however, separates the stories of Yates and
Fortune as climbers of mountains. Violet Fortune did not know the exact
shape of her husband's dream, but she knew that whatever it was, she
supported both it and Amos Fortune. Yates's parents knew the shape of
her dream—her desire to be a professional writer—yet opposed her out
of love, concern, and the conviction that writing was wrong for a girl in
her well-heeled station in life. Speaking as paterfamilias, Harry Yates
told Elizabeth, " 'Writers, like artists and musicians, are born. Such
talent is not in our way of life. For you to try to be one might only be to
break your heart. Your mother and I want you to be happy' " (145–46).
Declaring " 'It applies to people in our position,' " Mary Yates suggested
that her word-hungry daughter might want to add "dilettante" to her
vocabulary (103).

These instructions did not fall on deaf ears, and therein lies the
dramatic tension at the heart of *My Diary, My World*. Like many young
adolescents, Elizabeth Yates both questioned and needed the approval of
her parents, but the rigor of their standards and the force with which she
felt and to a large extent internalized them mark her situation as
exceptional. A number of the entries in *My Diary, My World* record
Elizabeth's reactions to parental expectations, but the one which follows
is paradigmatic in its outline of her response:

> As usual, Father asked me if I had been at the head of my class
> today.
>   It's nice when I can say yes, because Father's smile and the
> twinkle in his eyes mean more than the gold star on my report
> card, but I had to say, "Not in arithmetic."
>   He looked so sad that it made me resolve to try harder than
> ever tomorrow. (19–20)

Not "good," not even "excellent," but "the best," the status of "head
of the class" is what's required. And not on some occasions, or most
occasions, but on every occasion. The penalty for failure is all the more
severe for its apparent mildness. Her father's "twinkle" is replaced by his
sadness. Conscious of causing pain, and not merely displeasure, Eliza-

beth strives to do better rather than to question a standard which is nearly impossible to meet.

When she does question a standard, her subsequent remorse prompts her to add her own self-punishment to the reprimand that has already been delivered:

> When Mother lectures me her words hurt more than a hundred bullets, and why can't I ever say anything in my defense? Why can't I ever do anything right?
>
> Maybe I am selfish and inconsiderate. If so, I'd better do some kind of penance the way monks did in the old days. When I went to bed I decided to sleep on the floor, rolled up in a blanket. (41)

Only an overriding need could withstand such opposition from without and questioning from within. Day after day, the diary shows Yates's conviction that she *was* born to be a real writer, not an amateur decorating the society pages with her pen:

> December 6, 1918
> The part [in *The Blue Bird*] I like best is the Kingdom of the Future, where Father Time says that each child born in the world must bring something to the world.
>
> I think I came with a pencil in my hand. (36)

> June 11–15, 1920
> Could someone take the pencil out of my hand, tear up my notebooks, say I was to write no more? No! Then and there I vowed an awesome vow that what I had to do I would do, and that no one would stop me. (66)

> October 14, 1921
> [from a passage describing a lesson with her teacher, Miss Watkins]
>
> She talked to me about my mixing of metaphors and asked me to bring her a single sentence that would be explicit. I worked hard and this is what I brought to her: "The forge of the years is before me: I know that only on the anvil of persistence with the hammer of hard work can I shape my dream into reality."
>
> Keeping her red pencil in her lap and smiling, she said, "You're really serious about your work, aren't you?"
>
> Of course I said yes. (93)

Given the influence of her parents, the "awesome vow" Yates made in the second of these three diary entries would have had little chance of fulfillment if it had not been in league with a faculty (sometimes deliberate, but as often unconscious) for subverting or revising any efforts to deter her from her ambition to write. Elizabeth's spirited imperative to create versus her family's desire that she assume a position of social privilege is the subject of the remainder of this essay.

My Diary, My World begins with a muffled act of rebellion which signals the imminence of Elizabeth's fall from the Eden of childhood harmony with her parents. The muffled aspect of Yates's rebellion is literal as well as metaphoric; the reader first meets young Elizabeth as she ignores "them calling my name" and continues to write while snuggled in her father's clothes closet, a spot she calls "one of my secret places" (7). As a closet writer, she defines her private space not only in terms of the psychic space created by the act of composition (cf. the implications of the title *"My Diary, My World"*), but also by the seclusion the physical space affords. In the beginning, this seclusion is secure, containing as it does reassurances that Elizabeth is not really cut off from her family—in particular, from the source of its authority, her father. The smell of his costly suits and shoes, an almost palpable reminder of his person, keeps her company.

Closets confine as well as protect, however, so it is not long before Elizabeth finds herself in open conflict with her parents. Pleased with the acquisition of a new term, and sure that the word "must mean something brave and strong," Elizabeth proudly announces at dinner that her teacher called her a "heretic" (20). When Mrs. Yates responds with the dictum that religion and politics are not appropriate for discussion at a meal, Elizabeth explodes in anger and she and her new word are banished from the table. Reconciliation with her parents follows shortly thereafter, but from here on in, Elizabeth is a fallen creature propelled by words from childhood's state of grace.

Setting the terms of discussion is a time-honored method for assuming control of a situation or argument. Mrs. Yates did not limit her use of this technique to the conversation at dinner. She redefined words as needed in her efforts to direct her daughters' energy and skill (first the older girls', then Elizabeth's) toward the proper management of a well-established family's home. What less euphemistic households call "chores" or "housework," Mrs. Yates called "privileges." Defining housework as a privilege is more than an act of verbal dexterity; it establishes the primacy of the domestic sphere and asserts that participating in the activities for its maintenance is a noble vocation in and of itself.

Mrs. Yates's use of the word "privilege" reflects her belief that her daughters need not look outside the home to find fulfillment.

Although Elizabeth nowhere voices an overt challenge to her mother's view of housework, her acceptance (at times enthusiastic) of various household "privileges" is linked to their fostering her development as a writer. Elizabeth's knack of turning drudgery to good account was all the more effective for appearing to have been less a conscious process than an instinctive response. When she initially concedes that her mother might be right about housework, it is "because something besides the doing is always there, too" (22). That "something" (a curious circumlocution on Elizabeth's part, as if she were imitating her mother's art of linguistic camouflage) is storytelling, either by the servants who work with Elizabeth, or by Elizabeth herself as she wonders and weaves histories in her mind. Later, helping to serve at one of her parents' dinner parties, she listens to the conversation and picks up "actual knowledge" which she subsequently puts to use during an exam at school. Her high score wins her a copy of *The Autobiography of Benjamin Franklin,* an excellent text for inspiring an ambitious girl (61–63).

Even more inspiring to this particular girl was her adored older sister Jinny, who looked like a Greek goddess, didn't "get into trouble," and would be "a very great writer someday" (17). The girls' parents encouraged the younger sibling's identification with a sister who "had been good in everything whether she liked it or not" (53). Jinny gave Elizabeth reading lists and shared with her the description she wrote of her dreamed-of "well-beloved" (49).

The trouble with Jinny, however, was that in being good in everything, she was also good at being bitter about bowing not once, but twice to the superior force of her parents' wishes over her own. She had wanted to accept a position as instructor at the women's college from which she'd graduated. Her parents wanted her home in Buffalo as a debutante, so home she went. She met and fell in love with an impoverished but romantic riding instructor whom her parents sent packing. Less than three months later she was married to a "rising young lawyer" (124). Home visiting, Jinny found and read poems which Elizabeth had sent secretly to a publisher. The editors returned them with frank but friendly criticism; Jinny chose to vent her own frustration and sense of failure:

"They're sentimental drivel. Juvenile. What's more, you've plagiarized. Love! What do you know about it? All your friends are girls."

"Someday you'll be sorry for saying things like that about my
poems."

"Someday! Don't you know it never comes?"

Before my eyes she closed her hands around the pages and
crushed them, then dropped them into the wastebasket. (133)

For the coup de grace, Jinny then told the family the news that
Elizabeth had been rejected by a publisher. Elizabeth's younger brother
Bobby was the only one who didn't add words of discouragement to
those delivered by the rest of the family. The portrait of Jinny is chilling
indeed. Rather than help her younger sister, she seems to have been
determined to crush her spirit just as thoroughly as she crushed each
cherished poem. Jinny is less sister to Elizabeth than she is her mother's
surrogate in the family struggle to subdue Elizabeth's desire to write.

Facing cruelty more often galvanizes a courageous spirit than corrodes
it. Smoothing out the pages of her poetry in the "sanctuary" of her
room, Elizabeth Yates pondered the significance of the family crest
engraved on the ring she wore on her little finger: "Sois Feal. But what
does one do when fidelities conflict? No matter what the cost, I know I
must keep faith to the urge within me, but I hope I can do it without
hurting other people" (134). Jinny set a powerful negative example of the
consequences of failing to keep faith with herself; in pleasing her parents
she left herself no reservoir of joy or self-respect.

Elizabeth's persistence in holding onto her dream finally prompted her
parents to switch tactics. Their earlier attempts at dissuasion had appealed to Elizabeth's sense of duty: she must not disappoint her parents'
expectations—which were, of course, based on their superior knowledge
of what would make her happy. The girl must be made to see that her
idea of happiness was misguided. A family trip to Europe and a good
look at the pleasures afforded by such travel might make their headstrong
daughter think twice about the consequences of abandoning their way of
life for that of a struggling writer.

There is, however, more than one way of looking at a trip to Europe.
While Mr. and Mrs. Yates seem to have thought of travel as a means of
leaving behind a problem from the past (in this case, Elizabeth's desire to
write), their daughter considered travel to be "the biggest kind of
experience. Now I really have become a Ulysses 'always roaming with a
hungry heart' " (151). The full significance of Elizabeth's identification
with Ulysses becomes more apparent when set beside her interpretation
of Tennyson's poem of the same name: " 'Ulysses has become to me
almost a prayer—. . . a suggestion, half a promise, that we too may leave

our well-ordered homes behind and strike out upon the waves *to strive, to seek, to find, and not to yield*' " (141–42). For a young woman with this view of "Ulysses," ignoring and resisting parental pressure to conform had become a point of honor.

In fact, Elizabeth's resolve was so strengthened by her travel that she was appalled, rather than reformed, by the example of a distant relative who lived in the fashionable Kensington area of London. Telling Elizabeth that she and Cousin Bella had much in common, Mrs. Yates arranged a meeting between the two. Cousin Bella confided, " 'indeed I have written many stories, but no eyes other than mine have seen them. . . . I could not have endured it if they had been rejected' " (150). Elizabeth's bafflement in the face of this attitude is only natural, since she had already withstood and survived rejection, not from strangers, but from her own parents and sister.

Real lives are seldom as dramatic as the "lives" in fiction, and their plots digress at will. There is no one point at which Elizabeth Yates could declare the issue of her vocation settled; she returned from Cousin Bella's to meet her mother's reiteration of the importance of filling one's station in life. *My Widening World,* Yates's second diary, continues the story of her deepening awareness of self and her growth as a writer during the years 1925 to 1929.[3] The book also continues the story of Mr. and Mrs. Yates's resistance to their daughter's choice of authorship as her station in life. Herein lies the real significance of Yates's story: her understanding that the dreamer's hardest task is not to find her dream, but to keep faith with it once found.

Notes

1. Elizabeth Yates, *My Diary, My World* (Philadelphia: The Westminster Press, 1981), "Dedication," n.p. Subsequent references to the book appear in the text.

2. Elizabeth Yates, "Climbing Some Mountain in the Mind," in *Newbery Medal Books: 1922–1955,* Horn Book Papers I, ed. Bertha Mahoney Miller and Elinor Whitney Field (Boston: The Horn Book, 1955), 361.

3. Elizabeth Yates, *My Widening World* (Philadelphia: The Westminster Press, 1983).

II.
Surviving Social Upheaval

8.

Survival and the Imagination in Depression-set Fiction for Children

DEANNA ZITTERKOPF

When Franklin Delano Roosevelt announced that Americans "have nothing to fear but fear itself," his words provided only a modicum of consolation for the children who populate a substantial body of children's fiction set in the 1930s. Their fears are not abstractions that can be vanquished by a big dose of positive thinking. Their fears stem from the daily reality of a life marred by physical and emotional misery. Hard times have, of course, long been a stock item of children's literature. From fairy tales to Horatio Alger to contemporary ethnic literature, the struggles of the downtrodden have attracted the talents of numerous authors intent on depicting the fortunes and misfortunes of individuals coping with poverty. Seldom, however, has a body of fiction treating a particular era of American history focused so exclusively on the problems of physical and emotional survival as does a recent group of twenty-odd novels set in the Great Depression.[1]

Collectively, the books are geographically representative of the United States. Although about half are set in the rural South, the remainder take as their landscape the large urban city (*Duffy's Rocks* and *No Promises on the Wind*), the small town in the Northeast (*Dotty's Suitcase*), the Midwest (*The Growing Season* and *The Dark Didn't Catch Me*), and the West (*Pistol* and *The Velvet Room*). Perhaps because of the stark subject matter, only a few (*Her Majesty, Grace Jones, Ida Early Comes Over the Mountains, November's Wheel, Nothing Rhymes With April, The Good, the Bad, and the Rest of Us,* and *Scaredy Cat*) are written for younger children, and in these, the harshness of life in the Depression is softened somewhat. The remainder of the works are intended for older children and adolescents, and as such, are the focus of this chapter.

With the exception of Mildred Taylor's books, these Depression-set novels are the products of authors who themselves lived through the era either as children or young adults. Violet Olsen, whose *The Growing Season* treats the fortunes of a Danish-American family on an Iowa farm, herself was reared on an Iowa farm in the 1930s. The youth of Timothy Brennan, hero of *Duffy's Rocks,* loosely parallels the youth of its author, Robert Fenton. Fenton, who grew up without a father, spent a year of his adolescence on the bum in New Orleans, "often subsisting for whole days on bananas, which in those depression days were the cheapest thing you could get."[2] Georgia writer Robert Burch says that in his novels he hopes to give young people "a glimpse of what it was like to have lived during the Depression years, when almost everyone was poor. At the same time, I try to show that we sometimes had ourselves a pretty good time back then and that there are lots of things more important than money or material wealth. . . . It was just that in my boyhood we had no choice: we had to get along without any, or much money."[3] Another child of the Depression, Zilpha Keatley Snyder, comments: "While not autobiographical, (*Velvet Room*) is in many ways a reflection of my own childhood in rural California. . . . Few things that happened to Robin ever happened to me, but writing about her responses tipped the memory-invention scales way down, in favor of memory."[4] And Crystal Thrasher knows firsthand the desperate poverty of the Robinson family depicted in *The Dark Didn't Catch Me.* As the fifth of seven children in a family who lost their farm, Thrasher moved with her family to Green County, Indiana "to wait out the Depression, or starve, whichever came first. And for a while, it was a toss up whether we would survive it or not." Her older brothers and sisters left home to work on farms for their room and board. Thrasher went to school barefoot and in ragged, misfit clothes: "Everyone in Green County was poor. But it seemed to me that we were the poorest of the lot."[5]

The commonality of the authors' memories and experiences undoubtedly accounts in part for the commonality of incident and perspective found in the novels they produced. Poverty, joblessness, bank closings, mortgaged homes, illness, death, grueling work, cardboard innersoles, outgrown clothes, a sparsity of Christmas and birthday presents—these elements are constants in the books which treat growing up in the 1930s. The passage from childhood into early maturity is usually difficult under the best of circumstances. But when it is compounded by the harshness of survival and uncertainty about the future, the experience takes on new dimensions of bewilderment and fear. Somber as the Depression works are, however, they seldom degenerate into total despair. The children depicted in this fiction not only survive, but cautiously look to the future with courage and hope rather than crumbling before the bleakness of their lives. In large part, their survival is linked to the resources of their imaginations, their fantasies and daydreams, which provide them with an escape from the adult world until they have matured sufficiently to cope with it.

Certainly escape is in order, especially since so many of the traditional sources for security in hard times are either absent or defective. Families, for example, are seldom the conventionally warm, strong units who count their blessings and cheerfully prop each other up in times of crisis. To be sure, the more fortunate children, such as Cassie Logan, the narrator of *Song of the Trees,* have loving, fiercely loyal families. But most fictional Depression children are less lucky. Improper diet, overwork, and the lack of money for medical care cause the death of a number of the parents; others are endangered. Absentee fathers are commonplace. Some, such as the one in *Duffy's Rocks,* simply desert their families. Others, such as Queenie Peavy's, are in jail. Still others are frequently absent because out-of-town jobs provide the only family income. (Interestingly, mothers absent themselves only by dying; they may or may not suffer in silence, but they never desert their children.) Even when physically present, however, the parents in Depression fiction are usually so embittered by poverty or so preoccupied with survival that they fail to perceive their children's needs and fears. These parents are not inherently cruel nor ill-natured. They love their children and in normal times would be more attuned to the problems and pain that beset them. On a day-to-day basis, however, worry and exhaustion seem to cause emotional isolation, benign neglect, or misplaced anger that often borders on child abuse.

Although his responses are extreme, Stefan Grondowski, the Polish immigrant father in *No Promises in the Wind,* typifies the plight of the family head victimized by the Depression. Without a job, he finds that "his industry, his shrewdness and thriftiness were worth nothing. He was powerless to save his home, to feed his family properly, to feel an ounce of pride or confidence in himself" (16). In anger and frustration he lashes out at his family, until his tirades force his son Josh to leave home. Likewise, Enie Singleton, the heroine of Mildred Lee's *The Rock and the Willow,* finds herself at odds with a bitter father who demands unquestioning obedience and hard labor from his children and who is hostile to his daughter's desire for an education. Enie's mother shelters and helps her children when she can, but when the mother dies, Enie is saddled with all the family's domestic responsibilities and a morose, often illtempered father. Family tensions also mar the home life of Seely Robinson, heroine of *The Dark Didn't Catch Me.* Seely's mother complains that

she has "nothing to look forward to, nothing at all" (62). Whenever
Seely's father comes home from his out-of-town job, he stays only long
enough to exchange his dirty clothes for clean ones and rejects his
children's bids for affection: "He never seemed to notice us kids unless
we walked between him and the newspaper. We were just as happy that
he didn't. We knew we were more apt to get the back of his hand than a
pat on the head if we were within touching distance" (63). Usually, the
tension between parent and child lessens when the circumstances of life
improve. But all too often, prosperity is not just around the corner, and
quarrels—or the fear of them—cripple the quality of family life, causing
it to be an additional source of anxiety rather than a buffer against the
world.

Religion, another conventional mainstay for the oppressed, provides
curiously little consolation for the victims of the Depression. For many
families, religion simply is not a part of the fabric of life and is seldom
alluded to. For others, the outward trappings are there—they attend
church, say grace at meals, and observe taboos against swearing—but
there is little sense of faith as a shield against calamity, at least as far as the
children are concerned. Seldom do the latter regard God as a source of
refuge and protection. In *Dotty's Suitcase,* for example, when Dotty
Fickett and her friend Jud are lost in a snowstorm, they repeat the Lord's
prayer, hoping for help: "They waited, silent in the storm, holding their
breath so, in case God decided to send them an answer, they'd hear it.
None came." The children are not surprised (83). For Enie Singleton, in
The Rock and the Willow, God and grace are remote concepts. She knows
she is expected to join the Pleasant Grove Baptist Church, but she
postpones membership because she vaguely "wasn't ready" (27). Occasionally Enie recalls her mother's admonishment that "God moves in
mysterious ways His wonders to perform" (140), but typically she lacks
her mother's spiritual acceptance of adversity and deals with her misfortunes independent of outside help. Other children, such as Marie Carlsen
in *The Growing Season,* try to reconcile their understanding of God with
the tragedies of life but end up more depressed than ever. When a
neighbor and a baby die, Marie concludes: "If there was a God, he didn't
care. And if he didn't care what happened to people, then there just as
well not be any" (147). It is a frightening realization for a child.

Given a world dominated by poverty and want, parents who often
misunderstand, neglect, or abuse, and a God who is apparently indifferent to them, it is inevitable that the young people who inhabit the
fictional terrain of the Depression should turn elsewhere for solace. Some
are buoyed by the bond of love and sympathy that exists between

brothers and sisters. For others, friends or a sympathetic teacher help make misfortune bearable. For almost all the children, however, the force that most commonly sustains the spirit is the imagination. It manifests itself in a number of ways: mere wishful thinking; prolonged, elaborate daydreams; creative ventures via writing and music; and the losing of self in the magical stories of others. But whatever its form, the imagination supplies children with a rich inner life which compensates for an impoverished outer existence. It replaces ugliness, fear, and failure with beauty, security, and accomplishment. It offers a haven from harshness until the circumstances of life improve. And by providing an alternative existence—whether fleeting or prolonged—it prevents entrapment in a mentality of despair and hopelessness.

The ready-made imaginary worlds of others are extremely attractive to the children of Depression fiction. Books in particular represent a passport from reality and are prized for the release they offer. Because of their poverty, however, most characters own few if any books. Libraries are usually nonexistent in rural communities and school holdings are often meager. As a result, the children read—and value—almost anything that is available to them. Some of their fare is traditional: *The Secret Garden, Ivanhoe*, poems such as "O Captain! My Captain!," and fairy tales such as "The Ugly Duckling." But they are just as likely to be caught up in *The Forsythe Saga*, the comic strips in the *Des Moines Register*, a dictionary ordered from Sears Roebuck, or pulp fiction in magazines that come their way by chance.

Oral stories also provide an uplift for the spirit. Robin Williams, for example, is enchanted by the historical tales of Bridget, an elderly, eccentric neighbor. Enie Singleton and Marie Carlsen find the drabness of their lives relieved by the imaginative resources of two Depression drifters who do farm work in exchange for room and board. Enie's unhappiness is lessened by Seedy Culpepper, a young man who sits on the porch after dark, playing a harmonica and spinning "incredible, yet irresistible tales" (113) derived from his life on the road. After he has lived with them for a short while, Enie realizes that "Seedy had put a spell on them all. . . . Even Papa" (117). A tramp named Nick does the same for Marie and her brothers and sisters. Marie realizes that Nick's tales about giants, wizards, movie stars, gangsters, and his own adventures are a mixture of fact and fancy, and she appreciates them as such. They give her life an element of excitement and enchantment—and they make the long days in the field pass more quickly.

More commonly, however, the children of Depression fiction live in worlds of their own making and their involvement in these worlds is intense and often sustained. Typically they have "secret" places—caves, willow-lined creeks, woods, city streets, pig-house roofs, deserted houses—where they isolate themselves from family tensions and the deadening responsibilities of the real world. It is in these retreats that they have the freedom and the leisure to construct rich fantasy lives which range from futures as famous fashion designers and writers to reunions with idealized, perfect fathers. As the characters begin to make the transition from childhood to maturity, however, they also begin to realize that they cannot live out their lives in escapist fantasies and idle daydreams. Although the world of the imagination remains vital to their existence, it takes on new directions and dimensions. In some cases, precious dreams are painfully relinquished. More typically, however, the dreams are amended, not abandoned; often they are converted into goals which offer the possibility of future realization. Hence, because the imagination continues to sustain the spirit, the children continue to be able to face life. In varying degrees, this pattern emerges in virtually every novel examined for this study.

Dotty's Suitcase is not as grimly realistic as some of the Depression novels. Nevertheless, its heroine, Dotty Fickett, has good cause to live a wildly imaginative fantasy life. Her mother is dead. Her father is a loving, but taciturn man who frequently works late, and her best friend, Olive Doherty, has moved away. Dotty also worries about her father's financial struggles, and "couldn't imagine what it would be like to have enough money or—praise be!—too much" (38). But Dotty can and does imagine what she'd do with vast sums of money: she would buy a monogrammed suitcase and depart for an exotic landscape such as Africa, with its mango trees, ostriches, crocodiles, and dancing girls with diamonds in their belly buttons. Dotty would like to be pretty and glamorous, an aspiration which leads to Hollywood fantasies of Greta Garbo, Katherine Hepburn, and Shirley Temple.

When she recovers a suitcase of stolen money, Dotty tries to translate her dreams into reality by traveling to visit Olive. Unfortunately, the dreams cannot be sustained. Olive's father has died and the Dohertys live in dismal squalor. Olive spends most of the reunion crying, and a count of the suitcase money produces only $200, not the million or trillion Dotty had assumed was there. Touched by Olive's plight, Dotty leaves the stolen money under her friend's pillow. On the bus ride home, she feels "strange, as if she had been asleep for twenty years, like Rip Van Winkle" (141). Awakening to the significance of her adventure, she realizes that despite her genteel poverty, she is rich compared to many people. Looking at her reflection in the bus window, Dottie also finds her movie star fantasies punctured. She is merely a "sappy-looking girl," not a Shirley Temple look-alike (145). Armed with these insights, Dotty prepares for a reunion with her family and further confrontations with a less than perfect existence. The fantasies which earlier had buoyed her spirit are not totally cast aside. She alights from the bus still pretending to be a movie star. But simultaneously she is now a more mature child, and she has less need for the suitcase escape. Accordingly, she resolves to place the suitcase under her bed and not use it "until the depression is over and the sadness goes. I'll keep it until Olive smiles again and forgets the bad things and we can go somewhere together." Significantly, the "somewhere" will not be to the India or Nile of Dotty's fantasy, but "maybe just to Utica. Or someplace where they had a skyscraper" (145–46).

Robin Williams, a fourteen-year-old member of a migrant family, likewise uses her imagination to blot out the ugliness of her life. Desperately unhappy with her gypsy-like existence, Robin gains access to an abandoned Spanish ranch house in which she discovers a "Velvet Room" filled with books, elegant furniture, pictures, and the diary of a young girl who had lived there in the 1890s. Palmeras House satisfies Robin's need for permanence and beauty by permitting her to escape into the past. Her parents are not insensitive to Robin's misery, but nevertheless, protest her proclivity for "wandering off" and her trance-like reveries when she is present in the family's tenant shack. As Robin's responsibilities grow so does her withdrawal. During the apricot harvest, she works in a hot pitting shed ten hours a day, seven days a week. As the days drag by Robin retreats mentally to the Velvet Room, recreating its cool, silent peace. "The picture was so clear sometimes, that for whole minutes it shut out everything else: all the dirt and heat and wind; all the tired dust-colored people; all the crying babies and scolding mothers. Sometimes it could even shut out the flies that crawled up the backs of Robin's sweaty legs and the smarting cuts on her fingers" (127). When Robin must choose between leaving with her family or remaining on the Palmeras ranch, she discovers that she *can* live in the real world, rather than having to retreat to the safety of the Velvet Room. Admittedly, Robin's imagination almost causes her to "wander off" permanently from her family and reality. But simultaneously, it seems unlikely that she could have survived unscarred without the solace it provided.

On the outside, Catherine Peavy, the heroine of Burch's *Queenie Peavy,* appears to be a child solidly grounded in reality. Only an eighth grader, she chews tobacco, kills and skins squirrels, does chores on a broken-down farm, and expertly imposes punishment on children who torment her about her jail-bird father. Queenie's outer composure is, however, merely a tough facade for a wounded, confused girl trying to make the passage to maturity. By nature, Queenie is a doer and not a dreamer. Nevertheless, even she indulges in daydreams of a more perfect world. After reading "The Barriers to Moonlight," a pulp romance with an improbable happy ending, Queenie visualizes herself as the story's heroine, newly married, rich, and envied by her class tormenters to whom she waves from the deck of an ocean liner. A trip to the spring with the buttermilk elicits a fantasy of the future in which she can afford an electric refrigerator. But Queenie's favorite dream is of a united family. She longs for her father's release from the penitentiary, and idyllically imagines his return will solve all her problems. When her father does in fact return, he is irresponsible and insensitive, not at all the loving, supportive man of Queenie's dreams. Saddened, Queenie realizes her loyalty to her father has been misplaced and that he "was not the father she wished him to be. She must not lie to herself about that or anything else" (145). Older and wiser, she gives up the unrealistic fantasies which had sustained her in the past and resolves to face life as it is—and to make something of herself and her future.

For Seely Robinson, life is a series of sharp reprimands, parental bickering, desperate poverty, and bewilderment about her own physical maturation. Unlike their mother, who hates the remoteness and dark hollows of the southern Indiana hills, Seely and her brother Jamie regard the terrain as a magical wonderland. In spring, the wildflowers provide an element of beauty in an otherwise drab existence. More importantly, a sheltered cave beside the rushing Lick Creek offers the children a special secret retreat from the adult world. There Seely and her friend Doris pretend they are in flight with Amelia Earhart or at dinner with the Roosevelts. Seely also finds solace in writing, and through her creativity transforms the hollow shelter into a cave like Ali Baba's. Seely's prag- matic mother has little use for wishes or stories, which she terms "lies." For Seely, however, the stories aren't "really lying. It's just seeing things the way you want them to be or telling the story different from the way it really happened to make it funny and happy" (106). Unfortunately, Seely's life is not a story she can provide with a funny, happy ending. Jamie drowns in the creek, economics force the family to move again, and the dreaded menses begins. Simultaneously, however, Seely realizes that life has changed and she has changed; without Jamie she no longer wants to remain a child forever. Their loving, imaginative play in the woods fortified her in past days of darkness and helped her tentatively face a more promising future: "There's a kind of light in the woods when you know where to look for it. They are not all shadows and darkness. If you stand back and look at the woods, you can always find a path through them. I've roamed these hills and hollows from one end to the other, and the dark didn't get me" (171–72).

City children also employ the imagination to make the unbearable bearable. Timothy Brennan hates Duffy's Rocks, a shabby milltown suburb of Pittsburgh, Pennsylvania. He loves his stubborn, Irish grandmother, but resents her prejudiced, rigid values and chafes against her determination to keep him separated from his father, whom he last saw at age seven. Timothy's need for independence rather than constriction compel him to seek a substitute existence in escapist daydreams. Each Saturday he dresses himself in a suit and tie, takes his weekly $1 earnings from emptying furnace ashes and goes to downtown Pittsburgh. Sometimes he visits museums, hotel lobbies, or restaurants. But his favorite pastime is a pretend game in which he picks, from each store window, the one item that he most wants for himself. His outings are his salvation: "The whole week, to him, was a trough between his Saturdays. It was the thought of them that made it possible to endure all those dreary weekdays which led up to them" (16). In his fumbling efforts toward maturity he sometimes attempts to merge his pretend world with the real one. Certain that he belongs in the world of an affluent matron whom he casually met at a symphony concert, Timothy manages to arrange an invitation to lunch. The visit does not go well. Timothy's lower class background and attitudes clash with those of his hosts and he once again finds himself alone. Following a bitter confrontation with his grandmother, Timothy goes to New York on an unsuccessful quest to locate his father. But the trip does have its benefits. From a series of interviews, he learns that his father is not the ideal of his daydreams but a charming, irresponsible cad who ties himself to no one. When he returns home to his dying grandmother, Timothy realizes that rather than living in an imagined world where beauty, love, and material comforts are magically given to him, he must explore himself and use his resources and talents to acquire the things he wants. In short, he accepts the reality of his unpleasant existence, but he retains his dreams of a better future.

If dreams can sustain, the lack of them can also destroy, particularly if the child is forced to sacrifice them prematurely. Such is the case in Irene Hunt's *No Promises in the Wind,* a grim slice of life which focuses on a set of characters who often are deprived of dreams and hope. As the book opens, Josh Grondowski can endure his father's rages and the family's poverty because of his mother's love and the refuge provided by music, particularly his piano improvisations. Once circumstances force him to leave home, however, Josh is forced to relinquish the imaginative and creative outlets which served as an antidote to cynicism and despair. Initially—and naively—Josh, his brother Joey, and a friend, Howie, believe they can support themselves as itinerant musicians. But Howie is killed when the boys are hopping trains and in the days which follow the two brothers experience the ugliness of robbery, the anger of the dispossessed, and the humiliation of scavenging for food. As he reflects on his bleak existence, Josh realizes that hunger has replaced hope in his life: "[Before] there had always been the dream of playing in an orchestra, dreams of the recitals which I would one day give, of the praise and acclaim my art would inspire. With Howie I had sometimes planned to run away, to roam the world . . . to see sights and have adventures and come back heroes. . . . Not anymore. There were no dreams now, no hopes, no interests except in finding food enough to keep Joey and me alive" (71–72). True, Josh is fortified by his attachment for Joey and the two boys do encounter a number of kind, caring people as they bum their way through the Midwest. More often than not, however, it is anger, pride, and fear that keep Josh going. Powerful though these emotions are, they do not sustain him for long. As his positive inner resources decline, so does his health. Ill and desperately hungry, he drives Joey away from him and comes close to dying. Fortunately, he is given sanctuary by an Omaha trucker and as he slowly begins to recover his physical and mental health, he also begins to recover some of his old dreams. Josh is matured by his experiences; he is willing to forgive his father and to return to Chicago. He is also prepared to convert earlier idle fantasies of a career in music into reality. One wonders, however, if Josh's early maturation is worth the suffering he endured. His story— almost a tragedy—is that of a child forced to give up his inner imaginative world before he had developed other resources which could sustain his spirit.

Depression-set fiction possesses no monopoly on hard times and the use of the imagination as a coping mechanism. The motif commonly appears elsewhere in children's literature. But it appears with greater frequency and intensity in the novels which treat growing up in the 1930s and, in fact, seems to serve as a common denominator for this subgenre of historical fiction. Despite its seemingly narrow perspective, the literature about the Depression era carries important implications for children. Both individually and collectively, these books encourage young people to imagine a better world, even if it is a wildly fanciful one. The novels tell youthful readers that life can be hard, and children can be victimized by poverty. But they also stress that even in the worst of times, the imagination can and does nurture and sustain the spirit. More importantly, they suggest that when childish things must be put away, escapist elements can be discarded without violating the basic dreams and hopes that make endurance possible.

Notes

1. This group of novels includes the following titles:

Branscum, Robbie. *For Love of Jodie*. New York: Lothrop, Lee and Shepherd, 1979.

Burch, Robert. *Queenie Peavy*. New York: Viking Press, 1966. And *Ida Early Comes Over the Mountain*. New York: Viking Press, 1980.

Engel, Beth Bland. *Ride the Pine Sapling*. New York: Harper and Row, 1961.

Fenton, Edward. *Duffy's Rocks*. New York: E. P. Dutton, 1974.

Green, Constance. *Dotty's Suitcase*. New York: Viking Press, 1980.

Hunt, Irene. *No Promises in the Wind*. New York: Follett, 1970.

Karp, Naomi. *Nothing Rhymes with April*. New York: Harcourt, Brace, Jovanovich, 1974.

Langton, Jane. *Her Majesty, Grace Jones*. New York: Harper and Row, 1961.

Lee, Mildred. *The Rock and the Willow*. New York: Lothrop, Lee and Shepard, 1963.

Milton, Hilary. *November's Wheel*. New York: Abelard-Schuman, 1976.

Olsen, Violet. *The Growing Season*. New York: Atheneum, 1982.

Richard, Adrienne. *Pistol*. Boston: Little, Brown, 1965.

Slaatten, Evelyn. *The Good, the Bad, and the Rest of Us*. New York: William Morrow, 1980.

Snyder, Zilpha Keatley. *The Velvet Room*. New York: Atheneum, 1965.

Taylor, Mildred. *Song of the Trees*. New York: Dial Press, 1975. And *Roll of Thunder, Hear My Cry*. New York: Dial Press, 1976.

Thrasher, Crystal. *The Dark Didn't Catch Me*. New York: Viking Press, 1975. And *Between Dark and Daylight*. New York: Viking Press, 1979.

Waldron, Ann. *Scaredy Cat*. New York: E. P. Dutton, 1978.

2. Doris de Montrevilla and Donna Hill, eds., *Third Book of Junior Authors* (New York; H. W. Wilson, 1972), 83.

3. Annie Cammine, ed., *Something About the Author* (Detroit: Gale Research Co., 1982), 1:39.

4. *Something About the Author,* 28:194.

5. *Something About the Author,* 27:222.

9.

The Survival of the Spirit
in Holocaust Literature
for and about Children

LEONARD M. MENDELSOHN

In June 1944 Allied troops massed for what was to be a successful assault on the beaches of Normandy. The days of the Third Reich were numbered, yet five months later in Budapest a twenty-one-year-old girl stared resolutely into the faces of three Nazi riflists, who casually readied themselves to snuff out her life. Inside of a year from the monumental landing in France, Germany had surrendered. Between two titanic episodes in which epic designs were soon to be matched by achievements of illustrious proportions was this event, dwarfed in significance by the saga-like circumstances on either side. For all its lamentable properties, the death of a young girl before a firing squad appears to be in the wrong company, mismatched in tone, in substance and in relevance.[1]

It was, to be sure, a tragic incident; a small, inevitable part of the fall out from great conflicts. The execution of the little known Hannah Senesh can be put down as yet another outrage which any legitimate historian, properly endowed with antiseptic emotions, knows should be consigned to footnote, biography, or family chronicle. For organization's sake, it was best bundled with a multitude of like barbarities, or, better still, sanitized as a statistic. Anecdotes, like multicolored weeds, can wrench the appearance of an otherwise meticulously tended garden of wisdom. Besides, not every Greek merits mention simply for spattering his guts on Troy's walls. In the interests of scholarly decorum, one could declare Hannah's fate a tear-soaked digression from a stately narrative relating the liberation of a continent.

Yet there remains a lingering suspicion that this private atrocity belongs narratively right where it stands chronologically, equidistant between the outcome and the design of the largest collective commitment of armament, manpower, and intellect in the twentieth century. If it disturbs continuity, then it is because the epic tenor linking an Allied onslaught with an Axis defeat is more tenuous than it seems. The homely, if sad, tale of the girl from Budapest provides a stern challenge to any presumed tonal connection between two towering events. It is a wedge in the truest sense, separating a pair of entities which for all their apparent affinity, just might not belong together. If such is the case, then the death of Hannah Senesh would prove an episode of crucial import, carrying with it the power to endow relatedness upon two separate episodes, or else to expose associations and grandeurs which did not in fact exist.

Hannah Senesh, despite what she herself would wish, calls into question the logic of linking encounters simply because they both happen to be epic-sized, and then shaping them to fit a theme of heroic victory over satanic intent. If there was such a triumph, then there must be a demonstrable degree of continuance, and the continuity should involve more than advancement of plot or sustaining of tone. There must be evidence of survival, not necessarily of the principals or of their group, but of their ideals and spirit. Without the survival of Hannah Senesh perhaps it could be said that D day simply marked the conclusion of the military domination of the Third Reich, and that Nazism, far from suppressed, merely moved into a new arena of activity.

It is the likes of the obscure and finally futile efforts of Hannah Senesh, far more than any dynamically enforced capitulation of Nazi Germany, which provides encouragement in the often frustrating search for hints of the triumph of the spirit. At the same time, it must be admitted that accompanying her remarkably unflagging idealism is a nagging doubt, one which she herself never entertained. Perhaps the commendable principles for which she willingly staked her life were themselves eloquent and emotive statements of the ultimate vanity of human endeavors.

The real fate of Hannah Senesh, the determination of whether or not she did survive in a spiritual sense, carries with it more than casual implications for any verdict on the outcome of the Great War. The assessment of her accomplishments may not have been completed, and she may not loom large in the annals of military history. Still, like a fishbone in the throat, she may be a small intruder to the great and complex body; but she must be dealt with or there are likely to be modifications in existence itself.

There are other, more obvious reasons why Hannah Senesh cannot be ignored. Unlike the overwhelming majority of her martyred coreligionists, Hannah eluded anonymity. She left a scattering of letters, poems, and a diary, sufficient testimony to an articulate and sensitively dedicated soul. From an early age (the writings which remain date from the age of twelve and the recollections of her mother extend back still further), she was inflamed by selflessly intense feelings, a sensibility which by no means precluded a confident sense of self worth. Her poems are decidedly optimistic concerning the purpose of human life, and her loving fortitude never wavered, even when she stood knowingly near the shade of perpetual eclipse.

But eulogies, however deserving, simply conceal for a brief moment an uncomfortable and self-centered concern with Hannah Senesh. The stark query inevitably reemerges. Are admiration and fine words enough to convince any of us that Hannah has survived? It is not for her sake that we probe her writings, and meditate on the known fragments of a promising life aborted by a clash of ideologies in which, initially at least, she took no part. Did the spirit of Hannah Senesh triumph, or was she simply another of those devotees who ascended the terrestial soapbox and mouthed sentiments to the winds?

The life and the fate of Hannah Senesh pose discomfiting suggestions concerning the significance of the grand events which dominated the world during most of the scarcely more than two decades of her existence. Can anyone truthfully maintain that such spirit, heeded by few even during her lifetime, could prove resilient more than forty years after her demise?

Survival is a shifty term, one often invoked as a euphemism whenever continuity is subject to doubt. The notion is sure to surface in any consideration of literature of the holocaust, a subject riddled by queasy uncertainties. During these superlatively bleak times even the inspiring examples of human conduct, and there are many of them, inevitably prove as worrying as the ever prominent bestialities. Were noble efforts and unflinching self-sacrifice evidence of the vain endeavors of the virtuous when matched against the might of the wicked, aided by the innumerable hordes of the uncaring? The psalmist's oft-stated question of why the wicked flourish while the good suffer hovers ominously over the entire genre. Here there are few answers offered, but a minority of them satisfactory, and perhaps none to console the reader. Certainly there is nothing at all resembling King David's unshaken confidence that the elusive rationalization of a divine plan is attainable, if so far hidden.

Ebullient faith to those who don't share it can be woefully distressing, and cynicism can provide a flimsy but palliative barrier against despair. *The Diary of Anne Frank* is rendered all the more unnerving through her incessant manifestations of a zeal for living. Her capacity to sustain such appealing and quintessential human passions despite prolonged existence within cramped conditions and exposure to the pessimism and selfishness of a number of her companions in hiding, argues eloquently for the durability of the spirit. On the other hand, a knowledge of her fate is likely to dampen the reader's assurance that survival was attained.

Unquestionably, she proves capable of dealing with even those always painful adolescent hostilities, though deprived of such temporary balms as space and solitude. Restrained but apparently undeterred by the extended nightmare of Nazi occupation of Holland, she maintains the conviction that people are basically good, and the reader does not know whether to laud the conviction of an emerging saint (who just happened to have been gassed at Bergen-Belsen before her sterling spiritual properties could fully mature), or to choke upon a naivete which might underline a fact that beautiful attitudes necessitate perversions of reality.

Holocaust literature implicitly raises queries which send readers scurrying after philosophic exits, escape routes as spiritually confining as those garrets, sewers, and bunkers where untold thousands sought the means of extending their lives and their sensibilities. The literature penned by children as they experienced horrifying conundrums which even quieter hours cannot resolve is particularly unnerving. In fact, holocaust literature is singular in that its material composed by children contains a compelling intensity. In it, the artistic efforts of the young often achieve an eloquence and stylistic facility equal to the poignancy of the perspective.

It is well established that the amorphous genre known as children's literature comprises but few documents of quality that were written by children. Compositions of the very young can be compelling, and they are unquestionably useful in probing an awareness adults seem to have lost forever. But for obvious reasons such writing lacks elements of style and technique which more often are the fruits of experience than of talent. Chukovsky parades a substantial number of stunningly apt utterances which he culled from a lifelong professional involvement with children. These are suggestively clever, at times naively astute. But they are never sustained. Every parent has a compendium of verbal facility and quaint entendres distilled from close exposure to their offspring. But a finished literary expression of the voice of childhood has been largely supplied by those who have left it behind, and who have called upon recollections to recreate attitudes long lapsed.

The literature of the holocaust contains a number of novel length recollections, such as *The Upstairs Room* by Johanna Reiss and *Upon the Head of a Goat* by Aranka Siegal.[2] Whatever their achievement, however, they pale before the austere majesty of the output of the young who wrote as they endured the world's supreme atrocity. The holocaust is laden with superlatives, and it is fitting that it should have induced a body of literarily competent material actually penned by children and adolescents. It is to these documents that we turn in a search for a survival of the spirit.

Perhaps the most searing and haunting of these compositions is to be found in a small volume containing, quite literally, the sole remains of children who passed through the concentration camp at Terezin. Although not officially designated as a death camp, Terezin was a way station for Auschwitz, a place where fifteen thousand children resided for a while, of whom about one hundred were alive when the war was over. Because of the peculiar circumstances at Terezin, there exist today more than four thousand drawings executed by child inmates, as well as forty-two manuscripts and twenty-four typed pages of their poetical compositions. They are an affecting record of the confrontation of childhood with a world gone mad.

The landscape was appropriate for the bizarre rendezvous of that vibrant onset of life that is childhood, with a demonic determination to root out every trace of life force. Terezin the fortress considerably preceded the twentieth century. It was established by decree of Emperor Joseph II, Mozart's patron, and it was named after the emperor's mother, Maria Theresa. Even in that day the methodical Germanic mind was fully employed, engaging Italian architects whose modified plans resulted in the twelve ramparts which enclose the locale in the shape of a star.

This eerie military outpost was posited in the middle of a countryside distinguished for gentle blue hills, green meadows, a variety of fruit trees, and tall poplars. It is thus an ideal left dismal, yet still hedged by a backdrop of unobtrusive pastoral lushness. Through its component parts, it emerges as the sort of place one would duly avoid while still acknowledging the manifestations of the surrounding beauty. To continue its paradoxes, it is a site suited to innocently pleasurable and inconsequential pursuits, but dedicated to the deadly business of suppressing all human joy, indeed to exterminating life itself. With such a confluence of opposites, it is no wonder at all that it was intended as a grotesque paradox, a model concentration camp. That it became the source of an extensive amount of artistic and literary endeavors on the part of Jewish children was also a reflection of the brutal mentality in its efforts to conceal the truth from an all-too-willingly credulous world. Over ninety-nine percent of the already flowering literary prodigies were eventually stuffed into Hitler's ovens.

Jiri Weil captures the full terror of a design which barbaric minds extended as a diabolic sop to soothe the selective demands of the Red Cross and, not so incidentally, to substantiate the declarations of a still vocal number who declare that the holocaust is a myth, and that Buchenwald and the like were in reality the country clubs of war-torn Europe. "Everything in this small town was false, invented; every one of its inhabitants was condemned in advance to die. It was only a funnel without an outlet. Those who contrived this trap and put in on their map, with its fixed timetable of life and death, knew all about it."[3]

To further the pretence of life as normal, children in Terezin went to school and were encouraged to draw and to express themselves in writing. Although unaware that their future had been predetermined, the children quickly grasped the contrast between the hint of beauty in the surrounding landscape and the unrelenting aura of death that constrained them in their assigned world. The attempt to coordinate these irreconcilable opposites was pursued with a degree of success which renders ghastly support for Thomas Mann's hypothesis that the ruthless workings of destruction motivate artistic creation.

Miroslav Koshek, a ten-year-old native of Bohemia, penned the following lines about a year before taking up residence in Auschwitz. The manuscript is in the characteristically immature lettering of a child's hand, but without a single grammatical aberration.

> Terezin is full of beauty
> It's in your eyes now clear
> And through the street the tramp
> Of many marching feet I hear.
>
> In the ghetto at Terezin
> It looks that way to me,
> Is a square kilometer of earth
> Cut off from the world that's free.
>
> Death, after all, claims everyone,
> You find it everywhere.
> It catches up with even those
> Who wear their noses in the air.
>
> The whole, wide world is ruled
> With a certain justice, so
> That helps perhaps to sweeten
> The poor man's pain and woe.[4]

The lines are remarkable for their refusal to succumb to pessimism despite the deathly discouragements which hem in the youthful poet. Excruciating reality leads to a set of universal truths, especially in the recognition of the undeniable agent who unifies high and low, victim and victimizer. A world amok is, incredibly, viewed as one yet governed by justice, although there is a prudent reluctance to elaborate on how such justice operates to sweeten the poor man's woe. I fear it is indulging in barbarity to applaud a wisdom and an artistic achievement undoubtedly derived from appallingly brutal circumstance. It is but a shade shy of the abominable practice of legitimizing Nazi experiments by pointing out some universal they might document. Yet is it not quite in contradiction to the Nazi intent to show that the spirit marked for annihilation did in repeated instances continue to manifest itself?

Terezin, according to Miroslav Koshek, becomes a microcosm of the worldly condition—beauty is everywhere apparent but universally unreachable. The nearness of death was a reality reinforced daily as carts, each pulled by two Jews, made their rounds through the camp to collect the between the 106 and 156 who found the hundred hour work week, the less than minimal nutrition, and the one-and-a-half square meter per capita of living space inadequate for further continuance. Terezin really didn't need gas chambers. Yet instead of giving in to self-pity at being yanked from his home and placed in this strange and unpromising proximity to dying and degradation, the young man finds the acquired awareness of the equality of all men to be a mite reassuring.

The poem is not really stoic, as there is no absolute disparagement of the human condition. Beauty and joy remain realities, fully apprehensible if inaccessible from the ghetto in which Miroslav is confined. The fact that he is curiously equal in fortune to those whose consistent arrogance inflicted pain and humiliation upon him and his people, does demonstrate a sophisticated recognition that conditions are not wholly what they seem. Even in a bizarre world there is revelation of the equal status of the human condition despite the obvious disparities which confront him at every turn.

It remains a morbid function to praise a ten-year-old, one apparently lingering on in some degree of health and sanity, for being so precocious in learning to die well—a skill he would exercise to the ultimate in a matter of a few months. It could be pointed out that for all his perceptiveness Miroslav probably had no idea how well off he was in the bleakness of Terezin. Soon he would experience Auschwitz in all its fullness, his gassing taking place about one month prior to the day on which Hannah Senesh faced her firing squad. One wonders if he, like

Hannah, would have been encouraged in knowing of the military reverses his German tormentors were then undergoing, or if he shared her conviction that even the feeblest inhabitant of human flesh could become an agent in freeing the inscrutable and divine qualities of the human condition. The impending fate of Miroslav Koshek lends a frightfully ironic possibility to one of Hannah's brightest poetic lines. Or, conversely, could it be said that the fate of Miroslav is partially ameliorated in our eyes by her perspective? "Blessed is the match consumed in kindling a flame. . . . / Blessed is the heart with strength to stop its beating for honor's sake."[5]

Whatever conclusion one chooses to reach, sardonic speculations are stifled to some degree by the cautious buoyancy of the articulate ten-year-old. A grotesquely accelerated maturity is to be decried. But as much as it hurts to say it, the statement as it comes down to us shows a spirit, however subdued, still very much intact.

Fourteen-year-old Hanus Hachenburg spent most of the year 1943 in Terezin, prior to perishing in Auschwitz on December 18. His poem speaks of a lost childhood and refers without elaboration to the hatred he has learned. Still the poem is remarkably free of bitterness, and even plays with the notion of childhood regained.

> I was once a little child,
> Three years ago.
> That child who longed for other worlds.
> But now I am no more a child
> For I have learned to hate.
> I am a grown up person now,
> I have known fear. . . .
>
> But anyway, I still believe I only sleep today,
> That I'll wake up, a child again, and start to
>   laugh and play,
> I'll go back to childhood sweet like a briar rose,
> Like a bell which wakes us from a dream, . . .
>
> Somewhere, far away out there, childhood sweetly
>   sleeps,
> Along that path among the trees,
> There o'er the house
> Which was once my pride and joy,
> There my mother gave me birth into this world
> So I could weep.[6]

It is nothing short of incredible that the bleakness of the sentiments still makes of childhood something real, not an illusion. The realm of tears which he suffers with such biting poignancy is the illusory realm.

In spite of grimest realities, pain, aborted childhood, bewilderment—the most bizarre of circumstances, the perspective somehow manages to remain a step, if barely, ahead of cynicism. Here the spirit is put to the acid test, and the abhorrent experiments of the brutal German captors, regardless of their fabled methodical thoroughness, fail to douse completely the spirit's capacity to envisage something beyond the diabolically contrived present from which there was but the scarcest hope of reprieve. Most of the Terezin documents continue to depict a world far better than the one where rank injustice is inflicted upon the innocent. And, unlike Christian utopias, this better world existed on earth.

Even so, a reader of these utterances by innocents in hell must ponder his own capacity to maintain that the spirit survives. Is there not mockery in knowing that the hiss of cyanide supplies a part of the creative drive for some of these prodigies? There is little question but that inspiration was force fed on a diet of bestiality. It is almost a relief to return to Hannah Senesh whose cruel end had in it a strong element of self-determination.

Hannah was a child of wealth and prominence. Her father had been a noted author and a respected columnist for a newspaper in Budapest. The family was completely assimilated, although they acknowledged they were Jews. Perhaps acknowledged is too strong a word, since they had no choice. In school Hannah was admired by teachers and well accepted by classmates. Nonetheless, her widowed mother had to pay three times the ordinary tuition simply because of her Jewishness. And Hannah, the prize student, was proscribed by law from claiming awards to which achievement entitled her. Neither the protests of her teachers, nor the hesitancy of the Christian girl given the prize in her stead could do anything to override this injustice. But how inane such injustices appear when contrasted with the denial to Jews of life itself. It was such circumstances, however, which molded the determination of a young girl to the degree that she, regardless of the relative comforts of her situation, would venture even life itself to achieve absolute freedom not only for herself, but for a people to whose ways she had been but marginally exposed.

It takes a peculiar metal to forego language, nationality, and family standing and to relocate elsewhere. Her mother remained in Hungary, survived the war, and apparently even escaped internment in any of the death camps. Her closest encounter with torment and destruction came from the efforts of Hannah's German captors who were trying to wring from the staunchly loyal girl the secret code through which they might destroy her fellow underground fighters. The daughter did not relent, despite her enormous affection for her mother, and, surprisingly enough, the elder Senesh was neither tortured nor imprisoned, an indication that Hannah herself might have escaped her fate had she chosen to live quietly and inconspicuously in the Hungarian capital.

But Hannah had emigrated to what was then Palestine, and the city girl found fulfillment farming on a kibbutz. Her tie to her people was so intense that she volunteered for a rescue mission which involved parachuting into Yugoslavia and then making her way into Hungary. The mission was a disaster. She was seized by the Germans almost immediately after reentering the land of her birth, and was tortured severely, although maintaining fortitude enough never to give away the slightest information. Because of her fear of torture, she had earlier contemplated ways of suicide should she face capture. Yet she proved stronger than even she had supposed she would be. Witnesses attest to the fact that she steadfastly refused to beg for mercy from her captors in order to escape the death sentence. She even disdained the offer of a blindfold as she faced her executioners.

No one should imagine that such heroism was guided by bravado or a desire for martyrdom. Nothing in her writings betrays the faintest desire for bold endeavors, least of all the courtship of the grim reaper. Before making the fated jump behind German lines, and while still secure "in the land, freedom . . . and fresh air" of Israel, she wrote:

> To die . . . so young to die. . . . No, no, I do not [wish to die]
> I love the warm sunny skies,
> Light, songs, shining eyes.
> I want no war, no battle cry,
> No, no, not I.

> But if it must be that I live today
> With blood and death on every hand,
> Praised be He for the grace, I'll say,
> To live, if I should die this day. . . .
> Upon your soil, my home, my land.[7]

Although she did not live to witness the destruction of the Nazi stranglehold upon her Hungarian homeland, it was through such perspectives as hers that there was something around to liberate. But what of the yearning sentiments of those hopelessly confined in Terezin? Do they too attest to a triumph of the spirit? Here the matter is considerably more complex, a complexity reflected in a poem by Pavel Friedmann, composed in 1942, little more than half a year after Terezin was turned into a death laden ghetto restricted to Jews. The lyric loveliness and bright colors contrast sharply with somber realities. Neither optimism nor negativity secures total domination of his world view.

> The last, the very last,
> So richly, brightly, dazzlingly yellow.
>> Perhaps if the sun's tears would sing
>> against a white stone. . . .
>
> Such, such a yellow
> Is carried lightly 'way up high.
> It went away I'm sure because it wished to
>> kiss the world goodbye.
>
> For seven weeks I've lived in here,
> Penned up inside this ghetto
> But I have found my people here.
> The dandelions call to me.
> And the white chestnut candles in the court.
> Only I never saw another butterfly.
>
> That butterfly was the last one.
> Butterflies don't live in here,
>> In the ghetto.[8]

To confront holocaust literature is to become involved with discomfiting issues. For the sensitive, there exists a frantic compulsion to search out conclusions long before they can become validated by logic, fact, or experience. It would be false comfort to hide behind theological niceties or to take refuge in despair. At such intellectual and emotional dead ends, it might be appropriate to convert Keats's concept of negative capability from an aesthetic to a moral imperative, and so sustain doubts and uncertainties while foregoing any irritably premature reaching after truth and fact.

Assuredly Pavel Friedman, wracked by the disappearance of almost all that was familiar and beautiful, stands startlingly secure upon a tightrope strung between rosy rejection of harsh reality and outright despair. The notion of loss receives a firm if simple acknowledgment, and he does not shrink from indulging in the brilliant colors he so longingly recalls. That the spirit remains operative in so unimaginably bleak environs is, to say the least, an encouraging sign that it might survive anything.

But while refraining from any rationalized suggestions that the spirit survived, it would seem a sacrilege to proclaim that it did not. To do so while residing safely beyond the walls of Terezin is essentially a proclamation that even the desire to see the yellow butterfly is gone. Pavel Friedmann maintained that butterflies do not live in the ghetto. But the statement clearly acknowledges that they do live elsewhere. More important, the human spirit which finds joy, inspiration, and longing in the dazzling yellow flight of a creature quite fragile, gives expression to such poignancy in quiet defiance of the dehumanizing web into which he has been pulled.

The experience of the death camps seems to indict all aspects of human conduct. But it must not. There are not only butterflies, there are Pavel Friedmanns who will apprehend them, no matter where, no matter under what duress, no matter for how short a time. And for the reader, these are the scraps of a reward for the necessary encounter with children's literature of the holocaust. No dreams of butterflies, no Pavel Friedmanns. No ability to imagine beyond tragedy, then there can be no epics. And without epics we are left with nothing but tired scribes composing tedious chronicles of events not worth recording. Surely it is a duty to show that the Nazis were unable to asphyxiate desire itself, and that their frame of reference should never dominate or confine our thoughts.

Notes

1. Hannah Senesh, *Hannah Senesh: Her Life and Diary* (New York: Schocken Books, 1972).

2. *The Upstairs Room* (New York: Crowell, 1972); *Upon the Head of a Goat: A Childhood in Hungary, 1939–1944* (New York: Farrar, Straus and Giroux, 1981).

3. *Children's Drawings and Poems: Terezin, 1942–1944* (Prague: Statui Zidovske Museum, 1959), 59; also published as *Only I Never Saw Another Butterfly* (New York: McGraw-Hill, 1954).

4. Ibid., 17.

5. *Hannah Senesh*, 256.

6. *Children's Drawings*, 22.

7. *Hannah Senesh*, 249.

8. Pavel Friedman in . . . *I Never Saw Another Butterfly* . . . Children's Drawings and Poems From Terezin Concentration Camp 1942–1944. New York: McGraw Hill Book Company, 1954.

10.

The Triumph of the Spirit
in Nonfiction for Black Children

JIM HASKINS

In the stories of successful blacks, the triumph of the spirit is a given. Even for those successful blacks who are thirty or younger and who were born into a society far more hospitable to them than that with which their parents had to contend, being black in America has always required a strong spirit. Sadly, not one of the many black personalities whose biographies for children I have written has not been touched by racism, and few have escaped that assault on their spirits at a very young age. Sadder still, not one of the black children who has read, or will read in the foreseeable future, one of these biographies will escape being touched by racism. They will not have to contend with affronts like "white" and "colored" drinking fountains and having to board municipal buses from the back. They will not be subject to laws forbidding blacks and whites to play checkers together in public and they will not be denied access to the "public" library, as I was as a child in Demopolis, Alabama. But they do, and will, grow up in all-black housing projects and attend all-black schools. They are, and will be, taught by white—and middle-class black—teachers who cannot or will not understand their particular needs. They are, and will be "tracked" into slow or Special Education classes by the educational system. They are, or will be, judged not by the content of their character but by the color of their skin. In short, they are, or will be, at a disadvantage in our society unless they can somehow outwit the forces that are stacked against them, unless they can somehow will their spirits to triumph over those forces.

Fully aware of how infinitesimal is the effect on their young spirits of whatever books of mine these children may read, I nevertheless make every effort to include in each biography I write for young children some sense of the difficulties the subject had to overcome as a child. Given the limits of space in a biography for young people, which must cover the entire life of an individual in about 150 pages (my limit, not one necessarily incorporated in publishers' editorial instruction sheets), it isn't possible to dwell on the individual's childhood, much less on those incidents that shaped the person's character. But to the extent that I can, I try to include some incident or experience in the individual's childhood that a young reader can relate to personally, or impersonally, as a black. I tread lightly on the latter point, knowing full well that black kids today will not really understand what it was like for Martin Luther King, Jr., to grow up in the South of the 1940s. I can only hope that the children who read the book will be able to make that time leap, for it is important that they have some sense of Afro-American history to understand the triumph of the spirit that the life of a man like King embodied.

Martin Luther King, Jr.'s, first direct experience of racism occurred when he was about seven, when his best friend's mother informed him in a hesitant voice that perhaps he should not come around anymore. He and his little (white) friend had played together, ridden their bicycles together, and been welcome in each other's homes for several years, for in the white southern mind small black children were not a bad influence on small white children. By about age seven, however, children began to be aware of racial and social differences, and at that point white parents ceased feeling benevolent toward their children's black friends.

Ralph Bunche's first shattering experience of racism came at age thirteen when, as a *Los Angeles Times* delivery boy, he was invited to an outing in nearby Venice and, with the other black delivery boy, was denied entrance to the pool. But this experience did not affect him as profoundly as his denial of membership in the city-wide scholarship honor society in his senior year of high school. At the Venice pool he had not been discriminated against personally, but as a Negro. In high school, however, he had excellent grades and because he was one of the few blacks in the school his academic record was well known. Not being named to the honor society was, in his opinion, discrimination against him personally.

The cancer of racism is so all-pervasive that it has a way of infecting even its victims. Katherine Dunham's first encounter with racism came at the hands not of white strangers but of her own relatives. When Katherine was three, her mother died and she and her older brother Albert were taken into the home of their much older half sister, who had children of her own. Their half sister was very light-skinned and so were her children, and though Katherine was too young to understand color prejudice very well she knew that because her skin was brown and her hair was tightly curled she somehow did not belong in the family.

Nor is color prejudice strictly a matter of color. Stevie Wonder, being blind, could not see colors, but from an early age he knew he was different not just because he was blind but because he was black. He'd heard his brothers and their friends talk about white kids and without ever having seen the color of his own skin he was ashamed of it and concerned that he was one of the few black kids at the special school for the blind that he attended. "I remember when I was a little kid," he recalled, "I used to listen to this black radio station in Detroit on my way to school. Like I was the only black kid on the bus, and I would always turn the radio down, because I felt ashamed to let them hear me listening to B. B. King. But I *loved* B. B. King. Yet I felt ashamed because— because I was *different* enough to want to hear him and because I had never heard him anywhere else."[1]

Many black children are sheltered from direct experiences of racism by virtue of de facto segregation: they live in black neighborhoods, attend all-black schools, and rarely come into contact with the white world except through indirect experiences—hearing their parents talk about racism, for example. But they are conscious of being different just the same and are frightened of coming into contact with whites. When young Bob McAdoo (basketball star, now with the Los Angeles Lakers) learned that as a result of court-ordered school desegregation he would have to attend a previously all-white high school in Greensboro, North Carolina, he was terrified. Never in all his thirteen years had he been to school with a white youngster, and even though he knew that most of his friends were being transferred to the same school, he spent the summer after graduating from junior high school imagining a small, scared group of black kids suddenly thrust into an otherwise all-white student body. "I thought there was going to be just a handful of black kids there," he recalled. "But it wasn't like that. There was a whole group of black people there, and I let out a big scream of happiness!" Maybe integration would work after all, he thought. But he was wrong. "The first two or three days the number of black and white students was about half and half. By the fourth day there were only two whites in the whole school. I don't actually know where they went. They just left, and never came back."[2] So, while McAdoo was saved the pain of being one of the few blacks in a white school, he came to understand in no uncertain terms that because he was black he was regarded as a virtual "untouchable" by the parents of the school's white students. Worse, the teaching staff of the school remained all white and unprepared to deal with the black students.

Like McAdoo, Earvin "Magic" Johnson, the Los Angeles Lakers star, fell victim to school desegregation. Having grown up in an all-black neighborhood and attended all-black elementary and junior high schools, he had always looked forward to attending the local black high school, which had an excellent basketball team. When he learned that he was one of the black students who would integrate the predominantly white Everett High School, he was devastated, and for the first year or so he had problems adjusting. According to his high school coach, George Fox, "there were reflections of racism around, and I don't think Earvin was as pleasant a person when I met him as he was after he blossomed into a more mature individual. He was a little moody and sulky and he would become despondent over little things."[3]

Shirley Chisholm was ten years old when she and her sisters left Barbados, where they had been cared for by relatives, to rejoin their parents in Brooklyn, New York. The first neighborhood in which they lived was predominantly Jewish, but there was little racial tension; the difference she remembers most vividly was religious, not racial. When they moved to a larger apartment in the Bedford-Stuyvesant section of Brooklyn, however, they found a much different racial climate. The neighborhood was fifty percent black, reflecting an influx of blacks, mostly from the South, and the Jewish residents, feeling threatened, were openly hostile. "The Jewish children would tell me their mothers had forbidden them to play with me," Chisholm recalls. "I was not used to black being used as a derogatory word."[4]

Being born black in America also carries a greater chance of being born poor, another condition that requires a strong spirit to endure, and to escape. For former boxing champion Sugar Ray Leonard, awareness of his family's poverty caused him to be a loner at school in Washington, D.C., where other kids had new clothes while he had to wear hand-me-downs from his older brother. Other kids could afford the dollar everyone was supposed to bring for class field trips but Ray, not having the dollar, had to stay home.

Stevie Wonder remembers when he was very young that he and his mother and brothers would go to a drydock and steal coal to keep warm. He says that, being blind, he could not see the things he did not have—on television, for example—and so was lucky in a way. But he was still aware that his family was very poor. He enjoys mimicking voices and sometimes does the voice of a "little urban white kid," which undoubtedly comes out of his own past: "My dad makes twenty-five hundred dollars a week. He gets us all the things you could ever want to eat. Our pantry is stacked with food, man. We're *never* hungry."[5]

Diana Ross could see television and for her, her father's surprising the family with a television one Christmas had an effect he did not intend. Living in an all-black housing project where "You had to be poor just to get in," and attending all-black neighborhood schools, Diana had not realized just where she stood in the societal pecking order. Seeing the beautiful clothes and fine homes of the white people on television, and noticing that except for Eddie "Rochester" Anderson on *The Jack Benny Show,* there were no blacks on television, made her feel that because she was black she was a nobody.

What caused these people to determine to succeed in spite of the handicaps presented by their race or poverty is so complex and dependent on so many different factors that it is not possible to surmise why they became successful while others, who grew up under similar circumstances, did not. In most cases, however, the key seems to lie in some of the circumstances of their childhoods.

The presence of a strong and dignified adult role model is a crucial factor. For many successful blacks, that strong and dignified role model has been a parent. Martin Luther King, Jr.'s, father, "Daddy" King, was for him that role model. Whenever he went to downtown Atlanta, Georgia, the elder King would take one of his children with him so that they could witness the way he dealt with whites. He always drove his own car, which was out of the ordinary because most black Atlantans rode the city buses. The sight of a black driving a car in the downtown section often signaled "uppity" to white Atlanta policemen, who would sometimes stop the driver on some pretext or other. Young Martin was with his father once when this happened. "Listen boy—" the policeman began. The Reverend King interrupted him. "That," he said, pointing to his small son, "is a boy. I am a man." The Reverend King also refused to shop in the back of downtown stores, as blacks were expected to do. Martin was with him when they went to a downtown shoe store and a clerk politely reminded the elder King that blacks were served in the rear. The Reverend King pointed out that the shoes were the same and he had no intention of moving. If the clerk insisted, he would take his business elsewhere. From Martin's earliest memory, his father would fix him with a piercing stare and say, "You are just as good as anybody else."[6]

Vandalia McAdoo was a member of a black parents group that met with white teachers at her son's school and tried to persuade them that black children could indeed learn. Former congresswoman Barbara Jordan's father impressed upon his children the following dictum: "No man can take away your brain." And thus, while she could say matter-of-factly to her high school homeroom teacher, "I am big and black and fat and ugly, and I will never have a man problem," she was an exceptionally confident teenager. She had every intention of being successful at something. "I always wanted to be something unusual," she says. "I never wanted to be run-of-the-mill. For a while I thought about being a pharmacist, but then I thought, whoever heard of an outstanding pharmacist?"[7]

The parents of other successful blacks, while they did not actively, or pointedly, stress dignity to their children, nevertheless encouraged the self-reliance and independence that enabled them to acquire their own sense of dignity and self-worth. Diana Ross remembers that when she was just a little girl she would sometimes wander away from home, "just to see what the rest of the world was like." As one of seven children who yearned for her parents' attention, Diana may have been testing her mother, seeing how far she could go until her mother came after her. But her mother let her try out her independence, and by the time Diana entered school she was absolutely fearless. She thought nothing of getting into fights with much older and larger children, and even when she was knocked to the ground she would scream defiantly, "I may be down but I ain't down!" The others knew exactly what she meant.[8] Earvin "Magic" Johnson also came from a large family—eight children—and learned early how to take care of himself.

In the backgrounds of successful blacks who did not have parental role models to look up to, there is always some other adult who served a similar function. Ralph Bunche's parents both died when he was young, and his grandmother raised him. It was she who decided they should move to Los Angeles, where they encountered as much racism as they had lived with previously in Albuquerque, New Mexico. After leaving one white neighborhood because their landlord, who had rented to them not knowing they were black, refused to renew their lease, they moved to another neighborhood that was largely white. Bunche wrote years later, "One day Nana sat rocking on the front porch when a neighbor strolled by and said mockingly, 'Good morning, Auntie.' Nana studied her intently for a moment, then replied. 'You must be mistaken. I have no nieces or nephews that look anything like you. My name, incidentally, is *Mrs*. Lucy Taylor Johnson.' Word of this incident got around, and from that day on Nana had no difficulty with her neighbors."[9] Ralph's grandmother always told him, "Never let anyone lowerate you," and her actions taught this lesson as well as her words.

Katherine Dunham's stepmother listened to young Katherine when she complained that her high school music teacher was teaching his students to sing songs with lyrics about lazy, shiftless, or stupid black people. Annette Dunham went to the school principal, and thereafter the music teacher was demoted to band leader and the objectionable songs were banned.

For Sugar Ray Leonard, the adult role model was a local recreation director named Dave Jacobs who, having given up his dreams of a professional boxing career because of his responsibilities as a husband and father, lived out his dream through the youngsters he trained to box. Ray's own father had been a middleweight of some promise while in the Navy but, like Jacobs, had given up his dream in favor of family responsibilities. He put his hopes on his son Roger, Ray's older brother, because he did not feel that his youngest son had what it took. It was some time before he even consented to attend amateur matches in which Ray was competing, but after seeing his son win he began to take an active interest in him.

Stevie Wonder's interest in music was encouraged by a number of adults—a local storekeeper who gave him a harmonica, a neighbor who moved and, not wanting to take her piano, gave it to Stevie, who was seven at the time. When it arrived, he ran his hands all over it, feeling the pedals, the keys, the strings. What color was it, he asked his mother. "Dark brown," she answered; and since, he had been told, his skin was a sort of dark brown too, he began to feel much better about his skin color.[10] Three years later, when Stevie was ten, Berry Gordy, president of a new black record label in Detroit that would later be called Motown, and others associated with the company became like a second family to Stevie.

Most of the successful blacks about whom I have written biographies have gone to college or, like Diana Ross, wish they had. The majority of the athletic stars enrolled in college primarily because they could pursue their athletic careers, while their parents considered the long range educational value of college more important. When Earvin Johnson left college to sign with the Los Angeles Lakers, his mother made him promise to complete his degree. Vandalia McAdoo was unhappy about Bob's leaving college to sign with the Buffalo Braves, but her husband had recently suffered a heart attack, their daughter was in college, and she was nearing retirement age. Bob signed with the Braves under hardship status, a category that enabled pro teams to sign players who had not completed their degrees but who could not afford to remain in college. Though the category was much abused by pro teams, McAdoo felt he could truthfully sign a contract on these terms.

People like Martin Luther King, Jr., Shirley Chisholm, Ralph Bunche, and Barbara Jordan enrolled at college because they were eager for more education and because they were aware that, as blacks, they needed as much education as they could get to attain a footing anywhere near even uneducated whites. All had found in books a way to be proud of being black. Reading was greatly stressed in Shirley Chisholm's family—she and her sisters received books as birthday and Christmas gifts, and her mother shepherded them to the library every week and expected them to read the three books each had checked out before they returned to the library the following week. After a time, Shirley became interested in biographies of blacks and read them avidly. She found in them the pride in her racial identity that she could not get at school, where black history was not taught and the only time blacks were mentioned was when slavery was discussed. By the time she was in high school "I had managed to find some books in the public library about our African heritage that few people then studied or talked about; I knew about the Ashanti kingdoms, for instance."[11]

My primary purpose in writing nonfiction for young people is to encourage them to read by providing them with material on their level that interests them. My secondary purpose, in writing biographies of successful blacks, is sharing with young readers what I have learned about how individuals become successful and hoping that readers will be inspired by their stories. I get feedback in the letters I receive from youngsters who have read the books, sometimes under duress: not a few contain the confession that they read the book and wrote the letter as a school assignment. However, sometimes I get a letter like the following from a boy in East Pennsboro, Pennsylvania: "I am a sixth grade student at the East Pennsboro School. I don't really have an interest in reading books but I am trying too [sic]. I really enjoyed your book *Babe Ruth and Hank Aaron: The Home Run Kings*. Your [sic] really are my favorite author. . . .I wanted to know how did you get your interest in being an author? How many books about sports did you write?"

Most of my "fan mail" is about my sports biographies. The majority of correspondents write that the particular star is their favorite athlete or that the particular sport is their favorite. I get no sense that they were inspired by the story. But once in a while I get a letter like this one from a boy in Torrance, California about my biography of Earvin "Magic" Johnson: "I really enjoyed this book because it showed how Earvin Johnson got so great at basketball. I also liked it because he was in a family of eight so he had to take care of himself a lot of the time. It made me feel good that no matter what kind of family you are from, you can still make it big in sports. . . . I learned from this book that practicing very much will help me reach my goals and I shouldn't give up. I should keep going until I reach that goal."

A girl in Orlando, Florida got the same message from my biography of Diana Ross: "Before reading this book, I didn't know very much about Diana Ross. All I saw was the glamour and fame. Now I've realized the struggle she had getting started and how poor she was in the beginning. I also saw an undying determination. She never gave up."

And a girl in Bellville, Texas was able to appreciate the struggles of Martin Luther King's early life: "The things that interest me the most in this book are that it tells the history of the black people. It tells how they were treated in the stores, on the bus, and at the soda fountains or eating at lunch counters. Also, it tells about the Christian life of the late Rev M. L. King Sr. . . . I am really proud of you for writing this great biography of the late Rev. King, Jr."

Receiving letters like that gives a little lift to *my* spirit.

Notes

1. James Haskins, *The Story of Stevie Wonder* (New York, 1976), 27.

2. James Haskins, *Bob McAdoo, Superstar* (New York, 1978), 26–27.

3. James Haskins, *"Magic": A Biography of Earvin Johnson* (Hillside, N.J., 1982), 21.

4. James Haskins, *Fighting Shirley Chisholm* (New York, 1975), 37.

5. *The Story of Stevie Wonder,* 26.

6. James Haskins, *The Life and Death of Martin Luther King, Jr.* (New York, 1977), 15–16.

7. James Haskins, *Barbara Jordan* (New York, 1977), 13–14.

8. James Haskins, *Diana Ross: Star Supreme* (New York, 1985), 5.

9. Jim Haskins, *Ralph Bunche: A Most Reluctant Hero* (New York, 1974), 24.

10. *The Story of Stevie Wonder,* 31.

11. *Fighting Shirley Chisholm,* 48.

11.

Death and the Human Spirit
in Jill Paton Walsh's "A Parcel of Patterns"

MARY SHANER

A dreadful plague in London was
In the year sixty-five
Which swept an hundred thousand souls
Away; yet I alive!

The above bit of doggerel concludes Daniel Defoe's *A Journal of the Plague Year,* an account of the Great Plague of 1665. This chronicle of horror and pity was published in 1722; Defoe had been about five years old in 1665. But although the *Journal* does not reflect Defoe's personal experience, Watson Nicholson clearly established in *The Historical Sources of Defoe's Journal of the Plague Year* (1920) that Defoe fictionalized but little in this work. The madness and despair, the appalling death rate, the helplessness of doctor and patient alike—all are there in Defoe's sources. There also is the inevitable question "Why?" and the usual but unsatisfying answer. "It is the will of God." Defoe, as a religous Dissenter, thought this answer the obviously correct one: God was angry with the sins of seventeenth-century society and had sent the plague to bring men to repentance. By God's wrath, thousands died; by God's mercy, others survived. It is not for complex religious argument that one reads *A Journal of the Plague Year,* but rather for the pathos of the human condition when confronted by, as Defoe said, "Death itself on his pale horse." Yet surely many during that fateful year questioned, even rebelled against, the more-than-usually mysterious ways of God. It is on the level of this spiritual struggle that the universality of the experience of England in 1665 is most clearly seen. In *A Parcel of Patterns,* Jill Paton Walsh transcends the merely morbid fascination with human catastrophe by exploring the conflict between unquestioning faith in God and the unrealistic human expectation that life will be fair and that death will have meaning.

Walsh, like Defoe, bases her novel on historical fact. In 1665, when the plague broke out in the village of Eyam in Derbyshire, the villagers voluntarily chose to isolate themselves from their neighbors rather than to risk spreading the disease. The magnitude of this courageous act can be best understood in the light of Defoe's *Journal* and his sources: remaining in the vicinity of plague victims was deadly. It seems beyond doubt that the spread of the plague throughout England was partly due to the flight of people (many of them unknowingly already infected) from London, where the plague first appeared. The villagers of Eyam, by closing their parish boundaries, not only protected the unwary outsider from wandering into danger, they declined to carry it beyond their borders. By so doing, they also shut themselves off from the hope of escape by flight from the plague; they locked themselves in with death.

Around this central historical incident, Walsh constructs her moving novel. The narrator, Mall Percival, is a teenaged girl of the Puritan faith through whose eyes we watch the inexorable progress of the plague and in whose mind we see the erosion of faith, hope, and certainty. Eyam is predominantly Puritan and, in the as-yet-early years of the Restoration, hostile and resistant (although mostly passively so) to the new laws and the new parish priest, Parson Momphesson. The Puritan minister, Parson Thomas Stanley, is forbidden under the new laws to preach, or to live within ten miles of his former pulpit. He conforms to the first requirement but not the second: he continues to dwell in Eyam, with the full approval and support of his former congregation. It is to Thomas Stanley that the villagers look for leadership, advice, and spiritual consolation when the plague comes to Eyam, brought, apparently, in "a parcel of patterns" sent up from London to a tailor in the village who had been requested to make a fashionable dress for Catherine, Parson Momphesson's wife.

These two ministers, both of them devout, honorable, brave, and good, represent opposing views both of the significance of the plague and of the appropriate religious attitudes and duties of the Christian faithful in coping with it. Parson Stanley says the plague can touch no one unless God wills it, and if God wills it, human precautions against it will do no good. Momphesson argues that people should not "tempt God" by exposing themselves unnecessarily to danger. He encourages people to take every possible precaution against the plague.

A Parcel of Patterns is, like most historical novels, full of irony created by the disparity between what the characters can understand about their own experiences and ultimate fates and what a modern audience knows of these things. We are aware, as no seventeenth-century person could be, that the bacteria of the plague were carried by the fleas of the black rat, but could also be transmitted from diseased human to human by contact with the fluid from a burst swelling if one had a cut or scratch, or, if the plague became pneumonic, through the exhalations of the victim. Therefore the best advice given in the book is that of Parson Momphesson, who would have the villagers scrub their houses with rue steeped in water to drive out fleas, and burn the beds and bedclothes of the dead. To the villagers, these seem feeble gestures against the violence of the plague. A grimmer irony still is the panic fear of house pets later during the plague. The villagers fear the plague may be carried by cats and dogs from house to house, so they kill the very animals that help to keep rats down.

At first, Mall has absolute confidence in Parson Stanley and his teachings. Like her mother, she is angry and horrified when Parson Momphesson rebukes them for visiting the sick; like the other Puritans, she has faith in the literalness of the promises of Psalm 91, especially verses 5–7:

Thou shalt not be afraid for the terror by night;
nor for the arrow that flieth by day;
Nor for the pestilence that walketh in darkness;
nor for the destruction that wasteth at noonday.
A thousand shall fall at thy side, and ten thousand at thy right
    hand;
but it shall not come nigh thee.

Mall feels secure in these promises and in Parson Stanley's theory "that the Plague of God was in the land for the new mixture of religion that was commanded in the church. And still all who heard him were comforted; for those of us who stood in the bitter cold to hear him were those who much misliked the changes, and would fain have kept the old ways of worship still, and so we surely stood in less danger than those folk of Eyam whose hearts went with the changes!"[1] But this security is shortlived. The plague takes Puritans, Anglicans, and Quakers alike; the good and the sinful, the cautious and the reckless, all die in great numbers.

Like abused children bewildered by the violent rage of their heavenly Father, the villagers take the blame for the plague upon themselves. They search their souls for little faults, repent and beg forgiveness, but the plague rages unabated and God (who they dare not doubt is in control of this horror) remains apparently unappeased. Some, like Mall's father, reject the contention of both parsons that the cause of the plague is the sinfulness of the people: " 'Child,' [Mall's father] said to [Mall], 'if none know a thing, and none can know it, it were best none claimed to know it' " (67). But when father dies of the plague, Mall's mother fears that he has been punished for this speech in which he doubts God's Providence.

The extremes of this search for guilt in one's self and one's neighbors is most clearly represented in the sick madness of Agnes Sheldon. This sour woman takes each death by plague to be evidence of some terrible secret sin on the part of the deceased, however apparently virtuous their lives may have been. On the other hand, Walsh also shows the ugly indifference of those who scorn the harsh, simple faith of the Puritans, although less directly. The Squire's family, the haughty Bradshaws, "left their fine half-builded hall . . . and all their carpenters and masons departed. With them went many chances for poorer folk: sales of broth and brews and salats by cottage wives, sales of parcels of nails and iron braces from the forge, work helping and making and feeding workers and setting things to rights, which had helped put groats and shillings in many plain family purses. All this ceased and left us [the villagers] fallen on harder times" (52). The gentry, being wealthy, can flee the plague, abandoning a community that is partly dependent upon them and toward which they have at least some social responsibility. Of course, it would be unreasonable to expect them to stay and die to complete the social contract; but they might have at least tried to ease the suffering of the village by gifts of money and food to compensate for the economic losses caused by their flight. Parson Momphesson is aware of this self-centeredness of the upper classes, and uses it to strike a bargain with the Duke of Devonshire:

> "We will confine ourselves utterly within the parish bounds. And so I will promise the Duke. None shall cross the parish bounds, for life or death, until the Plague has run its course and departed from us. But where the roads cross the bound, we will use the boundary-stone to leave notes of requisition for all that we have need of, and the Duke will send us those things. . . . I will most humbly ask him for this favour; but I will tell him that unless he help us, we cannot remain within Eyam bounds, and if we cannot . . ."
>
> "From Eyam to Chatsworth [the Duke's estate] is but eight miles," said Robert Wood.

"And Plague no respecter of place and wealth," said Father, a grim understanding in his tone. (91–92)

The fear of the plague and the utter incomprehensibility of its cause bring out the worst in many, of whatever creed. In still others, a heroic courage and selflessness emerges. In many, including Mall, mere stubborn endurance becomes a kind of heroism. Although a Puritan, she sees the godly dying all around her, and begins to doubt Parson Stanley's words. She loves Thomas Torre, a man from another parish, but, even before Eyam closes its bounds, she begins to avoid him, fearing that she might somehow carry the plague to him. Her best friend Emmot, however, continues to meet with her fiancé from another village, using Parson Stanley's words to justify herself when Mall chides her for this. Mall, listening to Emmot, is torn: she has suffered and caused Thomas to suffer by her self-imposed estrangement from him. What if she has been wrong? On the other hand, as she says, "What harms will flow from it, if Parson Stanley in this be wrong!" (70). The possibility that the Puritan minister might be in error was originally unthinkable to Mall; but her independent mind will not shut out the evidence that the plague, as well as being no respecter of persons, is no respecter of creeds. She maintains the integrity of her own love and judgment, and, despite Emmot's arguments, continues to avoid Thomas.

When Emmot dies of the plague, yet another chink appears in Mall's armor of certainty. She, who in the beginning was horrified that Parson Momphesson's small daughter should be dressed in red silk and lace "fitting for a whore" (14), now sees "that life was like the flower of the field, that if you pluck it not today will not be found tomorrow. . . . For would not Emmot have done better to lie with Roland first, and made a marriage later, like the poorest girls in Eyam who go to the altar swelling with sin, and full of happiness, rather than to have waited for the proper season in her virtue, and been fed on nothing but withering hope?" (84). In the face of death, Puritan scruples suddenly seem petty, even foolish. This world and this life may be things of vanity, but how precious seem those vanities which we may lose in a moment. A little beauty, a little happiness are not so little when one is surrounded by death and grief.

Mall's mother is broken by the death of her husband and by the dreadful conflict between her faith and her grief. Her blunt, clear-thinking husband has sometimes horrified her by his views; yet she loved and needed him. She fears that God has taken him for his sins, and cannot answer back when Agnes Sheldon says so. But neither can she take

comfort any longer in Parson Stanley's teachings about the will of God;
she turns away when he comes to talk with her. Parson Momphesson's
cheery chit-chat about a new device for magnifying candlelight does her
more good, as does Catherine Momphesson's interest in her knitting
patterns. This light and worldly talk temporarily restores her interest in
living, and might ultimately have guided her past her grief to an active
will to live. But Catherine Momphesson is struck with plague and dies,
despite the prayers of Mall and her mother; and Mistress Percival,
although she has the plague but mildly, lacks the will to fight it,
especially after Thomas, believing Mall to be dead, enters Eyam, desir-
ing death too. Mistress Percival knows Thomas will take care of Mall,
and begs Mall to let her go. So Mall, in pity, ceases to beg her mother to
live, and she goes to her stern God.

In the midst of all this sorrow, Mall marries Thomas and enjoys a brief
respite from her sufferings. Her joy is yet another revelation to her of the
inadequacy of the teachings she has always lived by:

> I have heard both parsons say there is no joy in this world, and
> they are wrong, are wrong! Where man and maid are wedded to
> their own good liking, there is joy. And I have heard Parson
> Stanley say such earthly joy is but a trick, a feigning and all the
> devil's making, to lead poor souls astray. And by that I know it
> is a joy he hath not tasted, for none who in their own flesh knew
> it could mistake it so. It is from God; I think it is a foretaste of
> the rapture of the saints, given to be a beacon to us unto heaven,
> to whet our longing for our immortality. (124–125)

Thus Mall's earthly love for Thomas becomes a medium of reassurance
of the love of God. But this happy interlude is brief: Thomas, too,
contracts the plague and dies. And Mall's happy vision of a loving God
who gave us earthly joy as a foretaste of Paradise is blown out like a
candle. Suddenly, to Mall, the parsons "are right, are right"; no earthly
joy endures. Mall is further tormented by guilt, for Thomas was brought
into the village by a message she sent him saying that she was dead,
hoping that it would keep him away. So she believes her lie to him was
the cause of his death.

> The Lord our God is a harsh and a cruel God. How terrible the
> punishments he visited on the small sins of Eyam! Where was his
> mercy, when my neighbors died in torments for the theft of a
> thimble, or a wayward thought, or a careless unkind word! . . .

would the providence of an affronted God not then bring death
to me? . . . The Lord God withheld his hand from punishing me
in my death, since a more terrible punishment by far would be
my life. (129–30)

Thus Mall's spirit, buffeted by seemingly endless grief, plunges from
joy to despair. She wraps herself in the stained bedclothes from Thomas's
bed and sits down to await death. Like her mother before her, she takes
no comfort from Parson Stanley's talk of God. But Parson Momphesson
manages to sting her into at least a semblance of living: "If you are not
sick, Mall, you are well. Get up and wash for very shame! . . . What
would thy mother say, to see her kitchen thus?" (131).

"Like a dead thing," Mall cleans the house, then sits and waits for the
dust to gather that she might clean it again, and yet again. Meanwhile,
nearly a month goes by with no more deaths. The plague has passed
from the village. "And of our Eyam's sometime three hundred and fifty
souls, there were written [in the parish records] the names of two
hundred and sixty-seven dead, from George Vicars's name, 7th September 1665, until . . . October 1666" (134).

How does the human spirit survive calamity of such magnitude? Mall
has seen the deaths of friends, family, and lover. She has seen both faith
and science fail to combat the plague. What resources are left to heal this
"broken-backed life"? At first, Mall has only that pride which Parson
Momphesson pricked with his scolding, and then the mere habit of the
activity of living. Yet habit is a powerful ally to life; by habit one may
eat, even when one cannot taste food. By habit one may complete the
motions of a task the meaning of which one has forgotten. By habit one
may pick up again the necessities of life even when life itself seems no
longer necessary.

Underpinning Mall's habit of life is that same tough endurance that,
now bruised and beaten down, nonetheless has been hers all along.
Supporting that endurance is the gradual renewal of human contact,
even, cautiously, of human caring. Francis Archdale, who has also
survived the plague, has loved Mall since childhood. Although he knows
she does not love him, he begs her to marry him and come away with
him to New England to make a new life. She does marry Francis. But
when they try to leave Eyam, by whatever road, they are always driven
back, for Mall sees all about them the dead villagers and hears their
voices calling to her. She cannot leave. It is this that brings Mall to
another great resource of the human spirit: creativity.

A spell which the girls of Eyam had sometimes practiced, "a simple for heart's sorrow," required that one "name the source of trouble, carefully writing down the cause of grief upon a paper" (136). Then the paper should be hidden away or burned, and it would carry the sorrow away with it. Francis urges Mall to try this remedy. So Mall writes the story of the plague in Eyam, and the creation of this book eases her heart. That humanity can make art out of tribulation is an oft-proven fact; it is one of the triumphs of our nature, although not a cheap or painless one. Mall turns her saga of sorrow into a coherent story. She looks squarely at her losses and, while she cannot make them less wasteful and baffling than they in fact were, she can by confronting them finish them, give them closure. The telling of her story lightens Mall's heart; the exercise of her creativity sets her free.

But what of Mall's damaged faith? In the beginning, she had, like any good Puritan, certitude: she knew what would please and displease God, and was to some extent sure of God's very nature. But her experiences during the plague did not conform to what she "knew." Her expectation that the justice of God would protect the good from the plague while punishing only the evil proved false. Even her brief vision of physical earthly joy as a foretaste and promise of Heaven seemed a delusion in her despair at the loss of Thomas. At no point did she consider that there might not be a God, but in her despair she arrived at a darker, grimmer conclusion: there is a God, and He is cruel. Even her own survival seemed no mercy, but a refinement of that cruelty. Parson Stanley's own certainty concerning the goodness of God's will was an offense to Mall's sorrow. Parson Momphesson at least offered her no absolutes, no platitudes: "It may be, some day, there will be a physic found for Plague," he said. "And will God's will then cease to be done? Doubtless God wills all things, but it is not for us to know his reasons, or his way of working. As he hath reminded us in the Bible, we were not there when he laid the foundations of the earth" (130–31).

It is of significance that Momphesson quotes the *Book of Job* here, the only reference to that book in *A Parcel of Patterns*. Job's story, that of the righteous man stripped, apparently capriciously, of every earthly good save his life, is perhaps the most appropriate of all Bible texts to the events of the novel. For Job rejects the arguments of his false comforters that he must somehow have sinned and deserved his fate; he will not take the path of guilt and accusation that so many seventeenth-century Christians took. Nor will he follow the advice of his wife to "curse God and die," the solution which Mall very nearly arrives at. Rather, he demands an answer of God, and receives that quoted by Momphesson. We know less about God than we think. God's only defense against the accusations of humankind is just Himself, as it is His only answer to our question, "Why?"

Mall's faith, like her spirit, is somewhat healed by the telling of her story; but, also like her spirit, it is never to be the same again. She is still a Puritan; indeed, the move to New England is partly influenced by the strong Puritan presence there. The real difference in Mall is revealed in the prayer with which she ends her writing: "And may God better understand and love us, than we, in our weakness, can do him" (137).

It is a brief prayer, almost a bitter one. But, Job-like, Mall stands by what she knows, what the plague year has taught her. She knows she is unable to understand or love God fully; and she knows she needs to be understood and loved by Him. She declares a kind of truce between herself and God. If God's best answer to mankind is just Himself, so Mall's best answer to God is just herself, weakness, confusion, bitterness, and all. It is her triumph to stand just as a doubting, questioning mortal and to look at God's acts as straightforwardly as she can, acknowledging that, through human weakness, in some ways she cannot. It is not the rock-hard assurance on which her first faith was built, but that burned away; this is what survived the furnace. It will endure.

Notes

1. Jill Paton Walsh, *A Parcel of Patterns* (New York: Farrar, Straus and Giroux, 1983), 62. Subsequent quotes from this volume will be followed by the page number.

III.

Myth and Fantasy
and Some Real Life, Too

12.

Abused Children and Their Triumphs in Literature

FRANCELIA BUTLER

The old folktales are full of abused children who overcome disaster to win out in the end. Rejected by parents and cruelly treated by older siblings, the younger sons, and often the daughters, ride to triumph against all odds. The Cinderellas in hundreds of versions are dirty, poor, and overworked—mistreated by older sisters and a wicked stepmother and either neglected or lustfully pursued by a father—but they end up as whole and happy personalities. All this has been pointed out in detail by the Freudian critic, Bruno Bettelheim, and the Jungian, James Hillman. Such tales can not help but bring consolation and hope to downtrodden children of almost any age or circumstance.

My favorite among cruelly treated youngest sons is Prince Ivan, who goes in search of a firebird that has been eating his father's fruit from an orchard near the palace. The older sons are first commissioned to catch the firebird, but they fail, and it is only then that the father, who is the czar, gives Ivan the chance to catch the bird. Ivan not only succeeds, but in the course of his travels, also procures a golden cage for the bird, a horse with a golden mantle, and a beautiful maiden. All this he does with the help of a gray wolf which may be an externalization of his good intuitions.

But Ivan is too trusting. On his way home with his treasures, he falls asleep under a tree. His wicked brothers find him there, chop him into small pieces, and make off with the bird, the horse, and the maiden. At home, they take all the credit for the conquest.

Meanwhile the gray wolf finds out what has happened to Ivan and sends a raven to the ends of the earth for the waters of life. When the raven returns, the wolf takes the water he brings and sprinkles it all over Ivan. Slowly, Ivan rises, yawns, and stretches. "Ah, I have slept long!" he says. He is a whole man again.

When he returns home, the beautiful maiden who had been too

terrified to speak the truth tells the czar the whole story. The wicked brothers are thrown in a dungeon, Ivan and the maiden are married, and the old czar retires and makes Ivan his successor.

Similarly, Cinderella emerges from her trials a joyful human being, even though her experiences may have included sexual abuse or the threat of it from her father, as some of the old versions suggest.

In an early seventeenth-century tale in Giambattista Basile's *Il Penta-merone,* a widowed king pursues his beautiful daughter. A servant gives the girl a piece of magic wood for protection. Whenever her father approaches, the maiden slips it into her mouth and turns into a she-bear. On one occasion, the chase is so furious that the girl runs into the woods. A handsome hunter takes aim to shoot the seeming beast, but something about it makes him pause. Eventually, he makes a pet of it and takes it home.

From there on, the story is very much like that of the frog prince, in which an enchanted prince, turned into a frog, becomes a man again through the power of love. In Basile's story, the beast ultimately sleeps with the hunter (also a prince, or at least a prince of a man) and, lo and behold, in the morning he discovers a beautiful maiden in his bed with whom he instantly falls in love.

With most good stories, the reader identifies with the protagonist, at least partially. With one folktale I read as a child, I identified almost completely. Of all stories it was my favorite. It has the psychic components of many traditional quest stories. As a child of eight or nine, I used to read it over and over again. I read it intensely. Tears would come into my eyes as I read along, and then I would close the book at the end and feel great joy and comfort. That story was "East of the Sun and West of the Moon," the Norwegian version of the Greek myth, Eros and Psyche.

Now, as a grown woman, I read the story again to try to discover why it had such a strong hold on me. I think I have discovered some of the reasons, and you may think of others.

The story, as most readers may recall, is about a poor woodcutter and his wife, with many children, who sell their youngest daughter to a white bear in return for material comfort. To help out the family, the girl reluctantly goes home with the bear.

They go to a splendid castle, where she eats and drinks her fill of delicious food and then lies down in a lovely bedchamber. After she puts out the light, someone lies down beside her—she does not know who.

During the daytime hours, she enjoys every luxury, but she is always alone, so that after awhile, she grows lonely and asks the bear if she can go home for a brief visit. Reluctantly, the bear agrees, but he begs her not to talk privately with her mother, for something bad will happen if she does.

Now rich, her family is full of curiosity about her life with the white bear, and she talks of it in glowing terms, always careful not to let her mother be alone with her.

Finally, however, her mother has her way and gets the girl to speak with her alone. The girl breaks down and admits that after the light is out in the castle, somebody comes in and lies down beside her.

Disturbed by the account, the mother insists she take a piece of candle with her, light it, and find out who is sleeping with her. When the white bear comes to bring her home, he asks her if she has kept her promise not to talk alone with her mother, and she lies and says she has not said a word.

That night, after her bedmate is asleep, she lights the candle stub, and to her astonishment, a handsome prince sleeps beside her. In her excitement, her hand trembles, and she drops hot candle wax on his night shirt and he feels it as it burns his flesh.

"What have you done?" he cries. "It's all up between us now. I was under an enchantment for a year, and if you had only trusted me that long, I should have been free from it. Now I must return to the castle East of the Sun and West of the Moon, where my stepmother lives—the woman who has laid the spell on me—and marry a mean Princess there." Then, in spite of her weeping and pleas for forgiveness, he disappears.

Next thing she knows, she finds herself dressed in rags again and lying alone in the middle of the forest. But she does not go home. Instead, she begins a long search for her lover, inquiring as she goes if anyone knows the whereabouts of the castle East of the Sun and West of the Moon.

An old woman gives her a golden apple and directs her to her sister. The second old woman gives her a golden carding comb and directs her to a third sister. This one gives her a golden spinning wheel and tells her to ask the East Wind to help her. After many days, she reaches the East Wind who directs her to his brother, the West Wind, who tells her to go to his brother, the South Wind, and the South Wind sends her on still another weary journey to his brother, the North Wind. Finally, after a tumultuous trip of which even the North Wind is afraid, she reaches the castle.

Sitting alone under the castle wall, she begins to play with the golden apple. Her playing attracts the attention of the mean princess, who asks if she may buy the apple. The girl agrees to exchange it if she can see the prince that night, and the mean one agrees . . . but gives the prince a sleeping draught, so that he does not know he has had a visitor. The same thing happens the second night—she exchanges her golden carding comb for the sight of a prince so heavily drugged that he does not know she has been there. On the third night—that magical third night—she exchanges her golden spinning wheel for a visit to the prince. But this time she is lucky, for a servant who dislikes the mean princess tells the prince what is happening, so that he only pretends to drink the drug.

When the girl comes into the prince's chamber, the two embrace with great joy. But he tells her that he will have to marry the princess he does not love the next day unless some special circumstance arises. He has a plan: he will announce that he will only marry the person who can wash the candlewax out of his nightshirt. The mean one and her mother try and fail. Then he asks the girl in rags—his sweetheart—to come in and try. The wax comes right out. The wicked people in the castle all burst with anger and the prince carries his maiden off to another castle, where they live happily ever after.

As I look at this story now, I notice several things: first, the materialism of the girl's family and her willingness to go with the bear to help them out. She is a generous-spirited girl. They are impressed only with external reality—the mother is irritated that the girl is sleeping with a white bear. The kindness and gentleness of the bear and the girl's fondness for him are of no importance. The girl, still immature, should have said "No!" to her mother—as many of us should say to our mothers at one time or another—but she obeys her and looks at her sleeping partner. This lack of trust hurts him, as symbolized by the drops of burning candlewax that fall on his nightshirt.

He, at the same time, is possessed by a mother figure—in the Greek myth, it is his mother, Aphrodite, and he is Eros. Besides this, the girl's lie—that she had not told her mother—and then her concern with his appearance, induces him to break off the relationship. She should not have cared what he looked like but been more subjective in her affection. The fact that he was handsome should not have made a real difference.

At the end, he proves his sincere love by thinking of a way of resolving the romantic problem. She proves her love by long and fearsome travels and by cleverness. Finally, not he but she, is disguised (as a beggar girl), but he loves her for herself, and with his help they come together again. He has forgiven her for her breach of trust.

No wonder I read the story over and over again. It meant that one could be under a curse for a mistake one thinks one has made, but with courage and patience and trust, it was still possible for everything to come out all right.

Adults in religious and classical myth and history have always done a lot of abusing of themselves and of children. Abraham had the knife raised over the tied-up Isaac on the funeral pyre—he thought at God's command—until God told him he had proven his loyalty and need not proceed with the execution. Joseph's envious brothers dipped his coat-of-many-colors in the blood of a killed animal and told his parents Joseph was dead. Later he was rescued from the pit in which they had put him and survived to become a leader of the Jewish people. Oedipus was exposed on a mountain top. Atreus ate his children, albeit unknowingly. Medea did not treat hers with much consideration—she fed them to Jason. The Slaughter of the Innocents is a well-known episode in the New Testament.

Children have been devoured by Saturn and by Ugolino in Dante's Inferno, Canto 33—all things have been done to them. In "The Juniper Tree" of the Brothers Grimm, an envious stepmother asks her little stepson to look into an iron chest and then shuts it on his head. She dissects the body and serves him to his own father as stew. The father sucks the bones and throws them under the table, where the little daughter, weeping, gathers them in a silk scarf and buries them under the juniper tree out in front of the house where the little boy's mother is buried. From the earth springs a little bird. The bird flies to a shoemaker and sings:

> My mother killed me
> My father ate me
> My sister buried my bones
> Heh, ho. What a beautiful bird am I![1]

The shoemaker asks the little bird to repeat the song, and he agrees, but only on condition that he may have the tiny red shoes the shoemaker is making. The shoemaker hangs them around his neck and the bird flies off, sings his song from the juniper tree at home, and when his little sister runs out, drops the shoes.

He then repeats the process with a gold chain procured from a goldsmith on condition he will sing his song again, and this he drops over his father's neck. Finally, he brings a heavy millstone home, and when his stepmother runs out, he drops it on her, plop, and smashes her. At this point, he is reconstituted as a little boy and he and his little sister and his father embrace and live happily ever after.

Violent as this tale is, it jumps, as do many folktales, from reality into healing fantasy. The reality may be based on an actual occurrence for it has even happened in recent times. My husband, Jerome Butler, day city editor of the European edition of the *New York Herald Tribune* in the 1930s in Paris, actually witnessed the guillotining in 1939 of a man who had asked his little stepson to look out a door, slammed the door on the boy's neck, dissected him, and burned him on an ash heap in the backyard.

Some simple folk rhymes from China depict cultural abuse, including children beaten by jealous mothers-in-law. Such beatings are common to all cultures and may not always be totally unproductive if we are to believe Samuel Johnson, who said he wouldn't have learned anything if he hadn't been beat.

The Babes in the Wood are described in a sixteenth-century ballad repeated in a number of versions in the seventeenth century. The orphaned children are exposed by an avaricious uncle who then inherits their estate. In some versions they are killed by hired killers, in others, they die of exposure in the woods, lying in each other's arms.

> In one another's arms they dy'd
> As babes wanting reliefe:
> No burieall these pretty babes
> Of any man receives.
> Till Robin Redbreast painefully
> Did cover them with leaves.[2]

In the *Divine and Moral Songs* of Isaac Watts, published in 1715, there is Song 13, reproduced in various versions in *The New England Primer,* such as this one which appeared in the *Primer* as published by Ira Webster in Hartford in 1843. In this the behavior of children is controlled through fear:

> Tho' I am young yet I may die
> And hasten to eternity:
> There is a dreadful fiery hell
> Where wicked ones must always dwell.[3]

Hundred of stories attempting, like this poetry, to control the behavior of children through fear were published in the eighteenth and nineteenth centuries, including the Joyful Death stories of James Janeway, Cotton Mather, and lesser writers and the innumerable Sunday school booklets. One can also imagine the terror engendered in children by the poems in *Struwwelpeter* by Dr. Heinrich Hoffman, published in 1844 and still on the market. Here, for instance, is the painful tale of Little Suck-a-Thumb:

> One day, Mamá said, "Conrad dear,
> I must go out and leave you here.
> But mind now, Conrad, what I say,
> Don't suck your thumb when I'm away.
> The great tall tailor always comes
> To little boys who suck their thumbs.
> And ere they dream what he's about,
> He takes his great sharp scissors out
> And cuts their thumbs clean off and then
> You know they'll never grow again."
> Mama had scarcely turned her back
> The thumb was in—Alack, Alack!
> The door flew open, in he ran
> The great, long red-legged scissors-man.
> Oh, children! See! The tailor's come
> And caught out little Suck-a-Thumb.
> Snip, snap, snip, the scissors go.
> And Conrad calls out, Oh! Oh! Oh!"
> Snip! Snap! Snip! They go so fast
> That both his thumbs are off at last.
> Mamá comes home: There Conrad stands
> And looks quite sad, and shows his hands.
> "Ah!" said Mamá. "I knew he'd come
> To naughty little Suck-a-Thumb."[4]

Then there is the Victorian story of *The New Mother,* as traumatic in its way as anything that could happen to any child. The story is from Lucy Clifford's *Anyhow Stories* (1882).[5] In this story, which has sexual overtones, two children, Blue Eyes and Turkey, return from town and meet a strange girl. She is a gypsy with a guitar. The children beg her to play, but the mysterious and glamorous girl says she plays for naughty children. They tell their mother that they want to be naughty, and she says she will abandon them if they are naughty. She will send home a new mother with glass eyes and a wooden tail. But the children so much want to hear the gypsy music that they are naughty. They break their mugs and throw their bread and butter on the floor and stamp their feet with rage when their mother tells them to go upstairs until they are good.

This pattern continues after two more visits with the gypsy maid. Finally, the mother can stand no more:

"Goodbye, my children," she says sadly, kissing them. "The new mother will be home presently" (178). Just by the corner of the fields she stopped and turned, and waved her handkerchief, all wet with tears, to the children at the window. They have lost their mother and not even heard the strange music promised to them for being bad. The gypsy tells them they have not been bad enough.

> All through the afternoon they sat watching. Then, toward nightfall, they heard a sound as if something heavy was being dragged along the ground outside, and then there was a loud and terrible knocking at the door. In fear and trembling, Turkey put her back to the door. They see a strange light which they know is the flashing of two glass eyes. Together the children stand with their two little backs against the door, but with a fearful blow, the little painted door was cracked and splintered.

> How they wished they could tell their own dear mother just once that they would be good for evermore. But it is too late. The devil mother has come to stay.

The story of Elsie Dinsmore is even more violent because the violence is so submerged and the battle is so great between the little girl's love for her father and her religious strictures.[6] Published in 1868, written by Martha Finley, the book was followed by a whole series. It was enormously popular with children, probably because at one time or another all of them had felt abused. When she learns that her long absent father is coming home, "Elsie leaned against the wall, her heart throbbing so wildly that she could scarcely breathe" (63). She has a real crush on her father, and when he demands that she sing on Sunday for his friends, she is torn between her desire to please him and her religious prohibitions. He orders her to sit on the piano stool until she is ready to obey. He is determined to break her will. She solves the problem ultimately by falling off the piano stool: "She was a pitiable sight indeed, with her fair face, her curls, and her white dress dabbled in blood. It was some time ere consciousness returned" (246). He is always hugging her to his heart, kissing her on the lips over and over again, and she is always asking, "Do you love me?" This sexual pressure, too, is child abuse.

Amazingly, many of these literary children eventually lead reasonably contented lives. For all their sufferings, David Copperfield and Oliver Twist turned out quite well.

People who are abused tend to overcompensate by excelling later in life in fields that they know people will admire. Practically deserted by an indifferent father, Charlotte and Emily Brontë wrote with Ann and their brother the Gondal and Angria cycle as children. In adult life, these were transformed into *Jane Eyre* and *Wuthering Heights*. The germ of the classic children's story, *The King of the Golden River,* was planted in the imagination of a lonely little boy, John Ruskin. Beatrix Potter, deprived by her parents of a normal sexual life until she was a mature woman, did the pictures for the children of her imagination which are now in the Tate Gallery.

In order to survive, abused children find various ways of coping with a hostile environment. Besides actual physical escape, the most effective escape is often through the imagination. A striking example in fiction of the use of the imagination to stave off the most damaging affects of abuse is to be found in Frances Hodgson Burnett's *A Little Princess,* published in 1905. Sara Crew, reduced from being her father's beloved daughter and the richest girl in a London boarding school to being an orphan in the role of scullery maid, must bear the cruelty of the sadistic headmistress, Miss Minchin. Sara takes refuge in pretendings that bring her, eventually, to a very happy ending. Hers was indeed a triumph of the spirit over adversity.

Abuse takes many forms. It can be horribly physical or mental, overt and blatant—like children forced to receive injections of heroin until they are addicted, or burned and beaten. It can be subtle and elusive as well, discernible only to the child who is abused. One dreadful form is not visible to outsiders as abuse: the conditioning of a child by parents determined to make that child an extension of themselves, thus robbing him or her of identity and will to be a person.

The turn-of-the-century novel, *Rebecca of Sunnybrook Farm* (1903), demonstrates the twisted theory that abuse makes you better. Rebecca, an attractive gypsy-like child, is sent to live with her witch-like Aunt Miranda, because her father is dead and her mother can't support her. Miranda, whose heart has never been used for anything but pumping blood, takes on the burden reluctantly. The book hints that she had had a secret crush on Rebecca's glamorous, improvident, dead father, and rejection by him has not improved her attitude toward his child.

Rebecca senses, of course, that she is unwelcome. She keeps her room untidily and is scolded severely. Rebecca is made to feel perpetually guilty: "Something came over me," she says, "I don't know what."

It is needless to say that Rebecca irritated her aunt with every breath she drew. She continually forgot and started up the front stairs because it was the shortest route to her bedroom: she left the dipper in the kitchen shelf instead of hanging it up over the pail; she sat in the chair the cat liked best; she was willing to go on errands, but often forgot what she went for; she left the screen doors ajar, so that flies came in; her tongue was ever in motion; she sang or whistled when she was picking up chips; she was always messing with flowers, putting them in vases, pinning them on her dress, and sticking them in her hat; finally, she was an everlasting reminder of her foolish, worthless father, whose handsome face and engaging manner had so deceived her mother, Aurelia, and perhaps if the facts were known, others besides Aurelia.[7]

Ultimately, this delightful, personable girl is trained, but she remains a trained little girl, and never becomes a woman, though in the end there is promise she will marry the father figure whom she fancies. And she has become a sound businesswoman. When the railroad buys Sunnybrook Farm, there is little nostalgia for its beauty because financial problems have been taken care of. The chapter is simply headed, "Goodbye, Sunnybrook Farm." Rebecca will always be fixed now in her little girl state, even, one knows, when she is ninety.

Children are abused when they are brainwashed into supporting fanatical ideas. Witch-hunts in which imaginative children play a role have occurred not only in seventeenth-century England and in Salem, Massachusetts, but in Cromwell's army and Stalin's Russia and Hitler's Germany. More recently, the movie "The Killing Field," based on a *New York Times Magazine* article by Sidney Schanberg, describes the situation in Cambodia in 1980 where children were encouraged to choose the adults who were to be executed. Many books reflect the tricky kinds of psychological abuse that date from the post-Freudian era when parents learned to conceal the abuse which is often a product of their envy of the children who will ultimately replace them in life. As several authors have observed, movies like "The Bad Seed," "The Omen," "The Exorcist," and "Rosemary's Baby," clearly reveal the hidden envy of children on the part of adults.

In recent years, with the increased interest in the problem of child abuse, many books for children have come out which, although less universal than the folktales in treating the problem, are more specific in defining various kinds of abuse.

Emily Neville's *It's Like This, Cat* (1963) is about an adolescent youth whose father considers his behavior unsuitable for a socialized male. This is because the boy happens to like a cat as well as an eccentric old woman in his neighborhood, and he must fight his father for his right to be himself. Another good book of the period—this one for young children, but having to do with the same kind of abusive contempt—is 1972's *William's Doll* by Charlotte Zolotow. William is called "a creep" and a "sissy" because he would like to have a doll. His father is disgusted with him, but his understanding grandmother buys him a doll so that "when he's a father, he'll know how to care for his baby."

Robert Cormier's *The Chocolate War* (1974) is one of the best books of the period concerning the injustices that a child must sometimes put up with in a world in which childhood should be, but too often is not, a happy experience. In it Jerry, a high school student, defies the school bullies and lives to fight on. In Helen Forester's *Tuppence to Cross the Mercy* (1974) a girl struggles to achieve maturity in the midst of a ne'er-do-well family.

Foster families are an important element, for better or worse, in books about unhappy and mistreated children. Julia Cunningham's *Dorp Dead* (1965) is about an orphaned boy caught in a sinister environment with a violent foster father. Betsy Byars's *The Pinballs* (1977) is about three children from different families who have had a bad time of it with their own families. Thirteen-year-old Harvey's legs were broken when his drunken father accidentally ran over him. Tom, only eight, is a foundling reared by elderly twin sisters who can no longer care for him because of illness. Carlie, a teenager, has been brutally beaten by her stepfather. The Masons have opened their home to the three because they cannot have children of their own, and help the children to cope by confronting problems rather than running away from them. The children no longer feel like "pinballs," but now have a sense of control over their lives in the foster home they share.

The Great Gilly Hopkins (1978) by Katherine Paterson, is about a girl who confronts her mother's consistent and heartbreaking indifference with aggressive behavior. The book has a satisfactory but not a saccharine ending. Gilly finally learns how to deal more equably with disappointments when she goes to live with her grandmother who needs her. In *Dinky Hocker Shoots Smack* (1972) a girl deals with a "liberal" mother who is so devoted to good causes that she neglects her own child.

Many of the books that deal with the more violent forms of abuse place emphasis on the culpability of the mothers. There are some guilty fathers too, however. *Spare the Rod* (1981) is adapted by Elizabeth Levy from *Fat Albert and the Cosby Kids*. It is about a girl, Patrice, who is abused by her mother until Fat Albert gets her to report it to the teacher. The resolution finds Patrice's mother getting professional help, and

Patrice winning the freedom to grow up more normally. Willo Davis Roberts's *Don't Hurt Laurie* concerns the physical abuse of an older child (1977). Louise Moeri's *The Girl Who Lived on the Ferris Wheel* (1979) is about a girl who manages to save her life in a home where her mentally ill mother is trying to kill her.

In the same class, but of more literary merit than most, is Cynthia Voight's *Homecoming* (1981) in which children, deserted by their mentally ill mother, manage to make their own way in the world and achieve a happy landing.

Michelle Magorian's *Good Night, Mr. Tom* (1982), which won the Carnegie Medal in England, is a frightening story about the abused son of a single mother who finds a world of friendship through his own courage and the help of a great-hearted old man.

Didactic though many of these books are they fill a real social need. Through reading them, thousands of adults may become aware of the problems of child abuse in its many forms; adults and children may learn how to cope with it more successfully. Young readers may see that they are not alone in the problems they face, and gain a sense of how their spirits may bring them triumphant through the hardest of circumstances.

Notes

1. Adapted from the translation by Eleanor Quarrie, *Grimm's Folk Tales*. London: The Folio Society, 1965, p. 26

Her translation is:

> "My mother made a stew of me,
> My father ate it all.
> My little sister wept to see,
> Marlene, my sister small,
> Then gathered my bones in her silken shawl,
> And laid them under the Juniper tree.
>   Sing, hey! What a beautiful bird am I!"

2. From "The Norfolke Gentleman," The Second Part, collected in *The Roxburghe Ballads,* Vol. 2 (Hertford: for the Ballad Society, 1872–1874.) Reprinted in Francelia Butler, *Masterworks of Children's Literature* 1550–1739. New York: Chelsea House, 1983, p. 6.

3. Part of a longer poem, this selection is to be found in *The New England Primer*. Hartford, Conn.: Ira Webster, 1844, no pagination.

4. Heinrich Hoffman,. *Struwwelpeter*. New York: Frederick Warne & Co., Inc. nd p. 15–16.

5. Mrs. W. K. (Lucy) Clifford, "The New Mother," in *Anyhow Stories, Moral and Otherwise*. London: Macmillan and Co., 1882. Reprinted in Leonard de Vries, *Little Wide Awake:* An Anthology of Victorian Children's Books and Periodicals. Cleveland and New York: World Publishing Co., 1967.

6. Martha Farquharson Finley, *Elsie Dinsmore*. New York: M. W. Dodd, 1868. Quotations are taken from the edition of 1896, published in New York by Dodd Mead & Company.

7. Kate Douglas Wiggin. *Rebecca of Sunnybrook Farm*. Boston: Houghton Mifflin, 1903, p. 64–65.

13.

Andersen's Heroes and Heroines: Relinquishing the Reward

CELIA CATLETT ANDERSON

Hans Christian Andersen's fairy tales have sometimes been described as too adult or too pessimistic for children. For example, May Hill Arbuthnot in her classic *Children and Books,* although praising Andersen as an allegorist, notes that "because of the double meaning, the adult themes, and the sadness of many of these stories, the whole collection is usually not popular with children."[1] P. L. Travers found a "devitalizing element" of nostalgia in the tales.[2] Bruno Bettelheim has commented that the conclusions of some of Andersen's stories are discouraging in that "they do not convey the feeling of consolation characteristic of fairy tales," and Jack Zipes accuses Andersen of teaching lessons in servility to the young.[3] Andersen's tales continue, however to be published, read, discussed, and used as a basis for children's theater, and the most popular of them have an undeniable appeal for children. Furthermore, the most popular tales, such as "The Ugly Duckling," "The Little Mermaid," "The Steadfast Tin Soldier," "The Little Fir Tree," and "The Nightingale," include for the most part, those stories that were original with Andersen. His view of the world, then, the problems he poses and the solutions he offers must touch some nerve in us; there must be something more to them than simple pessimism, more than a servile call to compromise.

Andersen does indeed often deliberately undercut the facile happy ending that is the trademark of fairy tales, but are his many characters who fail to win a reward defeated in spirit? I would argue that they are not. Take the one that may be, perhaps, saddest of all his protagonists, the little fir tree (or pine tree as Erik Haugaard translates it).[4] The tree fails to appreciate its youth in the forest, is bewildered and frightened during its one glorious evening as a baubled Christmas tree, is exiled to an attic, and there is unable to hold an audience of mice who want to hear stories of "bacon or candle stumps" (232), not of "How Humpty-dumpty Fell

Down the Stairs but Won the Princess Anyway" (229). Hauled out into the spring sunlight, the pine tree is forced to recognize that it is a dead thing among the green renewal of the season and achieves its one brief moment of wisdom: "If I only could have been happy while I had a chance to be" (233). Finally the poor tree is burned, sighing its sap away in shots, and "Every time the tree sighed, it thought of a summer day in the forest, or a winter night when the stars are brightest, and it remembered Christmas Eve and Humpty-dumpty: the only fairy tale it had ever heard and knew how to tell. Then it became ashes" (233). The tree dies unfulfilled, yes, but in one sense undefeated. It never loses its vision of the possibility of beauty in the world. Like King Lear, the tree is ennobled by wisdom that comes too late.

When we read this tale to our son, then eight years old, he had tears in his eyes and commented that it was the saddest story he had ever heard. Initially, I judged this as a negative reaction, a rejection of the story, but I was wrong. He returned to the story again and again. Like the small boy who rips the golden star from the tree's branch and pins it to his chest, our son took something shining from the story and, for all I know, wears it to this day.

Of course not all of Andersen's tales end sadly. Even considering only those stories that are not simply retellings of old folktales (and therefore with conventional conclusions), we can find several types of endings. There are some which express religious optimism, and some which reward the hero or heroine with acceptance and love. Stories in the first group are rather self-consciously overlaid with Christianity and conclude optimistically. To mention only one of these, consider "The Old Oak Tree's Last Dream," a story quite different in tone and message from "The Pine Tree." The oak lives three hundred and sixty-five years, many of them as a landmark for sailors. It pities the mayflies and flowers for their short existences, but learns in a death dream of ascension into a joyous heaven that "Nothing has been forgotten, not the tiniest flower or the smallest bird" (548–49). The story concludes

> The tree itself lay stretched out on the snow-covered beach. From the ship came the sound of sailors singing a carol about the joyful season, when Christ was born to save mankind and give us eternal life. The sailors were singing of the same dream, the beautiful dream that the old oak tree had dreamed Christmas Eve: the last night of its life. (549)

At least for the believer, this conclusion is more encouraging than that which gives the pine tree only ashes of regret.

Another class of stories in Andersen does include more tangible rewards. In these, the protagonists win acceptance by remaining true to their natures and persisting in some quest or duty. "The Ugly Duckling" comes immediately to mind, but perhaps "The Nightingale" is an even better example. In that tale, the small bird is as plain and dull in plumage at the end as at the beginning, but its ability to remain natural, to sing a spontaneous, honest song finally wins it the respect of the emperor who has been saved by the power of its singing and now realizes the false choice he made in earlier preferring the bejewelled, mechanical bird who can sing only one song. Of all Andersen's stories, this may be the one in which the triumph of spirit over matter is most simply and directly presented.

Love is the ultimate form of acceptance, and the tale "The Snow Queen" most fully elaborates this theme. Bettelheim concedes that this tale belongs among the tales that console.[5] An allegory of reason versus love, "The Snow Queen" is, like all allegories, explicitly symbolic, and this very explicitness makes the story a good choice for analysis.

The childhood paradise of Gerda and Kai is blighted by Kai's growing away from Gerda into a cynical stage of adolescence (symbolized by the splinters of the mirror of reason that have entered his eyes and heart and by the numbing kisses of the Snow Queen who kidnaps him). Gerda, like the sister in Andersen's retold folktale "The Wild Swans," endures much suffering before she is able to restore Kai to his natural state as a warm-hearted, loving person. The story is a classic example of what Marie-Louise von Franz describes as the projection of anima—the suffering, brave woman as a projection of the man's problem with his feminine side. In this case the identification is very appropriately used since Gerda, in bringing about the union of intellect and emotion, is indeed a Sophia-like figure.

The story is one of Andersen's most successful blendings of Christian and folk elements. It contains not only many magical creatures (the Snow Queen herself, a talking raven, and a Finnish white witch), but also a hymn in place of the usual incantation, angels formed from the breath of prayers, and a wise old grandmother who knows both the language of ravens and that of the Bible. After Gerda, through her persistence, reaches the ice castle and frees Kai with her warm tears, the two retrace her steps and finally arrive back at the old grandmother's apartment. Andersen tells us that "as they stepped through the doorway they realized that they had grown: they were no longer children" (261). But the grandmother is reading "Whosoever shall not receive the Kingdom of Heaven as a little child shall not enter therein" (261). Kai and

Gerda understand the lesson and "There they sat, the two of them grownups; and yet in their hearts children; and it was summer: a warm glorious summer day!" (261). In choosing that particular text from the New Testament, Andersen voices a central theme shared by Christian theologians and writers for children. For the child, and for all of us, the test of spirit is to grow into intellectual wisdom without losing the capacity for emotion, for love.

Certainly this is a central theme with Andersen himself. Elizabeth Cook holds that "two of his strongest themes are the plight of the outsider, and the primacy of Love over Reason."[6] We see these ideas combined in two tales where the endings are unhappy and love must be its own reward. In both "The Little Mermaid" and "The Steadfast Tin Soldier" the main characters persist and suffer and do not win. These stories, along with "The Pine Tree," "The Little Match Girl," and that very complex Andersen tale "The Shadow," are probably most responsible for the author's reputation for pessimism. The mermaid *is* promised eternal life at the last minute, but in this story the Christian promise is not as successfully woven into the plot as it is in some others (the tale always seems to me to end with the mermaid's dissolution into foam). Are these stories, then, about the defeat of the spirit? As I said earlier, I think not. Neither the mermaid nor the tin soldier turn aside from their goal, nor do they become bitter or vengeful. Through many trials they continue to be humane and loving. Many of Andersen's heroes and heroines, though they suffer greatly, remain true to their ideals. If not rewarded, neither are they defeated. And the true triumph of the spirit, after all, consists not in winning the prince or princess, the kingdom or riches, or even immortality, but in being worthy of the winning.

Much that is written for and about children springs from the premise that the young need the hope and encouragement provided by the success of the hero in the stories presented to them, and that they cannot cope with models of failure. This may be true for certain ages and types, but it is in many cases a condescending and even dishonest attitude. Hope can help develop a child, but false hope can absolutely devastate. Hans Christian Andersen knew that when Humpty-dumpty fell, he didn't win the princess anyway and that a storyteller who claims he did is a liar and, further, that an innocent, like the foolish pine tree, who believes the lie will reap much unhappiness.

The child who comes to Andersen for spiritual sustenance will learn that we must both test our dreams and be tested by them and that in this world some bright dreams have gray awakenings. Will this harm or strengthen a child? I think it strengthened our own children, that our son drank courage, not despair, from the tears he shed over the story of the pine tree. In Andersen's tale "The Pixy and the Grocer" the pixy peeks through the keyhole and sees the turbulent visions that the poor student enjoys while sitting under the magic tree of poetry. Before such splendor, the pixy "experienced greatness. . . . He cried without knowing why he cried, but found that in those tears happiness was hidden" (426). So art redeems us; as Tolkien put it so well in his famous essay on children and fairy stories, "It is one of the lessons of fairy stories (if we can speak of the lessons of things that do not lecture) that on callow, lumpish, and selfish youth peril, sorrow, and the shadow of death can bestow dignity and even sometimes wisdom."[7] Hans Christian Andersen gives us in his stories "peril, sorrow, and the shadow of death" but also "dignity" and "wisdom."

Notes

1. May Hill Arbuthnot and Zena Sutherland, *Children and Books,* 4th ed. (Glenview, Ill.: Scott, Foresman, 1972), 313.

2. P. L. Travers, "Only Connect," *Quarterly Journal of Acquisitions of the Library of Congress* (October 1967); repr. in *Only Connect: Readings on Children's Literature,* ed. Sheila Egoff, G. T. Stubbs, and L. F. Ashley (New York: Oxford University Press, 1969), p. 198.

3. Bruno Bettelheim, *The Uses of Enchantment: The Meaning and Importance of Fairy Tales* (New York: Knopf, 1976), 37; Jack Zipes, *Fairy Tales and the Art of Subversion: The Classical Genre for Children and the Process of Civilization* (New York: Wildman Press, 1983), 94.

4. Hans Christian Andersen, *The Complete Fairy Tales and Stories,* trans. Erik Haugaard (Garden City, N.Y.: Doubleday, 1983). Page numbers for quotes from this edition are given in the text.

5. Bettelheim, *Uses of Enchantment,* 37.

6. Elizabeth Cook, *The Ordinary and the Fabulous: An Introduction to Myths, Legends, and Fairy Tales for Teachers and Storytellers* (London: Cambridge University Press, 1971), 43.

7. J. R. R. Tolkien, "Children and Fairy Stories," from *Tree and Leaf,* in Sheila Egoff, G. T. Stubbs, and L. F. Ashley, *Only Connect,* New York: Oxford University Press, 1969, p. 120.

14.

Mythic Consciousness
and Hawaiian Children's Literature

STEPHEN CANHAM

The first thing to understand is that "mythic consciousness" is a Western concept, implying the existence or at least the possibility of other types of consciousness distinct from those which are called "mythic"—say, perhaps, artistic, historical, ethical, or even technological. But to the ancient Hawaiians (i.e., people living in Hawaii prior to 1778), no such adjectives were necessary, or, I suspect, even conceivable. The supernatural and the natural were united in the actual; what was noumenal was every bit as epistemologically valid as what was physically concrete—in fact, the two partook of each other, were indivisible. All things were imbued with greater or lesser qualities of mana, a spiritual power analagous to that of "the Force" in the Star Wars serial. I intend no trivialization by the analogy, but rather an attempt to show how strongly we in the West seek the clarity and wholeness that the culture of the Hawaiians presented and which is still reflected in some of the best books for children on Hawaiian themes.

Mana is the power that links past to present through ancestors, all the way back to the gods themselves and first causes, as depicted in the great Hawaiian creation chant, the *Kumulipo*. Mana is sacred, potent, immanent; it can be constructive or destructive. It is the power which allows efficacy, whether in battle or in fishing; it is not unlike the concepts of quality and virtu rolled into one, and it is to be found in inanimate as well as animate matter. So, for the ancient Hawaiians, when Captain James Cook "discovered" the Sandwich Isles in 1778 (a good thousand years after the Polynesians, of course), during a festival on the island of Hawaii dedicated to the god Lono, it seemed clear that Cook was Lono—not an emissary or avatar, but the god itself. It was only a few days, however, before Cook and his men revealed their decidedly clay feet. Or, consider that the triggerfish with the wonderful name of *humuhumunukunukuapuaa* seen swimming off a coral reef might well be the great pig god Kamapuaa in his fish form—not an iconographic emblem of the god, but the god itself. Interestingly, in late 1984 the people of Hawaii voted the *humuhumunukunukuapuaa* to be the state's official fish. Somewhere, Kamapuaa must be grinning.

In Hawaii, the power, grandeur, and vitality of ancient spiritual concerns are still visible today, despite the commercial development and technological changes occurring throughout the islands. At the head of a trail or by a mountain pool, you might see a fresh green ti leaf carefully wrapped around a stone and placed inconspicuously near other leaves, now brown and withered after months in the rain and sun. Ti, which grows wild but is also cultivated as a yard plant, is sacred and the leaves are offered as propitiation to the local dieties *(aumakua)* which still inhabit and guard specific locations on all the islands. Aloha Airlines, one of the three primary inter-island carriers, boasts proudly that "the spirit moves us," with a play on "spirit" as the "aloha spirit" familiar to tourists (itself a powerful concept) and spirit as mana. An "easy-listening" Honolulu FM radio station sports the call letters KUMU; in Hawaiian, *kumu* means "source, foundation, master, teacher." Tourists go home with polymer lava tiki dolls replete with fake sapphire eyes glittering in shallow parody of the *ike,* or power of understanding and insight of the Hawaiian gods and kings. But even today in Hawaii one avoids looking directly into another's eyes, not only out of Oriental deference and politeness, but because to glare at a person can be construed as a serious personal affront. In ancient Hawaii, to look into the eyes of a king or queen was a violation of *kapu* (tabu or taboo), punishable by death for a commoner.

But what does all this have to do with children's literature? One more example. Recently I watched a group of 12 to 14 year-old local (i.e., part Hawaiian, non-Caucasian) youths arrive on the beach at Waimea Bay on the North Shore of Oahu for a day of bodysurfing in the 7 to 8 foot winter swells. They traveled light—bodysurfing fins and towels, but two boys had Walkman-type radios, eminently stealable while they body-surfed. "Ho, consider dem gone," one boy said loudly enough for me to hear. Then, quietly, another boy, complete with baggy "surfah" shorts, peroxided punk tail and digital watch, simply walked up and stuck the ti stalk he had been carrying into the sand in the middle of their pile of belongings. "Nobody going boddah dem now," he announced, and the troupe hit the waves. He was right, nobody did bother their things—the power of myth, of matters spiritual and sacred, is sometimes very close to the surface of life in modern Hawaii.

At the same time that a fourth-grader is learning the rudiments of volcanology, he or she is also learning in school the stories of Pele, the fire goddess who is as responsible for recent eruptions on the Big Island of Hawaii as is plate tectonics: alternate ways to truth. You realize their prevalence and intuitiveness in Hawaii when the announcer on the evening news opens the broadcast by saying that "Madame Pele put on a spectacular display last night, as fountaining on the east rift of Kīlauea Volcano reached one thousand feet. Geologists at the National Park predict. . . ." As Joseph Campbell notes, if we are to maintain our sense of wholeness, it is imperative that a dialogue between the old symbolic forms and the newer empirical forms of consciousness be achieved.[1] In Hawaii, old and new ways of knowing and perceiving seek continual accommodation, and it is in part through children's books that this process of evaluation and renewal occurs.

The primary means of transmission of the old ways and stories in Hawaii remains, as it does throughout Polynesia, the oral tradition in all its forms. These range from traditional genealogical and historical chants to the *mele* (songs) which accompany various types of hula, from popular Hawaiian music, to the ever-present capacity of the people to "talk story," or swap gossip and tales with one another. Formal Hawaiian studies programs in the schools and universities are also responsible for a great deal of the preservation and reinvigoration of Hawaiian culture, especially during what has been termed the "Hawaiian renaissance" of the 1970s and 1980s. But I would suggest that Hawaiian children's books are a substrate for this reinvigoration and that, perhaps unacknowledged, they have quietly provided children of all backgrounds with written texts of key concepts and stories for generations. A written text widens its audience beyond that of the oral reciter, and with this expansion come a number of key issues and questions.

Children's fiction based on Hawaiian materials falls roughly into two categories: those books whose purpose is to convey traditional myths, legends, and stories without major reference to the present and those which involve the present with the past, usually by means of a child protagonist. Into the first rudimentary grouping fall translations, retellings, adaptations, transcriptions of oral materials, and historical fiction; these works are often informed by a deeply felt desire to preserve and perpetuate the stories and ways of the past "as they used to be." Many of the works in this mode belong to an entire culture, not an individual authorial mind; their very existence derives not from the imaginative ability of a single person or consciousness but from the evolving needs and desires of an entire people. Thus, their continuance becomes an imperative if the culture from which they developed is to be considered

still viable. That such tales shift in Hawaii from the oral to the written—
and illustrated—tradition reveals a fundamental historical and aesthetic
change. Prior to the arrival of the Caucasian missionaries in the early
nineteenth century, Hawaiians had no written language, and, despite a
few sporadic printings of Hawaiian language primers, texts, and story
collections, it was not until the 1930s that books for children dealing with
Hawaiian themes began to appear in any number, and these were in
English.

Despite the slowness of the West to recognize it, the greatest Hawaiian
legends and stories—those of the gods and heroes Maui, Pele, Hiiāka,
Umi, for instance—touch, in Campbell's phrase, "themes of the imagination,"[2] nonhistorical renderings of absolutely fundamental matters and
principles such as birth, procreation, death, courage, loyalty, love,
jealousy, and greed. But even the best of the modern retellers sometimes
cannot resist the temptation to shape their material to fit narrative
patterns other than those of the ancient Hawaiians. As Martha Beckwith
noted in her classic study, *Hawaiian Mythology,* Hawaiian romances
typically ended in estrangement, and "stories which end with a happy
married life must be suspect as a foreign innovation."[3] And sure enough,
in 1981 Dave Guard, in the generally well retold and handsomely
illustrated story of *Hale-Mano,* seemingly could not resist the Western
lure of the happily-ever-after closure, and grants his lovers a very
atypical fairy tale ending. Is this "bad"? No, just untraditional, although
from one point of view, such tampering dilutes the authority of the
traditional material. In addition to Guard, names to look for among the
best of the retellers and adapters for children (and adults) include Marcia
Brown, Guy Buffet, Mary Kawena Pukui, and Vivian Thompson.

In the retellings of traditional material the usual critical and aesthetic
criteria apply: grasp of concept/material by author, accuracy of data,
including linguistic features, stylistic grace, appropriateness of material
for a given audience, and so on. Such criteria are familiar and have
nothing exclusively to do with Hawaiian children's literature. But in
evaluating the second grouping, those stories which engage the past and
the present, a new criterion begins to become evident and appropriate:
the quality of the mediation between the old and the new and frequently
between one culture and another. When I look at children's books about
Hawaii, I notice that most of the names of the authors and editors are
Haole (Caucasian): Berkey, Thompson, Guard, Buffet, Tabrah, Doyle,
Myhre, Brown—these are not Hawaiian names. Even the various "Tutu
Nenes," the Hawaiian translation of "Mother Goose," seem to be *Haole*
in disguise. Surnames of course are not necessarily accurate indicators of

ethnicity, particularly in Hawaii, but my own research suggests that the clear majority of fictional works for children written on Hawaiian themes has been done by non-Hawaiians. Why? In part because of the oral tradition and the educational oppression of the native Hawaiians in the nineteenth and twentieth centuries, and the fact that the printed English word, and especially the book form, was clearly and to some extent remains, the province of the non-Hawaiian.

During the nineteenth century a number of Hawaiians did adopt Western literary forms, and Hawaiian language newspapers from the last century are rich in as yet mostly untranslated folklore and fictional material, but this energy seems to have waned by the early part of the twentieth century. In the West the continuing importance of the printed word is unquestioned, and is even raised to the power of myth (consider the recent redemonstration of the power of Logos in "Raiders of the Lost Ark" [of the Covenant]), but such traditions simply do not exist in much of Polynesia; in ancient Hawaii, the arts of oral poetry and epic/saga were highly refined, but not the art of preserving them through transcription.

Mircea Eliade in 1952 identified what he called an "Oceanian paradise," a "dream of islands" in the historian Gavan Daws's later phrase, which has dominated the imaginations of many in the West: "for the last hundred and fifty years," Eliade wrote, "all the great European literatures have vied with each other in exalting the paradisiac islands of the Pacific Ocean, havens of happiness, although the reality was very different."[4] The archetypal desire for an earthly paradise I think accounts for a good deal of the interest of "outsiders" in the mythology and the mythographizing of Hawaiian materials. The outsider finds in the old stories not simply charming or quaint narratives of unusual customs or shocking behavior, but rather occasional glimpses of the unity, the centeredness, the wholeness, of culture and life itself which has long been lost in the West. Nostalgia, then, may well inform many of the children's books about Hawaii—and this is not all bad. When nostalgia is based on informed appreciation for its subject, the result can be a kind of reachievement, a temporary, conditional, aesthetic and imaginative "return" to modes of inner life now difficult to sustain; and the subject, the Hawaiian material, is strengthened for its renewed interpretation and transmission. But when the nostalgia is governed by what could be called literary tourism or aesthetic carpetbagging, in which the perception of the subject as quaint, curious, or marketable informs the fiction, then the subject becomes, almost inevitably, denigrated. When "Jack and the Beanstalk" becomes "Keaka and the Lilikoi Vine," or when the three little pigs are joined feebly with a Hawaiian shark (no wolf being available), as they recently have been, trivialization occurs. What was archetypal in one culture becomes merely cute or clever in the other.

More difficult to achieve is the story which results from a sensitive, informed grasp of the culture—be it inherited or learned. Consider, for instance, Ruth Tabrah's use of traditional Hawaiian belief and legend in *The Red Shark* (1970). In this novel for young teenagers, Tabrah uses Hawaiian concepts of guardian deities *(aumakua)* to craft a story of the lingering powers of the old ways. Like his ancestors before him, old Isaac Kaimana (his surname translates roughly to "spiritual power of the sea") has quietly served a shark god, marked by a sacred rock, which inhabits a shoreline pool, but when the god reveals itself to the young outsider Stanley Sasaki, old Isaac decides it is time to pass the responsibility on. As he slowly, spellbindingly relates the old stories of how the high prince could take both human and shark forms and of how dangerous it is for young women to swim in his pool, Isaac gradually crafts an elegy to Hawaiian culture and the waning of the old ways which his life has striven to perpetuate. "When I was six years old, [my grandmother] showed me the stone, she told me this story. No secret. Only people don't like to talk about such things. . . . They don't like to think about such things could be. . . . The islands, they coming different. Hono-lulu—Kona—Hilo—everyplace but here, they forget how to live. They cut down the old trees. They block off the beaches with big hotels. They hide the mountains from your eyes with tall buildings. . . . Not much left of the old island feeling, the true spirit."[5] Stanley, Isaac has come to believe, possesses "the feeling for this place," what in Hawaiian is called "aloha āina," or "love of the land," in which John Charlot has noted a "seamless joining of physical description and symbolic meaning," an integrity of self and all the dimensions of the sensed world often alien to the West.[6]

Tabrah's treatment of not only the traditional materials but also the potentially volatile political dimensions of change is both respectful and insightful. And, clearly, one primary aspect of "the old island feeling" is the dimension of life we call mythic, the unity of self and physical and spiritual contexts. For many of us, myth has become an academic subject, or a quaint, slightly exotic indulgence, rather than a living, vital element of being, for, as Carl Jung noted,

> You can know all about the saints, sages, prophets, and other godly men and all the great mothers of the world. But if they are mere images whose numinosity you have never experienced, it

will be as if you were talking in a dream, for you will not know what you are talking about. The mere words you use will be empty and valueless. They gain life and meaning only when you try to take into account their numinosity—i.e. their relationship to the living individual. Only then do you begin to understand that their names mean very little, whereas the way they are *related* to you is all-important.[7]

The contemporary storyteller Jane Yolen concurs: "Mythology, legend, the lore of the folk, those tales that were once as real to their believers as a sunrise, hardly exist today even as reference points. In our haste to update educational standards, we have done away with the older gods, so that now all that we have left are names without faces, mnemonics without meaning."[8]

Yet we still seem to need contact with the old ways, and Eliade speculates further that nostalgias "are sometimes charged with meanings that concern man's actual situation,"[9] instead of representing a desire for the past per se, for, as Jung says, "in former times men did not reflect upon their symbols; they lived them and were unconsciously animated by their meaning."[10] It is this "unconscious animation" of the archetype that I think attracts so many writers to Hawaiian materials, but not all are successful in dealing with it. Take two examples which treat the same motif, that of the penetration of an ancient Hawaiian burial cave by a Caucasian. In the first, *The Secret Cave of Kamanawa* by Helen Lamar Berkey (1968), young Llewelyn "Boy" McFarlane, having recently moved to Hawaii with his family, hears of a nearby secret burial cave of Hawaiian royalty *(alii)* from an old Hawaiian neighbor (the eccentric but kind Cat Woman), and sets out with his dog to discover it. He does, of course, against all odds—or, more accurately, his dog discovers it. "Boy" breaks the highest of the ancient *kapu,* formerly punishable with instant death, by penetrating the cave and desecrating it by taking a finger bone and other souvenirs to prove to Cat Woman that he has actually found the cave. Cat Woman is deeply distressed to learn that the bones of her ancestors have been discovered and disturbed, but she decides to safeguard the remains of the cave by donating them to the [Bishop] Museum. When "Boy" and a young anthropologist are unable to relocate the entrance to the cave after a remarkable four days of rain and tropical growth, Cat Woman is relieved and "Boy" chagrined. But for all of his encounter with things of great mana, "Boy" learns virtually nothing about either ancient Hawaii or himself; he seems capable only of drinking lemonade with the anthropologist and picking burrs out of his dog's coat, rather than realizing the experience he has undergone. This is clearly a superficial, "outsider's" story, and Ray Lanterman's dramatic, carefully accurate illustrations overshadow the text.

In another book by Ruth Tabrah, however, the penetration of an ancient cave is made to serve higher concepts of cultural awareness and self-realization. In *Hawaiian Heart* (1964), newly-arrived twelve-year-old Emily Fergus is urged from the outset to keep her "heart and eyes open" in order to truly understand her new experiences.[11] Emily meets a field archaeologist from the Bishop Museum who leads her family on an exploration of known burial caves in the Kohala area of the Big Island. Tabrah introduces the "superstition" of a mysterious "cave sickness" which can result from the removing of artifacts from a sacred cave. This belief has a corollary in the widespread notion that to remove rocks from the Hawaiian Islands is bad luck. Each year, the U.S. Postal Service in Honolulu receives dozens of packages of rocks from former tourists now willing to believe that the possession of Madame Pele's rocks caused their unusual bad luck. Mana, remember, is everywhere, even in the lava.

When Emily's younger brother sneaks a leg bone out of a cave and becomes suddenly and seriously ill, Emily, who fears caves to begin with, is called upon to surreptitiously return the bone to its rightful place. Her redescent into the cave marks a shift in the direction of her life, for Emily comes to grips with death as a process: "Emily poised the leg bone over the scattered bones at the rear of the alcove. Now she actually was here so close to the reality of all these 'old ones,' she was no longer afraid. Here was death as it came to everyone."[12] Emily has felt the power of the "old ones," and has learned to treat the dead, as well as the living, with respect. More importantly, by the end of the novel her encounters with the ways of ancient Hawaii have revealed her own place: "I'm a *haole*, Emily thought. The word no longer offended her. . . . She was a *haole*, as Alix was part-Hawaiian, as Dorothy was of Japanese descent, as Noelani was Hawaiian-Chinese, as Mrs. Dacuycuy at Hōnaunau was Filipino. . . . These names were only labels that told other people what part of the world you were proud to have your ancestors from."[13] Like various sister-heroes of European folktales, indeed like all archetypal heroes, Emily must descend into the world of the dead in order to better understand the world of the living; in her selfless act of saving her brother from cave sickness, Emily comes to terms with key aspects of her humanity—and it is ancient Hawaiian myth which shows the out-sider the way.

Yolen speaks profoundly in *Touch Magic* of the power of the old stories and of our continued need for them: "Storytelling is our oldest form of remembering the promises we have made to one another and to our various gods, and the promises given in return; it is a way of recording our human emotions and desires and taboos."[14] Like all great stories, Hawaiian legends and myths can remind us of these promises. No matter that the outward trappings may be unfamiliar—the point is to make them familiar, to discover the numinosity that Jung speaks of. Modern Hawaii prides itself on being a meeting point, a place where peoples and cultures merge and learn from one another. In our haste to learn of the technology and business skills of others, we—adult and child alike—should not forget the old wisdom embodied in the ancient Hawaiian tales, wisdom still accessible through the best of Hawaiian "children's" literature.

Notes

1. Joseph Campbell, *Myths to Live By* (New York: Viking, 1972), 5.
2. Ibid., 26.
3. Martha Beckwith, *Hawaiian Mythology* (Honolulu: University Press of Hawaii, 1970), 525.
4. Mircea Eliade, *Images and Symbols: Studies in Religious Symbolism,* trans. Philip Mairet (New York: Sheed and Ward, 1961), 11; Gavan Daws, *A Dream of Islands* (New York: Norton, 1980).
5. Ruth M. Tabrah, *The Red Shark* (Chicago: Follett, 1970), 77–78.
6. John Charlot, *Chanting the Universe: Hawaiian Religious Culture* (Honolulu: Emphasis International Limited, 1983), 62.
7. Carl Jung, *Man and His Symbols* (New York: Doubleday, 1964), 98 (emphasis Jung's).
8. Jane Yolen, *Touch Magic: Fantasy, Faerie, and Folklore in the Literature of Childhood* (New York: Philomel Books, 1981), 14.
9. Eliade, *Images and Symbols,* 17.
10. Jung, *Man and His Symbols,* 81.
11. Ruth M. Tabrah, *Hawaiian Heart* (Chicago: Follett, 1964), 14.
12. Ibid., 170.
13. Ibid., 180–81.
14. Yolen, *Touch Magic,* 25.

Additional Reading

Marcia Brown, *Backbone of the King: The Story of Pakaa and His Son Ku,* illust. Marcia Brown (New York: Charles Scribner's Sons, 1966; repr. Honolulu: University of Hawaii Press, 1984).
Guy and Pam Buffet, *Adventures of Kamapuaa,* ed. Ruth Tabrah, illust. Guy Buffet (Norfolk Island, Australia: Island Heritage Limited, 1972).
Guy Buffet, *Kahala: Where the Rainbow Ends,* ed. Ruth Tabrah, illust. Guy Buffet (Norfolk Island, Australia: Island Heritage Limited, 1973).

Padraic Colum, *At the Gateways of the Dawn: Tales and Legends of Hawaii,* vol. 1, illust. Juliette May Fraser (New Haven: Yale University Press for the Hawaiian Legend and Folklore Commission, 1924).

Padraic Colum, *Legends of Hawaii,* illust. Dan Ferrer (New Haven: Yale University Press, 1937).

Padraic Colum, *The Bright Islands: The Tales and Legends of Hawaii,* vol. 2, illust. Juliette May Fraser (New Haven: Yale University Press for the Hawaiian Legend and Folklore Commission, 1925).

Dave Guard, *Hale-Mano: A Legend of Hawaii,* illust. Caridad Sumile (Millbrae, Ca.: Celestial Arts/Dawne-Leigh, 1981).

Helen P. Hoyt, *The Night Marchers: A Tale of the Huakai Po,* illust. Susan Carter-Smith (Norfolk Island, Australia: Island Heritage Limited, 1976).

Ku'ulei Ihara and 'I. Johnson, *The Eight Rainbows of Umi,* illust. Marcia Morse (Honolulu: Topgallant Publishing Company, 1976).

Herb Kawainui Kane, *Voyage: The Discovery of Hawaii,* illust. Herb Kawainui Kane (Norfolk Island, Australia: Island Heritage Limited, 1976).

Eric A. Knudsen, *Spooky Stuffs: Hawaiian Ghost Stories,* ed. Sally Kaye, illust. Guy Buffet (Norfolk Island, Australia: Island Heritage Limited, 1974).

Mary Kawena Puku'i, comp., *Hawaiian Folk Tales,* trans. Laura Green, 3rd series (Poughkeepsie, N.Y.: Vassar College, 1933).

Mary Kawena Puku'i, comp., *Pikoi and Other Legends of the Island of Hawaii,* retold by Caroline Curtis, illust. Robert Lee Eskridge (Honolulu: The Kamehameha Schools Press, 1949; repr. 1971).

Mary Kawena Puku'i, comp., *Tales of the Menehune and Other Short Legends of the Hawaiian Islands,* illust. Richard Goings (Honolulu: The Kamehameha Schools Press, 1960; repr. Honolulu: Bess Press, 1983).

Mary Kawena Puku'i, comp., *The Water of Kane and Other Legends of the Hawaiian Islands,* retold by Caroline Curtis, illust. Richard Goings (Honolulu: The Kamehameha Schools Press, 1951).

Pilipo Springer, *Makaha: The Legend of the Broken Promise,* adapted by Robert B. Goodman and Robert A. Spicer, illust. Guy Buffet (Norfolk Island, Australia: Island Heritage Limited, 1974).

Vivian L. Thompson, *Hawaiian Legends of Tricksters and Riddlers,* illust. Sylvie Selig (New York: Holiday House, 1969).

Vivian L. Thompson, *Hawaiian Myths of Earth, Sea, and Sky,* illust. Leonard Weisgard (New York: Holiday House, 1966).

Vivian L. Thompson, *Maui-Full-of-Tricks; A Legend of Old Hawaii,* illust. Earl Thollander (Chicago: Children's Press, 1970).

Vivian L. Thompson, *Hawaiian Tales of Heroes and Champions,* illust. Herb Kawainui Kane (New York: Holiday House, 1971).

Margaret Titcomb, *The Voyage of the Flying Bird,* illust. Joseph Feher (Rutland, Vt.: Charles E. Tuttle, 1970).

Jay Williams, *The Surprising Things Maui Did,* illust. Charles Mikolaycak (New York: Four Winds Press, 1979).

15.

The Childlike Spirit
of the Avant-Garde
and Children's Literature

JAY LIVERNOIS

Fin-de-siècle Europe saw the dawning of a new spirit among artists and thinkers. They believed that they actively carried an advanced, modern sense of life and considered themselves "ahead" of society. A large part of this *esprit nouveau* which was held by the avant-garde was characterized by puerility or childlishness. This puerile spirit was used as a weapon to attack nineteenth-century European society, an attack intended to create new styles in art and in the way reality was seen. Many avant-garde artists were led not only into creating and using an imaginative, image-filled, and childlike spirit in their work, but were also brought to write children's literature out of their affinity for and indentification with this spirit.

In many ways the avant-garde artists at the turn of the century tried to bring back or reintegrate this childlikeness into European life from which it had been split off by Descartes and the rationalists. [1] They were largely successful in this because the solid, rationalist life of Europeans had already begun to break down in the face of modern, industrial existence. Dostoevski's short novel, *Notes from Underground,* clearly reflects European life cracking up before modern reality. [2]

The first writer to whom the avant-garde looked for inspiration was the poet Arthur Rimbaud. Rimbaud was not only their great predecessor or grandfather (he foreshadowed the avant-garde by thirty years), but also their "grand child." He wrote his major works when he was *"Encore tout enfant"* (still but a child), [3] about seventeen years old, and he completely gave up writing poetry when he was nineteen. Rimbaud was truly "un enfant terrible."

In his *Une Saison en Enfer* (A Season in Hell), Rimbaud invokes the spirit of children. He says, "I thought of us as two good children, free to wander in the Paradise of sadness." [4] The childlike spirit was what, in part, moved him to write. But Rimbaud's child is a mischievous child, and its spirit is perverse and not at all sentimental. Whenever Rimbaud presents a sentimental child image, he does so only to immediately pervert it. Here is a passage in which a pastoral childhood is invoked, only to bring with it the devil and stupidity: "Ah, childhood, the grass, the rain, the lake over the stones, the moonlight when the bell was chiming twelve . . . the devil is in the belfry at this hour. Mary! Holy Virgin! . . . —Horror of my stupidity."[5]

For Rimbaud "One must be absolutely modern,"[6] and in that modernity he says, "I loved . . . fairy-tales, children's books, . . . Oh! the life of adventure in childrens' books, to recompense me, I have suffered so, will you give me that?"[7] Clearly the child spirit was important for him and his work. The avant garde, which loved him, seems to have carried a similar spirit in their work including, most significantly, its perversity.

The first great avant-garde artist to integrate a childish spirit into his work was Alfred Jarry. Jarry's riot-starting play, "Ubu Roi" (King Ubu), was first performed with marionettes in 1896. Besides the fact that this anti-realist play was first performed in a medium thought appropriate only for the entertainment of children, it childishly, gleefully, set out to destroy adult conceptions of how a play was to be performed. The "adults" were so literally offended, they punched the adults who had put on such a childish play.

In this play Jarry brought a primitive infantalism to his main character, King Ubu, and even lived the role of Ubu (so much of the avant-garde's artistic theory was also acted out in their lives that it is difficult to separate the two). Jarry would stage tantrums in public to "hit" the bourgeoisie of Paris.

Jarry was good friends with Guillaume Apollinaire, and the childish role he assumed seems to have had a great influence on Apollinaire's stance toward art and life. Apollinaire said of Jarry on his friend's premature death in the summer of 1907: "Alfred Jarry was to a rare extent a 'man of letters'. His least actions, his childish pranks, were literary. For he justified himself through literature and through it alone. . . . These orgies of intelligence . . . were only possible during the Renaissance and Jarry, miraculously, was the last of these sublime debauchees."[8] Apollinaire was the first major figure in the avant-garde actually to write children's literature.[9] Although he wrote children's literature for money, Apollinaire's interest in it can also be related to his closeness to the child spirit found throughout his life and works. His personality, the spontaneous acting out of his life, seem to have lent itself naturally to his attraction toward writing for children. Apollinaire maintained a close touch with his subconscious life, and his truest, most childlike self, and this was easily translatable into the writing of children's fables. "What Apollinaire attained then, and what renders him so fascinating to a public which finds it hard to make any vital connection between art and life, is the automatic life . . . a way of acting in total response to one's deepest nature without rejecting the contradictions or paradoxes inherent in that 'nature.'[10] It seems Apollinaire learned this automatic or consistent life from Jarry.

At the same time that Apollinaire was shaping the attitudes of the French avant-garde, Filippo Marinetti launched Italian Futurism with his publication of the Futurist Manifesto in *Le Figaro*. In it Marinetti advocated a puerile, futuristic destructiveness, along with a "little boy" fascination of machines, bombs, and speed. In the manifesto Marinetti said: "We wish to extol the love of danger, the custom of energy and daring. We desire to destroy all the museums, the libraries, combat 'moralism' . . ."[11]

But the avant-garde movement which had probably the most child-like, playful elements in it was Dadaism. It took its name from the infantile pronunciation for father, which also means a child's rocking horse in French. Dadaism was founded in 1916 by a group of international exiles in Zurich who were avoiding the collective madness and slaughter of World War I. The central figure around whom Dadaism revolved was Tristan Tzara, a young Rumanian Jewish exile.

The Dadaists loved to shock society. Their actions often seemed like those of bad children. In one of their shows, they dressed a girl as if for her first communion and had her recite obscene poetry. Another example of this shocking playfulness can be seen in one of their paintings in the Zurich Kunsthaus. It depicts a fantastic geared machine which looks like a meat grinder. It is titled "une grate de poo-poo."

At the end of World War I, Tzara and many of the Dadaists moved to Paris (another group moved to Berlin). There they were joined by a younger group of French poets led by André Breton. Breton and company had admired Apollinaire as the leader of the older generation of the avant-garde, (which had helped develop the cubism of Picasso and Braque). They called themselves surrealists, a name they were given by Apollinaire.

Unfortunately, the surrealists seem to have had little of the childlike openness or humor of the Dadaists. Some artists, like Dali and Margritte, maintained a certain playfulness in their work, but Breton turned surrealism into a serious movement and set himself up as its dictator. Throughout the twenties he expelled from the movement anyone he disagreed with, including Philippe Soupault and Louis Aragon, two of the movement's founders. In 1930, Breton joined surrealism to the cause of Stalinism and, with ideological and political overtones, the childishness of the avant-garde ended.

One outstanding avant-garde figure, however, maintained her childlike sensibilities until the end of her life. Gertrude Stein had been one of the first of the English writers to use cubism in her work. Her *Three Lives* (1909) is a cubist novel, and her erotic cubist poem, *Tender Buttons,* was published in 1914. In 1939, Stein's major contribution to children's literature, *The World is Round,* was published by an unconventional young publisher, William R. Scott, who specialized in children's books. Miss Stein's editor for the book was Margaret Wise Brown, who was herself, over the period of the next decade or so, the author of about one hundred books for young children, which projected the childlike spirit of the avant-garde to an extraordinary degree, showing that spirit triumphant over (sometimes) sad reality. In her children's story, Stein broke down conventions in syntax and punctuation to get a rhyming, fantastic effect. She carried the reader along through the imaginative story-journey of a little girl, Rose. In this book, Stein used all her old tricks of analytical and synthetic cubism to come up with a story which is delightful, serious, and modern. But most importantly the heroine, Rose, is Gertrude Stein's own imaginary child, and unlike the city of Oakland where she was born, Stein is there there.[12]

The puerility of the avant-garde began with the inspiration of the "almost child" of Rimbaud, went to the shocking childishness of Jarry, Apollinaire, Marinetti, and the Dadaists, slowly melted with the outrageousness of the surrealists, and was crushed when Breton became a Stalinist. Its final end and triumph found expression in the reflections and cubism of Gertrude Stein's Rose. And after all "Rose is a Rose is a Rose is a Rose is a Rose."[13]

Notes

1. There is an interesting correlation between the rise of Cartesian philosophy in the seventeenth century and the distinct development (which I see as a fragmentation of Renaissance European culture) of children's literature (the idea of childhood as we know it was invented then), the occult, and the ideas of madness, the primitive, and the erotic. It seems as if these subjects developed out of the attacks by the Jesuit philosophers, Descartes and Mersenne, on the Renaissance Neoplatonic tradition. In Neoplatonic philosophy, they were inte-

gral parts of a way to understand life, but with the rationalists' war on this philosophy, it broke apart into separate although occasionally related subjects.

2. Rimbaud echoes this, "Yet, I was hardly thinking of the pleasure of escaping modern wretchedness," Arthur Rimbaud, *Une Saison en Enfer & Le Bateau Ivre,* trans. Louise Varese (New York: New Directions, 1945), 70, 71.

3. Ibid., 14, 15.

4. Ibid., 42, 43.

5. Ibid., 28, 29. Not long after Rimbaud's death, the theory of the polymorphous by perverse child was developed by Freud.

6. Ibid., 88, 89.

7. Ibid., 48, 49, 44, 45.

8. Cecily Mackworth, *Guillaume Apollinaire and the Cubist Life* (New York: Horizon, 1963), 98–99.

9. Apollinaire's children's writings have not been translated into English. Guillaume Apollinaire, *Selected Writings of Guillaume Apollinaire,* trans. and intro. Roger Shattuck (New York: New Directions, 1971), 7.

10. Ibid., 52–53.

11. Mackworth, *Apollinaire and the Cubist Life,* 99–100.

12. When Gertrude Stein was asked where she was from, she would say, "Oakland, a city where there is no there there."

13. Gertrude Stein, *The World is Round,* in *Sharing Literature with Children,* ed. Francelia Butler (New York: Longman, 1977), 426.

16.

Progression Through Contraries: The Triumph of the Spirit in the Work of Maurice Sendak

GERALDINE DELUCA

> Without Contraries is no progression. Attraction and Repulsion, Reason and Energy, Love and Hate, are necessary to Human existence.
>
> *William Blake*

The spirit in the work of Maurice Sendak is a contrary thing; it is that of fighter and aesthete, a child and a highly sophisticated adult, a brash teller of simple truths, and a repository of esoterica. It reflects a lover of spontaneity with an obsessive need to research, reexamine, redo; a champion of childhood with a (rightful) need for an appreciative audience of informed adults. It is Sendak's strength and his burden that his spirit of creation—and for him "the only thing that's miraculous is the creative act"—is tied to his childhood.[1] There is an urgency in his work to define once and for all the nature of childhood desire, longing, transcendence, and presumably from that definition to forge an artistic statement that includes us all.

The young child in Sendak is an egocentric, impulsive creature with a driving curiosity, great stores of energy, equally great needs for attention and autonomy, and a tendency to get stuck in rigid patterns of behavior. And that child's conflicts, what goes wrong and how it gets put right again, to some degree represent our own. Thus, in depicting the Oedipal dramas, the sibling rivalry, the drive toward control and creativity, Sendak is a humanist, understanding and celebrating the place of anger, rebelliousness, hunger, and recognizing the need to shape those drives to create the order, the decorum, the harmony that his own work at its best demonstrates.

We can begin, in talking about the triumph of the spirit in Sendak, with the body. Convention places body and spirit in opposition, but as any reader of Sendak knows, in his work they are integrated. Blake writes, "Energy is the only life, and is from the Body; and Reason is the bound or outward circumference of Energy. Energy is Eternal Delight."[2] One thinks of the "eternal delight" of Mickey in the sky of the night kitchen, of David floating voluptuously in *Fly By Night,* of the naked girl in the illustration for MacDonald's *The Light Princess.* When their spirits quite literally take flight in their dreams, their bodies become free as well. Sendak knows that young children love to take off their clothes, and he celebrates their lack of self-consciousness, the loveliness of their being, like Adam and Eve before the fall, unashamed of their nakedness. Theirs is a spirit of innocent sexuality; they enjoy what feels good. And Sendak insists quite justifiably that in certain contexts that deserves a place in their books. Anything else would be dishonest. In the case of David, in *Fly By Night,* it would also be unaesthetic. According to Sendak, the boy simply looked too awkward floating in pajamas: "He had to be naked. But I knew they'd say it was just like me, arbitrarily making somebody nude."[3]

Sendak's portrayal of children in the freedom and exploration of their dreams has gained him some notoriety, but it is very faithful to a child's sensibility and interests. The enduring popularity of *Where the Wild Things Are* and *In the Night Kitchen* attests to the astuteness of his instincts. Both books are now comfortably regarded as classics in which children neatly and imaginatively resolve their problems.

In a number of other works, small and large, Sendak depicts heroes whose irritated psyches don't take such active routes toward their own satisfaction, who, rather, are locked into rigid forms of behavior, usually nay-saying or devouring, and who need outside help to make their way past their own rigidity. Hector Protector, Pierre, and Jennie the dog are cantankerous, compulsive characters. The baby swallowing its mother may fit here too. They are all involved in antisocial behavior that will ultimately leave them lonely. The counter-example, it is worth mentioning, is the hero in *One Was Johnny* "who lived by himself and liked it like that." That seems to be a different issue. Johnny is an autonomous figure in a family-centered world. The other characters, however, are alienating themselves because they are stuck in their own bad moods. Something calamitous yet ultimately safe needs to happen to release them back to more comfortable selves who can live with the rest of us.

This is an important theme in Sendak—getting past one's own rigidity or neurosis—and its more elaborate working out occurs in *Higglety, Pigglety, Pop.* Its subtitle, "Or There Must Be More To Life," tells us that

Jennie is a dissatisfied soul, "unfulfilled" despite her devouring nature; devouring because of that unfulfillment. The book, Sendak makes clear in his conversations with Selma Lanes, is his attempt to reconcile himself to the loss of his dog Jennie and to prepare for the impending loss of his mother. Thus, he gives us himself as a baby who is separated from parents who have gone to "Castle Yonder," and Jennie, who is leaving an overindulgent master, also Sendak, in search of something more than the predictable "everything" she has gotten in Sendak's care.

Clearly allegorical, this book reflects a preoccupation with the spirit in its implication of other worlds, levels of understanding, depths, and transcendence. Allegory insists on interpretation and involves its protagonists in a search for answers. Jennie, stuck with her hunger for something more than dependency, must make her own small journey to the end of the night, reach the point of having "nothing," and in the process gain "experience." What is most important for Jennie is that, in taking care of baby, she subordinates her own needs to that of her charge (thus paying Sendak the master/baby back for all his love), and gains experience—which is also on one level sacrificing her life. The artist needs experience to create, and once Jennie has it, she is released from her bewildered compulsiveness to become the dog in the nursery rhyme whose creative act is, amusingly enough, to eat a mop made of salami every day and twice on Saturday. The other hero of the book, Baby, the compulsive nay-sayer who wouldn't eat, represents Sendak as an orphan. He finds his happiness by achieving immortality as Mother Goose, creative artist and spirit of childhood par excellence.

The spirit triumphs in this book by discovering what it loves best to do and then finding a socially acceptable way to do it. Of himself, Sendak says, "As a small boy, I pasted and clipped my bits of books together and hoped only for a life that would allow me to earn my bread by making books. And here I am all grown up—still staying home, pasting and clipping bits of books together."[4] One watches how children who are not given the space to explore and create become disruptive and irritable, and how, conversely, they relax when someone channels their energy by offering them something to do that they find genuinely interesting. Sendak knows that "laziness," rigidity, grumpiness can be seen as signs of unfulfillment, of the creative spirit thwarted in some way and needing release.

Although Sendak is exploring a double loss in *Higglety, Pigglety, Pop,* and although the book has a surreal, cryptic quality to it, it still has a clear sense of resolution that can satisfy both child and adult. In Sendak's *Outside Over There,* the sense of the infinite complexity of the artist's own

perceptions and memories work to the story's disadvantage. Reading
Sendak's conversation with Jonathan Cott, one finds association upon
association woven into pictures and text so that one feels this work insists
on its inability to be deeply understood. Obscurity becomes a kind of
end in itself. The spirit of childhood and the spirit of the artist in search
of an enormously suggestive way of recording his aesthetic and emotional experience come into conflict.

Perhaps some of this has to do with the subject matter, for the spirit in
Sendak's world is sorely burdened around the subject of sibling rivalry.
Sendak's perception is that children don't just learn to love the baby
because their parents tell them they should, and both the early *Very Far
Away* and *Outside Over There* convey clearly that this is one problem not
easily transcended. Because Martin's mother in *Very Far Away* has no
time for him, he decides to go "very far away" where someone will
answer his questions, and he meets a horse, a bird, and a cat who are
feeling as disgruntled as he is. Unfortunately, they discover that their
separate ideas of an ideal place are discordant, and Martin finally leaves,
disappointed and cranky, with no place to go but back to his still busy
mother. There is no triumph here. This is one experience that doesn't
transform anyone. Essentially Martin is no better equipped to handle his
feelings at the end of the book than at the beginning. Sendak himself is
critical of this fact.[5] But the book is an interesting one with a certain
amount of quiet humor and symmetry, and it is unfortunately true to
many a child's experience of what it means to have a new baby enter the
house. About *Outside Over There,* Sendak offered the following to Cott:

Appearances aside, we are really looking at only a minute's
worth of life. And if the mother is distracted for that minute, can
we draw the conclusion that she's indifferent or comatose? Or
isn't it just that she's unwittingly distracted, like any normal
mother who, at any given moment of the day, gets distracted
. . . and during that moment something happens to the child—
bad luck, bad timing?

My intention was to leave room for a break to occur: In every
child's life it happens that at a critical moment the mother . . . is
inattentive to the child. And the child is then given his or her
opportunity to make out for him- or herself, because there's no
mama there. . . .[6]

True enough, and Stephen Roxburgh argues eloquently that the drawings support this interpretation, but is this the perception the child is

likely to have in reading this book—that Mama was maybe just a moment before actively involved with Ida and the baby? Ida is a child in trouble. Her young spirit is burdened with jealousy and loneliness; she is charged with caring for the baby when she'd rather play her horn. The experience of the kidnapping—the ultimate horror and punishment for a moment's inattention—evokes momentary and not terribly convincing anger and ultimately a kind of bewilderment. That she endures and everyone survives is about as much triumph as we get in the book, and elsewhere I have argued that it is not enough. Sendak's own love for the book, as communicated to Lanes and Cott, has to do with issues, influences, and images that I find interesting but ultimately irrelevant to its meaning to children.

But I do think there is a consolation, and it comes to us through the spirit and presence of Mozart in the book. What Sendak offers Ida in this work is her own power to create, represented in her playing her horn to get rid of the goblins, and letting her pass by Mozart in the woods to show how close she is—though she doesn't know it consciously—to that music and its power. Ida may not be ready to understand the joy and sorrow of the human spirit embodied in the figure of Mozart at the keyboard, but it is one thing an adult can offer to a child whose problems cannot be acted out and conquered in a single dream. Sendak would argue, I'm sure, that the dream is the first form of creativity and is involved in everything creative that we do. Ida's experience is, on one level, all internal; but *Outside Over There* also suggests how the complex feelings of love, jealousy, fear, loneliness, and relief can find enduring and rich expression in a work of art—Mozart's music being perhaps the ultimate, sublime expression. And there is also, with all its difficulties, Sendak's lovely book itself.

Outside Over There is filled with folk motifs, and it is no surprise that Sendak, with his love of romanticism, of the dark recesses and the wildest flights of the soul, with his reverence for both the primitive and the consummately refined, would also find himself drawn to the spare and somber beauty of the Grimm tales. The genre bridges the gap between children's and adult literature and is filled with the primitive impulses and the deepest conflicts in all of us. His illustrations for *The Juniper Tree* give us the taboo side of the human soul, collections of characters smouldering, enraged, languid; the compression of the pictures, the claustrophobic sense of borders closing in telling us that this is all repressed but pushing against the surface. This is the fertile soil of our imagination, these are the patterns of our lives, though bizarre enough so that we may not own them. There again is Sendak's fascination with brash truths, the bare bones of things, and there again is the challenge to the conventional notions of what children's literature is supposed to be, of what Sendak the artist is supposed to be.

I find myself at once awed and distracted by the mannerist quality of those illustrations. The tales tell us of dream and metaphor and censorship; they are refined, elegant, and somber, and they haunt us as Sendak's severe drawings do. I wonder though, after considering the fairly harsh appraisal of Donnarae MacCann and Olga Richards, what those drawings might have been if Sendak had not done quite so much research, had not needed to be more romantic and Germanic than his German predecessors. For one misses in these pictures the spontaneity that MacCann and Richards rightly admire in many of his early illustrations for other artists. There—in Meindert DeJong's books, in the luminous paintings for Charlotte Zolotow, in the drawings for Ruth Krauss—one sees art that is much closer to the spirit of childhood, to the vulnerability Sendak so often mentions, the freshness, the honesty and directness. One misses those lovely, more tentative evocations of childhood, and wonders whether it was easier for Sendak to create with a lighter hand because he was working as an illustrator with other writers. Perhaps, with the shared responsibility, the artistic stakes were not as ominously high.

I find the ever-more-pressing need for elaboration, the quest for truth through endless definition in Sendak's work somewhat oppressive. His illustrations are gorgeous, dazzling, but also somehow wearisome. Sendak's movement into set design for opera and ballet, both art forms characterized by a high degree of artifice, precision, spectacle, and an almost super-human level of performance, may be a fruitful one for him. Perhaps there the desire to create works of high seriousness on a huge scale, to follow the path of his own artistic heroes, Mozart, Melville, and Conrad, will have freer play. For part of what keeps the spirit soaring, as his works tell us, is finding joy in the day to day work we do, which also means finding new paths to travel, knowing where one's creative spirit needs to go, and also receiving the recognition of a wider audience than has previously been his to enjoy.

Notes

1. Jonathan Cott, "Maurice Sendak: King of All the Wild Things," in *Pipers at the Gates of Dawn: The Wisdom of Children's Literature* (New York: Random House, 1983), 60.

2. William Blake, "The Marriage of Heaven and Hell," in *Complete Writings* (London: Oxford University Press, 1966), 149.

3. Selma G. Lanes, *The Art of Maurice Sendak* (New York: Abrams, 1980), 216.

4. Ibid., 270.

5. Ibid., 66.

6. Cott, "Maurice Sendak," 78.

IV.

Foreign Writers and Literatures

17.

Marguerite Yourcenar and Michel Tournier: The Arts of the Heart

MARGARET R. HIGONNET

Two of France's best-known novelists, Michel Tournier and Marguerite Yourcenar, have written children's books that sometimes shock by their inclusion of sexuality and violence, themes which are usually excluded from American children's literature. Yet both writers succeed in conveying the power of love and art to transcend all difficulties and to create new worlds.

Yourcenar's story *How Wang-Fo Was Saved,* inspired by a Tao apologue and condensed from a version written for adults (1936), depicts the arrest of the painter Wang-Fo and his disciple Ling by the Han emperor. This effete young emperor hates the painter, whose perfect works have made him realize the poverty of his kingdom. When he recounts the artistic wonders that have made him resolve to blind and cut off the hands of the aged artist, we realize the extent of Wang-Fo's genius. The devoted Ling springs to his master's defense. Envious of such loyalty, the emperor has him beheaded, then commands Wang-Fo to complete in his last moments of vision a landscape he had sketched in his youth. Slowly the artist begins to fill in the sea depicted in the picture. As he does so, the jade pavement becomes wet and the sound of oars is heard. While the courtiers remain ceremoniously frozen, Ling rows in and carries off his master. "So long as you were alive," he explains, "how could I die?" Their dedication to each other and to art draws the two into the painting, to the country that lies beyond the painted sea.

The mystical transformation that closes Yourcenar's tale (a pattern that recurs in her other *Oriental Tales*) also shades into all the metaphoric descriptions that so vividly evoke Wang-Fo's warm art and the emperor's chilly palace. We see, as if through Wang-Fo's idealizing eyes, the transfixed emperor, who floats "like a lotus" among the rising waters. Most striking is Yourcenar's treatment of her terrible events: "One of the soldiers lifted his sword, and Ling's head fell from his neck like a cut flower. . . . Wang-Fo in despair admired the beautiful red stain of his disciple's blood on the green stone floor." Even violence may occasion beauty.

Both the artistry and the terror of this story pose difficulties for the illustrator. Georges Lemoine has found remarkable visual equivalents to Yourcenar's devices. Perhaps to control the moment of shock, Ling's blood stains only a small part of one page, opposite an iris petal of the same fluid form and size, surrounded by text that suggests the continuity of life. By contrast, two full pages depict the inundated imperial hall, and the closing lines are suffused by the pale blue wash of Wang-Fo's liberating sea. Most significantly, Lemoine blends the face of Wang-Fo with his landscapes—a crescent moon shines in the artist's eye. Thus he prepares us for the mystical fusion of Yourcenar's conclusion. Image and word collaborate fully in this gem of aestheticism.

The transcendence of death, the legendary Oriental source, and the illustrations by Lemoine all link Yourcenar's tale to *Barbedor* (1980) by Tournier in the same Gallimard series. Tournier's ruler Barbedor faces old age and the unresolved problems of succession with serene indifference. What preoccupies him instead is the growth each day of a white hair in his beautiful golden beard; strangely, he is awakened from his daily nap by a thief who plucks out each new white hair. Finally Barbedor catches sight of the bird which has been stealing this token of his mortality and pursues it through town and country to its white nest, where he finds an egg. During his quest, he has mysteriously become a child again, and as he arrives at the imperial gates, the egg hatches and a fledgling bird heralds him as the new ruler. In such mythic cycles of youth and age, of course, death remains far less problematic than in *Wang-Fo*. Indeed, some readers have found in Tournier's plots for adults as well as children an unrealistic suggestion that we can reproduce by cloning, by repetition rather than change. But this unnatural model for reproduction may also be read as an allegory about artistic creation and self-recreation. Such a cycle is a way to represent the recovery of their own childhood that many writers of children's literature sense.

Tournier's narratives lie on the threshold between reality and dream, between the everyday and mythological, and between children's directness and adult innuendo. By his own account, Tournier's most successful book for children is *Pierrot, or the Secrets of the Night* (1981). "I would gladly give all my other works for this one." This story, which won the prize for best foreign book at the Leipzig fair for children's literature, combines powerful mythic oppositions with lighthearted subtlety. The tale on the face of it seems simple, yet it fuses many themes and provokes thought about major issues.

Pierrot starts from familiar, traditional materials, as does *Friday* (1967), Tournier's best known novel, based on Robinson Crusoe, which won the Grand Prix de l'Académie Française. In *commedia dell'arte*, Pierrot and Harlequin are rivals for the affections of the flirtatious and flighty Columbine. Just as Italian street actors used to localize each performance, Tournier has blended his traditional theme with details and language from provincial French life. His Pierrot makes croissants and brioches, his Harlequin paints houses, and Columbine is a washerwoman. Into this comic village romance, Tournier has inserted a scene evoked by the traditional French song, "Au Clair de la lune."

Pierrot, who bakes at night, loves from afar Columbine, who does her wash by day. One day, Harlequin arrives and seduces her by his bright colors and saucy manners, carrying her off in his gypsy van to enjoy the heat of the summer. Come winter, Columbine finds life difficult with her happy-go-lucky lover, and a love note from Pierrot persuades her to return to town, to relish the stability and warmth of the bakery. Harlequin soon follows, singing by moonlight his famous request: "Friend Pierrot, lend me your pen to write something by moonlight. My candle is out, my fire too. Open your door, for heaven's sake." Unlike the character in the song, Pierrot welcomes his rival and the three share an enormous loaf of bread that Pierrot has baked in the shape of Columbine.

Even a brief summary suggests the mythological overtones of the story. Pierrot is associated with night, Columbine and Harlequin with the day. Tournier deftly explores the ambiguous value of the two poles. Day is bright, gay, filled with flowers and song. The sun not only whitens and dries Columbine's wash, but brightens the colors of Harlequin's outfit. Day and summer are linked to happy conversation and fertility: social values. But Harlequin's pot of colors is also "gaudy," soon to fade, and "toxic." A vat of dyes gives off nauseating fumes, as Pierrot hastens to warn Columbine.

Nighttime, thinks Columbine, is obscure, filled with threatening beasts of prey like wolves and owls; she fears that Pierrot's cellar kitchen may be rat-infested, sooty, and black with the fumes from his oven. Through Pierrot, however, the child afraid of the night learns how to overcome such projections and comes to appreciate night. If Columbine and Harlequin are "children of the sun," linked by their gaiety, Pierrot is "brother" of the moon, and like her is silent, timid, and faithful. He knows that the moon is not flat and cold but smiles or grimaces, depending on what she sees; his night has its own colors of blue and its own dance. Like Tournier's shipwrecked Robinson in *Friday,* the solitary Pierrot is attuned to cosmic harmonies and elemental beauties.

Pictorially, the story starts from an apparent opposition between the colors of Columbine's day and the black and white of Pierrot's night. This stylized contrast is enhanced by Danièle Bour's cheery, doll-like figures, reminiscent of pantomime. We move on to an opposition between summer and winter, which dislocates the original contrast. Finally, we reach a more profound understanding with the opposition between the bright, transient colors of Harlequin's paints and the lasting, fresh blues and delicious golds of Pierrot's night and oven. The mythic balance between day and night from which we start is displaced by a more charged contrast between new and old, between ephemeral innovation and enduring tradition.

Ultimately, this new contrast has moral undertones. The unspoken echo of La Fontaine's "The Grasshopper and the Ant" enters into our judgment of Harlequin, the charming solipsist. Yet Pierrot's warm welcome to both Columbine and Harlequin takes us far beyond the harsh moralizing and self-righteousness of the fable. In Tournier's version, both figures are artists. In their contrasting skills we trace a threatening but ultimately creative rivalry, one which brings Pierrot to express his love and to create a new social circle.

Just as he invokes traditional oppositions and themes in order to make us question them in his adult fiction, Tournier in this classic tale for children sets into play and challenges our norms and values. This is especially evident in the ways he combines traditional, mythological motifs with modern sexual themes. Thus in *The Ogre,* the legend of the erl-king frames a study of pedophilia and Nazi terror. Rival desires, of course, are embedded in Tournier's *commedia dell'arte* source for *Pierrot,* and his success there lies in part in the breadth of his mythologizing impulse.

All children's literature has a double audience, child and adult, and some of our greatest works juxtapose ironic subtexts to their main texts. Tournier's tactic is rather to exploit ambiguities in level of understanding and to defy our expectations, leading the child–reader through a narrative process of redefinition.

Provocative ambiguity is evident in Tournier's basic characterizations. Pierrot and Columbine are half-way between children and adults. He is a baker's "boy" *(mitron),* yet he would like to caress her breasts. The sensuousness of Pierrot's love for Columbine may remind us of a child's response to the mother or to its own fresh body. We should note that Pierrot's affections are universal; he responds similarly to the roundness of the moon, as to "a cheek, a breast, or a bottom." Ultimately, with a wisdom and artistry born of respect, instead of fulfilling his desire to caress Columbine, he sublimates his passion in modeling the round breasts, cheeks, and bottom of her double, the Columbine made of bread. In all likelihood, children will respond in their own way to the terms of physical attraction (*fesses,* bottom, is an everyday term in French, related to *fessée,* spanking). Such details should challenge our conceptions of children's self-image as well as our patterns of censorship.

Through stylistic details that suggest constant cosmic regeneration, Tournier universalizes the sexuality of children (which Freud misleadingly calls polymorphous "perversity," because it is nongenital). The winds of day are "impregnated" with the labor of men; yeast "fertilizes" the bread Pierrot bakes at night.

Tournier's provocative restraint is most evident in the "primal scene" which follows Harlequin's initial welcome by Columbine. Pierrot discovers the painter's scaffold on Columbine's house, climbs up, and is so shocked by what he sees ("We will never know!") that he falls back, tumbling ten feet to the ground and injuring himself. While the sexual content of this scene is suppressed, its emotional impact finds expression in the labyrinth of pots and scaffolding through which the baker's boy staggers and the wound he receives when he "falls" from innocence. Pierrot, who must always work inside, by virtue of Harlequin's seduction of Columbine becomes an outsider, but by the end of the story brings the outside into his warm kitchen. Columbine, incorporated in the bread, incorporates it in turn. Both these inversions work to transform the conventional understanding of the sexual content of the scenes.

The ambivalence of sensuousness that merges into sensuality, depending on the degree of awareness of the reader, reaches a delightfully outrageous climax in the scene of Pierrot's night kitchen. Columbine betrays her narcissism in embracing her pastry twin. She spreads apart the breasts made of dough, and wiggling her tongue, "She plunges her eager nose into the golden neckline of Columbine." Then, delighted by her own delicious flavor, she invites her lovers to participate, to "eat me." Such a scene is at once mythological and erotically suggestive, by contrast to the more restrained symbolism of food and love in stories like *Higglety-Pigglety-Pop.* In the English tradition, Christina Rossetti's *Goblin Market* may come closest to Tournier's shock effect, when Lizzie urges, "Hug me, kiss me, suck my juices," and thus redeems her sister.

The final love feast marks Tournier's most creative departure from familiar mythological and psychosexual alignments. Pierrot's lunar wisdom transcends destructive jealousies and unites the three in a harmony at once infantile and mature. The Oedipal trio latent in the scaffolding scene is overcome by the child-man's expansive love. In the return to the ovenroom we see not only a presexual return to the womb, but at the same time the triumph of higher, more stable domestic values. Similarly, Columbine's self-delight and self-division wittily blend her flirtatious narcissism with maternal love. For the forms of sexuality Tournier celebrates are not binding or fixed but liberating and open to others, they are cosmic and metamorphic forms of love. Love, he suggests in *Friday,* may be vast as well as deep. He leads us from eros to agape.

For a feminist reader, Columbine, with her traditional volatility and her narcissism, seems problematic. Like Harlequin, she is symbol rather than realistic person; both lack the emotional complexity and rounded character of Pierrot. Yet Columbine's relationship to Harlequin and Pierrot suggests that her symbolism is not so simple as may first appear. These rival artists attempt to "capture" and define Columbine, each shaping this girl in his own image, as a "Harlequinette" or "Pierrette." Perhaps the "woman" who poses for these two women is simply a projection of their fantasies—a question we may welcome in children's literature.

The theme of the artist is crucial to our understanding of Tournier's methods. The novelist, as Tournier has said elsewhere, is something of a man-eater, "But cannibalism won't work without a good stomach that mashes, crunches, dissolves, digests, assimilates, and metamorphoses." The artist always kneads and leavens his materials. Indeed, his materials leaven each other. We see this when Tournier layers his narrative patterns—the *commedia dell'arte* tale of rivalry, the song of the unwelcome night visitor, the quite similar fable of the cricket visiting the ant, what Freud called the "family romance" of the Oedipal phase, and the Judeo-Christian shared supper. As the patterns fuse, they disrupt traditional lines of interpretation. The moments of slippage from one narrative to another offer us as readers freedom to reinterpret and to revalue their moral baggage. Thus each narrative, when inserted into another, becomes the germ of fresh insights.

Furthermore, Tournier reinterprets his own earlier themes. The folk motif of cannibalism, which figures in *The Ogre* through the voyeuristic protagonist's attraction to children, is displaced here into the spontaneous joy of the final feast. The identification of generosity with hunger (so like the combination of greed and self-sacrifice in Sendak's Jenny) carries into a realm familiar to children the theme of desire as self-sacrifice prominent in Tournier's adult fiction, where the "ogre" is also a Saint Christopher.

Within the story itself, the mirror opposition of Harlequin's reading of Pierrot and Pierrot's reading of Harlequin distances us from a simplistic acceptance of either. This is even more true of their representations of Columbine. As the characters learn to reinterpret each other, so does the reader reassess the oppositions of the tale.

Tournier's scrupulous verbal artistry supports our mastery of his most problematic and provocative themes. For his language helps us to realize the reasons for Pierrot's triumph. Words, as well as colors, can seduce Columbine. Harlequin "talks clothes" to Columbine, but Pierrot's poem wins her back. Their rivalry is verbalized as a battle in Columbine's head between two sets of words beginning with f, the first a swarm of hostile nouns like feebleness, folly, and famine, the second set comforting and encouraging, like flower, fire, flour, or feast. More immediately, these opposed sequences echo the "floof" sound of footsteps in snow and appeal to children's love of word-play.

Undoubtedly, Tournier's subjects are potentially quite demanding, and so is his style. He does not hesitate to use long words (fluviatile, for example, to describe Barbedor's undulating, silky beard) where they can mark a major visual feature, yet are supported by an explanatory context. He exploits the possibilities of mixing past and present tenses to give rhythm to his narrative. Indeed, *Pierrot* shifts to the present at the moment Tournier describes his secret knowledge of the night, thus lending special emphasis to the secrets of the title. Similarly, he uses pointers like "here," or "how," to give actuality to a scene, like theatrical pointers to a visual world that has the vivid quality of mime—or of illustrations. The contrast between Tournier's stylistic control and the potential violence of some of his material makes him a modern Racine.

Tournier says he does not directly intend to write for children, but discovers after the fact that what he has written, at its best, may succeed as children's literature. The underlying premise of this confession is that the greatest literature for adults has the simplicity and mythological structure of our traditional children's literature. Undoubtedly, Tournier has labored to achieve such clarity and structure in all his works. Purity of line is the first quality that will strike the reader of *Pierrot,* and it is one that is enhanced by Bour's translucent colors and simple outlines. At the same time, the text also has the fascination that stems from the disturbance of traditional attitudes. At a very simple level accessible to quite small children, Tournier exposes questions about sexual desire, jealousy, and sensual joy. It is adults rather than children who may be shocked by his material. For the shared community in the final scene of breaking bread offers a powerful affirmation of values that lie beyond the conventional representation of sexuality.

The cultural value of children's literature in France clearly emerges from these works by the first woman writer admitted to the Académie Française and by the man who has won a reputation as the most exciting living novelist in France, for his novels evoking the life of outsiders in impeccable, classic prose. Their works exemplify the thesis that great children's stories often spring from the germ of legend, rhyme, or pun. They challenge children's linguistic resources with word play, esoteric words, extended rhythmic phrasing, and surprising displacements.

Tournier has explained that in his effort to write "true philosophy" or a "true novel," he turns to the myths that are at once eternal and alive. Because they draw on myth, Yourcenar and Tournier confront major issues in their works for children. Tradition, however, must always be seen anew, as Jung recognized in his study of recurrent archetypes. *Pierrot* in particular stimulates fresh insights through Tournier's rich juxtaposition of motifs. He leads the reader through processes of reinterpretation by depicting the characters' own struggles to understand. His ambiguities leave open issues of value that more conventional writers foreclose. Thus he exploits children's own open spirit, to reopen our and their understanding of the central experiences of life-giving sexuality and death.

18.

The Victorious Monkey:
Favorite Figure in Chinese Literature for Children

GUO JIAN

Ask any Chinese child to name five best-loved figures, real or fictional, and you fill find Sun Wu-kong—the monkey hero of *The Journey to the West*—on every list. Though the language of a one hundred chapter narrative written five hundred years ago is by no means easy, many young readers have already attempted the original version, perhaps several times, before they reach the age of proper literacy. To meet his admirers, the monkey appears in storybooks, picture series, puppet plays, cartoons, and films—probably no other Chinese book has been so widely adapted for children. It is surprising, however, that the novel has seldom been observed by critics as a masterpiece of children's literature. Scholars and religious men have argued for hundreds of years about what is truly implied in the book, but no one seems to take this simple question seriously: if the book is so complicated, so difficult even for adult readers, why does it interest children so much? It is my belief that the attempt to answer this question will shed new light on the nature of the book.

Originally, the westward journey only referred to the historical pilgrimage of Xuan Zhuang, an admired monk in the Tang Dynasty, who spent seventeen years traveling to India and bringing back with him six hundred and fifty-seven volumes of Buddhist scripture. After the historical event took place, however, the image of the monk gradually entered the realm of myth and legend, in which the journey to India became an adventure through the lands of demons and ogres, and the monkey and some other animal figures emerged as the Tang monk's disciples and guardians. About five hundred years later when those stories were collected, recreated, and woven into the well-organized structure of *The Journey to the West* by a great storyteller (generally believed to be Wu Cheng-en, 1510?–1582?), the Tang monk's role in the narrative was, to a large degree, overshadowed by the monkey hero Sun

Wu-kong. With the fusion of a religious theme and popular legends comes a puzzling ambiguity. On the one hand, the pilgrimage depicted in the novel, with all the pilgrims canonized in the heaven at the end of the journey, seems to suggest a spiritual progress toward a supramundane state of going through ordeals and self-rectification. On the other hand, so dominant is the role played by the monkey with his attraction for fun, his love for freedom, his common sense and irresistable humor, his defiance of authorities, and his unmatchable courage that not only do the demons seem harmless, but the dignified power of the heavenly gods and the rectitude of the master pilgrim often seem laughable.

Since the author himself takes an equivocal attitude in handling his materials, the task of fitting the work into a coherent pattern of interpretation is extremely difficult for critics, and their views differ greatly. Some take the book as a manual for Buddhist, Taoist, or Confucianist doctrines, or for the unity of the three religions. Others believe it to be an allegorical rendering of the peasant revolutions against the feudal autocracies in ancient Chinese history. Still others hold that it is no more than a comic work embodying the author's cynical view of the world. The critics who favor either a religious or a political interpretation must risk the involvement of a moral judgment which the author seems either to avoid or feel it difficult to make. The judgment of the last group, on the other hand, is not sufficient for our need for a more profound knowledge of a work of art rather than a general statement about it.

If a Chinese reader can still recall his own enjoyment as a child from reading the book, that is, an impression not distorted by adult influence, he will understand why the story appeals to children's imaginations; not only is the story funny, but it allows a child to identify the daring spirit of the monkey with an imagined self in the unconscious battle against forces imposed by the adult world. Children's interesting responses reveal to us a new way of approaching the narrative. Seen from this perspective, the fundamental myth of *The Journey to the West* lies in the struggle of a natural being against civilized society. I believe that children's perceptions will enable us to reach into the philosophical depth of the novel, and gain a proper understanding of its ambiguity.

From the very beginning of the novel, we know that the monkey is born to challenge the divine order. Nourished by the essences of the sky and the earth, of the sun and the moon, a stone on Flower-Fruit Mountain becomes pregnant, and one day splits open to give birth to a stone monkey whose eyes project two beams of golden light toward the sky. The gods in the heaven are disturbed. The canonical doctrine "each is in his proper place" suggests a limitation of individual freedom, but the monkey has no intention of obeying such a rule; instead, he strives to liberate himself from any controlling power. First, he becomes a king of monkeys in the Water-Curtain Cave, a self-ruled kingdom away from the turmoil of the world. Then he sets out to obtain immortality and magic power. From his first master, he acquires an oral formula which enables him to fly a hundred and eighty thousand miles by one cloud-somersault. In the Dragon Palace of the East Ocean, he gains as his weapon a 13,500 pound Golden-Hooped Rod. Down in the Palace of Darkness, the Oriental hell, he crosses out his name on the register book so that his life will no longer be controlled by the Gods of Death. To restrain the monkey from lawless deeds on earth, the Jade Emperor hits upon the idea of pacification and receives him into Heaven. The monkey, however, is not satisfied with the position the Jade Emperor gives him as a horse keeper, and grants himself a bold title "Equal-to-Heaven Great Sage." Uninvited, he goes to a heavenly banquet ahead of gods and sages, and joyfully treats himself to immortal peaches, jade juice, as well as gold elixir. Then, various battles are fought, and the monkey is still uncontrollable. When the all-powerful Buddha Tathagata comes from the West to help the Jade Emperor, the monkey shows his rebellious spirit in a most blasphemous manner. He tells the Buddha:

> Many are the turns of kingship,
> And the next year the turn will be mine.
>
> If might is honor, let them yield to me,
> Only he is hero who dares to fight and win!

Although a striking contrast is drawn between the supernatural power and intelligence of the monkey and the bureaucratic pretention and incompetence of the deities, the supremacy of the gods' rule is not to be questioned. When the monkey's lawless and anarchic tendencies go so far as to challenge the unalterable principle, the Buddha decides to get him imprisoned beneath the Wuxing Mountain.

Five hundred years later, when the Tang monk's westward journey begins, we observe a change in the monkey's fate. The Buddha releases him from his confinement so that he will be able to escort the monk to the Western Heaven, and in doing so, to atone for his past misdeeds. He is forced to convert to Buddhism and deceived by the Buddha and the monk into wearing a "Tight Fillet" around his head. Whenever he disobeys his master, the monk recites the "Tight-Fillet Spell," or the "True Words for Controlling the Mind"; as a result, the fillet tightens and

causes unbearable pain in his head. From now on, he can no longer be a
free spirit, but we see little change in his character. Though his loyalty to
his master and his intention to save the local people from the demons'
torturing hands are quite sincere, he cannot help being humorous and
funny even when engaged in fierce battles. His impudence and assertive-
ness and his defiant manner toward deities identify him quite aptly with a
wilful, restless, mischievous, and disobedient boy. By instinct, he knows
the terms of the fight—kill or die—but, to his master, it means an
intolerable offense against the Buddhist commandment not to take
human life. Therefore, for several times after delivering the monk from
danger, the monkey is severely punished by his master's spell for his
killing the disguised demons. Despite the ridiculousness of the monk's
rectitude, however, the validity of the religious doctrine and the super-
iority of the monk as the monkey's spiritual guide are never questioned
throughout the book. Once when the monkey is banished by his master
because of his violation of the Buddhist injunction not to kill, he turns to
the Buddha Bodhisattva for adjudication. The Buddha immediately
justifies the monk's stern attitude, allowing neither disobedience nor
questioning on the monkey's side.

At the end of the journey, the monkey, along with his fellow
pilgrims, is canonized in the Western Heaven, which seems to suggest
that, in carrying out his mission of accompanying his master through the
eighty-one ordeals en route, he abandons his anarchic tendencies through
self-cultivation as well as the lessons he receives from the human monk.
However, when we read the monkey's last remark on the Tight Fillet,
we are likely to doubt if the spiritual transformation really takes place.
The monkey says: "Master, now that I am a Buddhist Sage myself, like
you, why should I still wear this golden fillet? Is there any reason for you
to recite the damned Tight Fillet Spell and torture me? You'd better chant
a loose fillet spell, get it off my head, and break it to pieces, so that the
damned Buddha can no longer tease others with it." For the monkey, the
Tight Fillet is merely a mean trick the Buddha plays on him, and he is
happy to get rid of it at last. The triumph of the Buddhist suppressive
power turns out to be a mockery to itself. The spirit of the monkey
remains intact, free of subjugation by any earthly or celestial forces.

Viewing the novel in this way, we can easily detect the human value of
the superhuman narrative: always present in the monkey story is a
reflection of the difficulties a human being has to encounter during his
spiritual journey from childhood to maturity. In this transitional stage of
human life, man's innocent and intractable self engages in the battle
against the civilizing forces of the world which are geared to putting

invisible fetters and shackles on him to make him an obedient member of society. Adult readers, already mentally subjugated and excommunicated from the world of nature, are likely to miss the real implications of *The Journey to the West*. Children's reaction to the book, however, is quite different. In the monkey story, they see immediately what they themselves are confronted with in their daily contact with the adult world. To them, the monkey's struggle against suppression is not fictional, but real; they are apt, unwittingly, to identify their own desires and feelings, frustrations and triumphs, with the monkey's. Though they can not escape the moral discipline—a real Tight Fillet—imposed on them by the adult world, they can at least find encouragement in the monkey's magic power and daring spirit, and hope to balance the odds in their imaginations.

This is not to say, however, that the author of *The Journey to the West* intends his book to be an epic of crusade against civilized society. In fact, he is dealing with a battle in which he himself can not take sides. His heart seems to go with the monkey's natural desire for freedom, and he is amused to see the fatuous and pretentious world rulers being fooled. As a civilized being, however, he can not disobey his social conscience, and can not help regarding the monkey's character as morally deficient. He feels obliged to bring his hero somewhat under the control of convention, symbolized by the subjugation of the monkey by the Buddha, fated to wear the mind-controlling Tight Fillet, and be finally canonized in the Western Heaven.

Still, the author is too cynical to allow a complete victory of the civilizing forces over his favorite hero. His reluctance to grant the championship is revealed paradoxically at the end of the narrative: the monkey's comment on the Tight Fillet does not show any sign of change in his mind; on the contrary, it suggests that the canonization is a completely false reward for him and that the wild spirit endowed by nature at the very beginning of his life is not, and can never be, suppressed.

It is a pity that we adults have already gone too far from where we were born, too far away from this triumphant spirit. Only children still have the privilege of discovering it at first sight.

19.

Instructive Animals
In Greek Children's Literature

LIA HADZOPOULOU-CARAVIA

The desire for learning is a trait common to human beings, but it seems to have been the main characteristic of the ancient Greeks. It was not, however, an accumulation of knowledge that was sought, but rather a foundation for the formation of sound judgment and social-mindedness. Therefore, considerable attention was given to the education of the young, and writings like Xenophon's "The Education of Cyrus" or "On the Education of Children" by Plutarch (or pseudo-Plutarch according to Albin Lesky) underscore societal concern for the education of moral citizens.

In the paganistic universe of ancient Greece, man was by no means the only being with an intellect and a psyche. Animals spoke to each other or discoursed with people, often setting examples of nobility and prudence. Inanimate objects were "animated" as well. In both the serious tracts of Homer and the witty parables of Aesop, Gods and the natural elements taught moral lessons to broaden sensitivity and understanding.

Spiritual triumphs in Greek children's literature were often portrayed through the behavior of animals, though few ancient works may be classified strictly as children's literature. Actually in ancient and medieval Greece, children's texts were limited to lullabies, songs, and a few teaching materials. A charming little song sung by children begging money at festivals is included in a "Life of Homer." Generally, children would read or listen to epics, myths, dramas, and fables. People were less age-discriminating. Even love stories like "Daphnis and Chloe" by Longus (about third century A.D.), which described the infancy and childhood of future lovers as well as their discovery of nature and their interrelationship with the fauna around them, were welcome fare for children.

The situation is not very different in our villages nowadays, or at least it was not so until the recent influx of televisions and comics ushered in a new era. Until then, any novelettes for grown-ups might be read by children, while a book for children would be read by adults, or even read to the illiterate among them by children. The generation gap is narrower where changes occur slowly.

Homer's epics were great adventure books, the equivalent of contemporary western and science fiction films, though the theology and politics in them might have been too complicated for children whose interests were caught by the glorious imagery, noisy battles, glittering ceremonies, and numerous familiar mythical animals. Throughout Homer's two epics we hear of oxen and sheep, deer and goats, boars and lions, leopards and wolves, geese, pigeons, eagles, snakes and bats, dolphins, sharkfish, seals, and, above all, dogs and horses. Sometimes they are flesh and blood animals in pastoral scenes, banquets, or sacrifices. At other times they appear miraculously to provide the hungry with a good meal. Often they appear in striking similes, and may be creatures of imagination or the personification of natural phenomena, like the Bitch (Scylla) and the Chasm, or perhaps the Storm (Charybdis).

What lessons were the young taught by all those animals? That they were gentle to mankind was only part of their significance. Most importantly, man, the most brutal of animals toward his enemies, was tamed when in the presence of these representatives from the natural world. In the din of a fierce battle in the *Iliad,* Pandarus, son of Laocoon, tells Aeneas that he came to Ilion on foot, leaving all his horses—no less than twenty—at home because they were used to good food and he did not want them to suffer. The remark sounds strange, as Pandarus had just wounded Diomedes after having wounded the son of Atreus. In the conversation that follows, Aeneas lavishly praises the horses of Troy, and Pandarus gladly rides with the leader of the Trojan army but will not hold the reins "as horses obey their own master most willingly."

Even a monster like Polyphemus, with his terrible appearance, thunderous voice, and predilection for human flesh, can be very tender and caring in what concerns his herd. Upon his return from the pasture, he leaves the rams and the he-goats out in the yard, takes the ewes and she-goats into his cave and partially milks them. Then he places each one near its own lamb or kid, "all in proper order." This part of the *Odyssey* has been a favorite for children since ancient times, and numerous editions focus upon this episode, while faithfully documenting the monstrous Cyclops in the illustrations. Yet the children cannot help feeling disturbed, even guilty. Of course we want Ulysses and his companions to escape, but how is the blinded Polyphemus to fare for the rest of his life? Compassion seeps in, no matter how "man-prejudiced" we may be, and we cannot easily rejoice in his plight.

In the *Iliad,* the immortal horses of Achilles, ridden to battle by Patroclus, weep with warm tears when they see their rider slain. They bow their necks to the ground and their proud manes are soiled, reminiscent of human mourners who used to soil their hair. They stand immobile, and neither soft words nor threats can budge them from the site. The image is so powerful that it has become a recurrent subject for sculptors, painters, and writers. Among the best poems by Constantinos Kavafis, the well-known poet from Alexandria, is one entitled "The Horse of Achilles" (1911). By such relationships between men and horses, Greek children were taught the virtue of devotion.

Dogs were similarly inspirational to mankind, especially in times of peace. Dogs, as well as canine statues, often guarded the master and his property. Hephestos himself sculpted the figures that stood adjacent to Alcinous's palace. They were majestic forms in silver and gold. In a similar situation from this same epic, Cirke's wolves and lions behave as loyal canine companions, complete with wagging tails, when their masters treat them to ceremonial foods. But it is Argos, Ulysses' dog, that has offered children and grown-ups alike a paradigm of noble endurance and fidelity. Having waited for his master's homecoming for twenty years, Argos, seeing Ulysses at long last, dies contentedly with a weak wag of his tail.

The *Iliad* and the *Odyssey* deal with animals seriously, as they do with the subject of war. It is a moral imperative to fight to the death for one's country, and if necessary to be cruel, relentless, and cunning. It seems strange to us now that a parody of the *Iliad,* called "The Battle of the Frogs and the Mice," could have been attributed to Homer ever since the Hellenistic period. In the 303 hexameters that are extant, we learn that the king of frogs, Swollen-cheek, a devoted friend of the mice, took one of them, Crumb-grabber, for a ride on his back in the lake. Frightened by a watersnake, Swollen-cheek dove, and the mouse was drowned. Fierce battles erupted as a consequence, and the heroic expressions seem particularly absurd when applied to these tiny animals, leaving us with an antiheroic and antimilitaristic story.

There are numerous descendents of the Homeric epics which mocked war while maintaining the grandiloquence befitting heroes though engaging small and humble animals. In the "Lives of Homer" (fifth century A.D.), Proclus labels writings of this type as "paignia," meaning children's games or entertainment. But they were certainly not written for children alone. We know the titles of some of them: "The Battle of the

Cranes," "The Battle of the Blackbirds," and "The Battle of the Spiders." None of them can be dated with certainty, though they were decidedly of the post-Homeric period when war was no longer glorified. Children were certainly amused by these battles. Even today they find the pomp of the frogs and mice very funny, and a performance of this poem was produced in Nicosia, Cyprus in June 1984, in which the children composed the songs, invented choreography, painted scenery, made costumes and masks, and of course changed the hexameters into dialogue, all of which provided for zestful antiwar humor.

Many centuries later we again find writings of this sort in the Byzantium period. But bridging these common forms were the fables of Aesop. His is perhaps the nearest we can get to juvenile literature. His fables are short and composed in an uncomplicated style. They entertain while presenting a moral principle. But Aesop's life story was also of interest to his public. A popular novelette already known to Herodotus in the fifth century B.C. relates the adventures of this slave from Phrygia in a passage through different countries to Delphi, where he was murdered. Though imaginary like the fables, these stories provided fascinating reading for the young, and not so young.

Countless editions of Aesop have been published through the centuries. There are beautiful as well as cheap ones. I consider myself lucky to possess a copy of a Venetian edition of 1816 by Nicolaos Glykys. Many of our best writers have translated Aesop's work. Still we are not quite certain what it is that has attracted young people to Aesop for over twenty-five centuries.

Again we must remember that in a pagan society the attribution of human qualities to animals or even to inanimate nature was more than just fantasy. It was a vehicle by which man in the early stages of every civilization, and also in the early stages of individual existence, could understand the world around him while moderating his egocentrism. For not only humans can reason and express emotions, virtues, and weaknesses. Leaves rustle, thunder roars, animals crow, grunt, bark, twitter, and croak. Are these not messages to one another, or to whoever is willing to listen?

There is an entire universe in Aesop's fables, from which neither man nor the gods are excluded. Aphrodite does not think it beneath her to help a cat in love (Aphrodite and the Cat). A camel, demanding horns from Jupiter, receives shorter ears as punishment for his insolence. Trees negotiate with man (The Trees and the Axe); they boast to thistles, which, however, are unable to answer intelligently (The Fir-tree and the Thistle), or they may scold travelers or quarrel among themselves. Jars speak to each other, wax experiences envy, and a pregnant mountain gives birth to a mouse.

Basically, Aesop's universe is "peopled" by animals. And there is little typecasting, except for deer which are always timid, snakes which are always treacherous, and peacocks which are always vain. Otherwise, most animals have their own personality, and individuals in each specie may not only differ from their fellows, but also metamorphose, for better or worse. Perhaps the greatest lesson that children learn is that there are innumerable shades between black and white. Such diversity develops a talent for judging cases individually.

No less than twenty fables are about foxes. With wonderful equanimity Aesop exposes their foibles and strengths, sufferings and wrongdoings, and their mordant wit that does not spare even themselves. They can act shamelessly in one fable and, in the next, give a bear an earful about its hypocrisy and greed. Though one cannot name all the animals in these fables, the fox cannot be overlooked, for it is the forerunner of a long line of foxes in literature: Bossuet's *Le Roman de Renart,* and stories by Chaucer, La Fontaine, and Goethe.

Stories about animals were popular wherever Greek was spoken. "A Narrative of Quadrupeds" states in its opening verse that it was composed on the fifteenth of September, 1364. Various manuscripts (Paris, Vienna, Leningrad) include in the title an adjective describing the language used as simple, amusing, and suitable for children. Though the "Narrative" was in fact refreshingly simple, it must have been entertainment for the whole family. In it a lion and his counselors decide to call an assembly of animals, with the intention of ending all warfare. Imposing a truce, they convene and make speeches which invariably praise themselves while criticizing their fellows. In disgust, the lion breaks the truce, and a homeric battle ensues. Written in free verse of fifteen syllables, the poem draws to a close as follows (in my own free translation):

> Then you should hear the groans and moans and
>   all the noise they made,
> then you should see them jump and run and chase
>   and seize each other,
> then you should watch them bite and fling and
>   kick all round with might,
> oh what a clamoring they made as they devoured
>   each other.

Unlike Aesop, this poet does not moralize on the ignorance of war. But how similar this poem is to Aesop's tale of "The Two Rucksacks" in which men carry two rucksacks which contain personal defects. One hangs across the back and contains the defects of the carrier, which consequently are unseen. The sack to the front contains the defects of others, which the carrier observes in every detail.

This theme of vanity and prejudice is echoed in another story entitled "Poulologos" or "The Story of the Birds," in which an eagle invites other birds to his son's wedding. Arriving in couples, the birds glorify their own specie while insulting the others. The eagle sternly chastises their boorish behavior and avoids further confrontations by repeating, and rephrasing, his invitation (my own free translation): "For I have not invited you to brag and to be boastful, I honored you, you honored me by coming to the wedding, to eat and drink and to enjoy yourselves and to make merry, but not to judge each other and to praise your noble race."

We wish that there might be an eagle around to lecture humanity on its similarly conceited behavior. The reconciliatory ending made this a welcome text for the young. Though manuscripts at that time were expensive, short texts such as "Poulologos" could be "mass-produced" and seven are extant—two in Leningrad, one each in Escorial, Constantinople, and Vienna, and two in Athens.

Occasionally such treasures are discovered in the possession of unsuspecting individuals. Thanks to W. Wagner, many were rescued from oblivion. In Wagner's "Carmina" we also find "The Book of the Honorable Donkey" which was written and first published in Vienna in 1539 as "The Beautiful Narrative of the Donkey, the Wolf, and the Fox." The verses rhyme in couplets. The pattern of fifteen-syllable verses is used, and survives as the most popular verse form in Greece. In fact, many peasants still correspond in this form.

Briefly, the wolf and the fox became partners and think that the donkey would be easy prey. They induce him to join them on a voyage and set off in a boat. Contriving by "confessing their sins," the wolf and fox relate their terrible misdeeds and absolve each other. The donkey, however, having little more to confess than an occasionally stolen leaf of lettuce, is condemned and sentenced to death. Cleverly, the donkey engages his own plan, and whispers a secret to the wolf. There is a magic mark under his hoof which, when seen, imbues the observer with tremendous powers. The wolf and fox decide that they must see this mark before the donkey's execution and, for their greed, become vulnerable to the donkey's hooves which promptly kick the two scoundrels into the water. The poem concludes (again in my own free translation):

"Well done, oh master donkey, sir, and bravo for your wisdom, through it you have escaped your foes and also won your freedom. You are no donkey any more, you should be praised aloud, and of your deed never repent, but feel forever proud." It must be remembered that the Greeks were under Turkish yoke at that time (1453 to 1825) and part of the success of "The Booklet of the Donkey" was that it glorified the underdog and inspired the humble and oppressed to ultimate victory.

Stories with animal characters are published to this day and abound in times of censorship. Foreign occupation and dictatorships, such as have been experienced in recent years (1967–1974) inspire innocent-looking stories in which a harmful beast is beaten or outwitted by tiny and supposedly weaker creatures. Censors may be duped, but a child will understand what it is all about. The clever animals expose the villain's weak point—his Achilles heel. Contrary to the raucous epic expressions of ancient and medieval battles, contemporary ants and mice, or whatever figures the writer chooses, will not overstate their cause, but be unified by their dedication. The readers about such hero-groups are reminded of those Spartan mothers who sent their sons to war saying "Bring back your shield, or be brought back on it."

In less crucial times in Greek history, animal-imagery can spur youthful imagination, disclose secrets of nature, or offer amusement. The dozens of aphorisms about animals convey moral messages to children. Even animals that are nonexistent in our region, like the lion or the bear, still exist in the world of children's stories along with butterflies and fireflies, bees and drones, lizards and porcupines. As long as such stories are written and read, the dialogue between man and nature will continue, proffering wisdom, moderation, and love of life.

20.

The Triumphant Transformations of "Pinocchio"

JOHN CECH

In the century since *Pinocchio* was published, first as a serialized story and then (in 1883) as a book, generations of fervent Italian fans, some believe, have bought more copies of his tale than of that other national classic, Dante's *Divine Comedy,* and perhaps even more than the Bible itself. The figures are debatable, but the part of the scholarly community which monitors such things agrees that *Pinocchio* has been translated into at least eighty-seven languages from its original Italian. Literally hundreds of television programs have been based, however loosely, on Pinocchio's adventures, and he has starred in a good half dozen feature films, ranging from the well known, animated Disney version to the obscure Soviet revision of the story which casts the puppet as a hero of the proletariat.[1]

Quite simply, *Pinocchio* has become one of those stories that we never tire of repeating or listening to and that, in every sense of the phrase, we won't let go out of print. In English-speaking countries alone, researchers admit that, finally, they can not count or possibly keep track of all the hundreds of variations on the theme of *Pinocchio* that have been abridged, condensed, or spun off from the original. It is no wonder, then, that some scholars (and perhaps anyone whose first exposure to the story was through Collodi's version) despair that this form of the tale has been hopelessly "desecrated" by the Disneys and other less talented interpreters and exploiters.[2] With some justification they fear that the authentic story may well be lost to future generations of children—particularly American children—because of the sheer volume of watered-down, censored, or otherwise distorted versions that have flooded the market.

Much as we might wish otherwise, Collodi's text will doubtless continue to be chopped up, sanitized, and changed. But, most importantly, the story of Pinocchio will continue to be *told*. It is part of what Carl Kerényi calls a "living mythology" which "expands in infinite . . . multiplication."[3] Something about it endures and can never be ultimately changed, and that is the essential nature of the story, its mythic core. For this is a tale about one of the most basic and universal of transformations:

the process of growing up, of moving toward conscience and consciousness. Pinocchio's journey takes him from that egocentric, undisciplined,
inexperienced world of childhood into an adolescence or young adulthood that is self-sacrificing, responsible, knowing. He begins, quite
literally, as just a wooden knothead who is helpless to follow anything
other than his own drives. But through the course of some excruciat-
ingly painful experiences, he evolves into a person of full, flesh and blood
humanity, with all its attendant vulnerabilities, but with all its ennobling
qualities as well. Pinocchio is, after all, the very incarnation of that
eternal figure of the child, that archetypal symbol we meet over and over
again in myth and literature. Pinocchio stands in that long line of child
heroes who are as old as the Greek baby Hermes, the Chinese monkey,
or the Japanese peach boy, Momotaro, and as young as Peter Pan, Pippi
Longstocking, or Maurice Sendak's Max.

The archetype of the child is a fascinating balance of paradoxical
qualities and complex tensions between strength and weakness, knowledge and ignorance, creativity and destructiveness, the finite and the
potential, the new and the old. In *The Golden Key,* at the very center of
the world "in the secret of the earth and all its ways," George Mac-
Donald locates the child and names him "the oldest man of all." He is the
spiritual guide who "can help everybody," especially those searching
souls who finally find him in his hidden grotto, playing his eternal,
mysterious game. We find a part of this archetype in the symbolic
embryo of future potential that awaits its birth at the outer reaches of the
universe in *2001.* Another time it appears in Shirley Temple's single-
handedly singing and dancing the country out of the Depression in *Stand
Up and Cheer.* Or in one of its more powerful recent manifestations, the
child archetype drops into our world as E.T., an alien creature from
another world whose meaning, of course, is rooted in our own. For Carl
Jung this mythic figure of the child embraces "all that is abandoned and
exposed and at the same time divinely powerful; the insignificant,
dubious beginning, and the triumphal end."[4] He could have been, and
ultimately is, describing Pinocchio—one of the thousands of youthful
faces that this hero has worn.

Yet Pinocchio's mythical geneology goes back even further, to that
most ancient of archetypal figures, the trickster, who, according to Paul
Radin, is part of the earliest stage in the evolution of the hero myth.[5] As
Joseph Henderson has noted, the trickster

> cycle corresponds to the earliest and least developed period of
> life. Trickster is a figure whose physical appetites dominate his

behavior; he has the mentality of an infant. Lacking any purpose beyond the gratification of his primary needs, he is cruel, cynical, and unfeeling. . . . This figure . . . passes from one mischievous exploit to another. But as he does so a change comes over him. At the end of his rogue's progress he is beginning to take on the physical likeness of a grown man."[6]

He then "appears as the founder of human culture—the Transformer, becoming a socialized being, correcting the instinctual and infantile urges found in the Trickster."[7]

The idea of Pinocchio as trickster springs immediately to mind if we think for a moment of Pinocchio's nativity in the novel. While he is still a piece of wood, before he has even begun to take on his final shape, he provokes Master Cherry and Geppetto into a brawl. Only a few moments of reading time later, the puppet is sticking his tongue out at the old woodcarver while giving him the "evil eye." Within a few chapters he has run away and, with absolute selfishness, has sold the school book for which his father has sacrificed his few meager savings to buy his way into, of all things, a puppet show! In quick succession, Pinocchio becomes at least partly responsible for Geppetto being thrown into jail; Pinocchio has forgotten his promises to the Blue Fairy that he will mend his ways; he has killed the talking cricket, his conscience; and he has allowed himself to be duped by the Fox and the Cat and hung out to dangle, slowly in the wind. On some level, Pinocchio is aware of what he should do, and he laments, alas after the fact, his not having done it. Ultimately, he is the scamp with the heart of gold, that figure Leslie Fiedler dubs "the good bad boy" in his discussion of two of Pinocchio's many kindred spirits, Tom Sawyer and Huck Finn.[8]

But Pinocchio's transformation from blockheaded rascal to responsible human being is a little trickier than Tom's, and in its way even more perilous than Huck's. In the process of his metamorphosis, Pinocchio completely loses his human shape and becomes, quite literally, an animal. In that horrific scene in which he and his friend Lampwick are transformed into asses, becoming what they already have been, he pays dearly for his earlier bravado. As so often happens with the trickster, he gets caught up in his own tricks and, like Br'er Rabbit in the tar, is stuck. However, Collodi does not provide Pinocchio with a clever escape from his new imprisonment. Instead, Collodi reminds the reader that one of the cruelly typical fates of a donkey in the realistic world of the peasant countryside is to be worked to death, as Pinocchio's friend Lampwick is, or else to suffer an equally hair-raising end, like being turned into the skin on the town band's new base drum—the poetic justice for Pinocchio's own loud, vain adventures. And still Pinocchio is not through with his journey into the symbolic underworld of his own and the collective psyche.

Like some juvenile Jonah in the belly of the whale, Pinocchio, consumed by the dogfish, repents of his past ways and truly undergoes a transformational experience. But he must languish there until he can find the opportunity to escape. Even this is not enough, for after being disgorged by the fish and, in a sense reborn, sloughing his ass's skin, he must save his father, and then demonstrate the truth of this transformation in very concrete ways so that there can be no possible mistake that it has truly occurred. Once he has dragged Geppetto to shore and has begun to search with him for shelter, he again encounters those unreconstructed reprobates, the Fox and the Cat. But this time he is armed, not so much with physical force (earlier, as you will remember, Pinocchio had bitten off the cat's paw when the animal had tried to pull the gold coins out of the puppet's mouth where he was hiding them), but rather with moral precepts, with verbal counters to ward off their temptations. When the Fox cries out, "Don't abandon us," Pinocchio replies: "Goodbye, old crooks! Remember the saying: 'Turn about is fair play.' "[9] The new moral and spiritual awareness that Pinocchio now has supports and comforts him, warding off the discouragement that could certainly be the natural result of the hard, back-breaking work he has yet to do to win his full humanity. Again Pinocchio is like a beast of burden, drawing hundreds of buckets of water from a well for just a cup of milk for sick Geppetto. He gives all the money he has managed to save from his meager earnings to the snail to take to the Blue Fairy who is ill in the hospital. These are the harsh realities and hard knocks of a more disciplined and committed phase of life into which Pinocchio is preparing himself to enter. He must learn there to put others before himself, to accept disappointments, and to freely choose to work toward higher goals. Now, at least, the puppet has his old form back, and soon his full transformation will be complete.

In his famous study of the trickster figure, Paul Radin notes that the trickster was viewed as an unconscious part of human nature "which it was imperative for both the individual concerned and, even more so, for [the community as a whole] to bring to consciousness lest it destroy him and those around him. No man can do this for himself. He must call his fellowmen and society to his aid."[10] And for this triumph of the spirit to be made clear, the former trickster must come to see "his own instinctual and irrational self, unanchored, undirected, helpless, purposeless, know-

ing neither love, loyalty nor pity."[11] Pinocchio is painfully aware of the
self-isolating experiences in his escapades, and by the book's end, he
recognizes in the Cat and the Fox the life that simply follows appetites
and instincts and so "leads inevitably to crime and the making of
irrational demands. Both must end in tragedy. But how can man be
warned against such an existence? . . . By depicting the inexorable and
tragic consequences that follow such a life and by holding it up to
ridicule."[12] Collodi weaves abundant warnings into the exploits of Pinocchio and the unfortunate endings of others who have followed the same
tricky path. When Pinocchio and Lampwick are changed into donkeys,
they each break out in uproarious laughter at the ridiculousness of what
has happened to the other. But when they quickly realize that they are
also laughing at their own misfortune, they are reduced to tears. Both
the ludicrousness and the tragedy of their plights have come home to
roost in one indelible moment.

Pinocchio's transformation is inevitable, despite Collodi's own cele-
brated attempt to do the puppet in. For Pinocchio is made of tough stuff,
like the puppet itself. Though the myth concerning the origin of the
string puppet attributes its creation to St. Francis, and though it was used
extensively as a visual aid for teaching the Scriptures during the middle
ages, by the late fifteenth century, puppets were banned from use in any
church service because these "little Marys," or marionettes, more often
than not stole the show. They were too magically distracting, too
intrinsically capable of disturbing the solemn seriousness of the service
with their fascinating, seemingly miraculous imitations of both human
and divine actions. So the puppet itself was driven out of the garden and
fell into the marketplace, where he became a secular amusement, the
plaything of the people, from Pulcinello and Punch to the Muppets.

Pinocchio also shares a number of basic qualities with that most secular
of literary forms, the folk fairy tale. As narratives, both Collodi's novel
and one of the paradigmatic forms of the fairy tale are concerned with
depicting the triumph of the proverbial little guy. He reaches his happy
ending because of his fundamentally good heart and his capacity to
endure misfortunes and finally pass the tests that fate dishes out. Though
he receives magical help along the way, as Pinocchio does frequently
from the Blue Fairy, in the end he proves, through the mettle of his own
character, that he has finally become a true, whole person, the worthy
recipient of the metaphorical and the real riches that life can bestow. But
it is the detail of the hero's struggle, and not its resolution, that makes
both *Pinocchio* and the fairy tale the target of frequent attack and revision.
Not only would some like to purge both of their more violent elements,

but also, and perhaps more importantly, cleanse each of conduct that might seem to be endorsing or presenting children with the wrong kinds of behavioral role models.

Still, it is precisely this tension that exists between Pinocchio's uncontrollable drives and actions and the morality he knows he should, but is initially helplessly unable to, obey that creates the reality of the story and the character with which we readily identify. Pope John Paul I, one of the more famous admirers of *Pinocchio,* grasped the story's significance when he wrote in an open letter to the puppet: "I was exactly like you when I was a boy."[13] For truly, like Pinocchio, as James Heising insists, "we are all of us, motherless children, whose task is to integrate our becoming with our origins."[14] Pinocchio's odyssey, the *Bildungsroman* of his young life, is not an easy passage—as no true mythic (or actual!) journey to a greater awareness ever is, whether it be the maturing of the child figure in *Pinocchio* or of the further, deepening passages of an adult traveler like Gilgamesh or Odysseus or Dante. The myth is part of our human need to "deal with the problem of growing up, aided by the illusion of an eternal reality."[15] No matter what future editors may do with Collodi's original, they can not alter the remarkable essence of Collodi's gift to the world's (children's) literature. He has given a name, a shape, and a story to this universal condition and this triumphant passage from puppet to person, from knot-headedness to knowledge, from being pulled by strings to embracing the stirrings of the soul.

Notes

1. Richard Wunderlich and Thomas J. Morrissey, *"Pinocchio* Before 1920: The Popular and Pedagogical Traditions," *Italian Quarterly,* 23, (Spring 1982), 61–72. See also "Pinocchio Lives at 100" by Dennis Redmont (for Associated Press), in *The Gainesville Sun,* 28 November 1980.

2. Richard Wunderlich and Thomas J. Morrissey, "The Desecration of *Pinocchio* in the United States," *The Horn Book,* 58 (April 1982), 205–11.

3. C. Kerény, "Prolegomena" in Kerény's and C. G. Jung's *Essays on a Science of Mythology: The Myth of the Divine Child and the Mysteries of Eleusis* (Princeton: Princeton University Press, 1949), 24.

4. Carl Jung, "The Psychology of the Child Archetype," in *Essays on a Science of Mythology,* 98.

5. Paul Radin, *Hero Cycles of the Winnebago* (Bloomington: Indiana University Press, 1948).

6. Joseph L. Henderson, "Ancient Myths and Modern Man" in *Man and His Symbols,* ed. C. G. Jung (New York: Doubleday, 1964), 112.

7. Ibid., 113.

8. Leslie Fiedler, "The Eye of Innocence" in *No! In Thunder: Essays in Myth and Literature* (London: Eyre & Spottiswoode, 1963), 257 ff.

9. C. Collodi, *The Adventures of Pinocchio,* trans. M. L. Rosenthal (New York: Lothrop, Lee & Shepard, 1983), 239.

10. Paul Radin, *The World of Primitive Man* (New York: Henry Shuman, 1953), 339.

11. Ibid.

12. Ibid.

13. Redmont, "Pinocchio Lives at 100."

14. James W. Heisig, "Pinocchio: Archetype of the Motherless Child" in *Children's Literature,* vol. 3 (Storrs, Conn.: Parousia Press, 1974), 168.

15. Henderson, "Ancient Myths and Modern Man," 112.

V.
Religious/Philosophical
Approaches

21.

Out of the Depths to Joy:
Spirit/Soul in Juvenile Novels

M. SARAH SMEDMAN

Stories in which the spirit triumphs provide readers a religious experience; they evoke a deep, aching, but welcome yearning for something bigger than oneself, accompanied by joy and tears. Spiritual yearning can never be satisfied by material things, indeed not even by reciprocal human love. C. S. Lewis names such yearning "Joy": "an unsatisfied desire which is itself more desirable than any other satisfaction," which "must be sharply distinguished both from Happiness and from Pleasure. . . . [No] one who has tasted it would ever, if both were in his power, exchange it for all the pleasures in the world. But then Joy is never in our power and pleasure often is."[1]

Perhaps Joy never is in our power. Still, some experiences are proximate occasions of it: Beethoven's jubilant "Ode"; sunrise over the silent snows of Lake Superior; the delicate grace of Botticelli's Venus; Madeleine L'Engle's *A Ring of Endless Light;* Ouida Sebestyen's *Words by Heart;* Robert Peck's *A Day No Pigs Would Die;* Katherine Paterson's *Rebels of the Heavenly Kingdom,* indeed all her novels. These masterworks quietly herald the triumph of the spirit.

Triumph of the spirit. The phrase conjures various images trailing clouds of connotations, some of them nebulous, others concretized in literalisms that betray impoverished imagination and shallow understanding. In the dualistic tradition "spirit" conventionally designates the impalpable but enduring component of humans housed in an ephemeral body, that corporeal component which roots us in time and place, in a "wicked" world. That the spirit "triumphs" conveys metaphorically an inevitable existential conflict with its "bonehouse": either the martial soul has waged war against and conquered the body, seat of concupiscence and other deadly sins; or the pure soul has escaped its fleshly bonds and fled to some figurative mountain where the real self can enjoy mystical communion with the divine.

Contemporary theologians and psychologists, however, point out that such dualistic conceptions of the individual and the cosmos have contributed to, if not caused, the demise of the spirit in our own time. John Spong attributes the death of the spiritual as a distinct realm to the alliance of spirit with God and the banishment of both by Western civilization to a world beyond that in which we consume our daily bread. If the spirit has no interest in this world, it has, consequently, no place in a culture as "blatantly earth-centered" as that of modern man.[2] The consequences, as Walker Percy portrays in *The Second Coming,* cluster about opposite poles: unbelievers who are crazy and believers who are insufferable fools. Like Percy's characters, many moderns search for an alternative. Jungian psychologists, like James Hillman, as well as theologians, like Spong, point such a way. They speak in different but equally apposite terms, for spirit has both religious and psychological facets. Spong advocates a return to the Hebraic-Biblical worldview. Rather than regarding this world as antithetical to God's realm, "heaven," the Hebrews looked upon the physical as good, to be enjoyed because it reveals the glory of its creator: "to be spiritual . . . meant to be alive to God and alive to the world. It did not mean to be pious or otherworldly. To have faith . . . was to have the courage to enter life, for that is where God is to be found, always calling us into tomorrow."[3] Those who would recall spirit, then, must immerse themselves in this world, rediscovering the holiness and sacredness which dualism has sucked from it. In "Peaks and Vales" Hillman argues that to restore the spirit we must regain the soul, return to earlier philosophies which recognized three human components—body, soul, and spirit—thus separating soul from spirit, a distinction lost to our culture at least as early as the eighth century.

It is of the nature of spirit, the archetypal *puer aeternus,* to long for something beyond, to yearn nostalgically, search restlessly, and chase wildly after self-transcendence. "We are defined," according to Hillman, "not by what we are or what we do, but by our *Sehnsucht.* . . . We are what we reach for, the idealized image that drives our wandering."[4] Nonetheless, if the spirit is not to remain impersonal nor be lost in madness, it must be reunited with soul, join forces with the dark, heavy, fecund faculty, each making concessions to the other, for the soul's need to be lifted up, not deserted, by the spirit is equally intense as the spirit's need for soul. The soul is that power which helps us focus our fantasies by creating images, the force which ties us to our earthiness, connecting us with our individual and cultural histories. To search for soul, we must go first to the images of our fantasies: "All consciousness depends upon fantasy images. All we know about the world, about the mind, the body, about anything whatever, *including the spirit* and the nature of the divine comes through images and is organized by fantasies into one pattern or another."[5] Because the "hatred of the image, the fear of its power and of the imagination, is very old and very deep in our culture,"[6] the soul, as Hillman understands it, has long been alienated from our culture, even by priests and psychologists. Soul is recognized, perhaps, only by artists, the professional imagemakers. Those artists who have lost touch with neither soul nor spirit may be contemporary prophets, proclaiming the triumph of the spirit. And the spirit does triumph in certain children's books.

A sine qua non for the joy which attends the triumphant spirit in a children's, as in any, book is literary excellence: powerful, precise prose, resonant with archetypal imagery and symbolism; compelling characters; themes of universal human significance. More particularly, the spirit triumphs in those books of artistic merit which honestly confront reality, with all its horror, its dreariness, its monotony, as well as its delights, and which simultaneously recognize within that reality a dimension beyond the physical. To prevail, to rise to the heights, the spirit must go through the depths: go through, not turn away from nor skirt, as do pious stories or those (to borrow a term from Elizabeth Enright) of "antiseptic coziness"; go through, not wallow—lingering in helpless fascination with their immediacy, as in the best of neonaturalistic juvenile fiction.

Children's books which courageously embrace an unwashed world and incarnate its dirtiness, ugliness, and festering sores, yet transmit the conviction that there is some meaning, some justice, some goodness in the face of so much contrary evidence, plunge into the valley of the soul. From its depths they create images which project the paltry and the evil in the fictional world, thereby confronting their existence in the actual world. The process is painful—for writer, characters, and reader. Little wonder a world striving to brainwash the imagination with sanitized fantasies of reality fears the soul. To ignore or blur the soul's existence, however, is to anesthetize the spirit or to drive it toward unnatural or illicit seeming-satisfactions. Katherine Paterson has epigrammatically suggested that the reason why many today cannot speak the word of grace is that few have descended into hell.[7] Heights and depths have been leveled. Grace, as Paterson among other writers depicts, is not magic; it is the faith, the hope, the love attendant upon the spirit's impetus to

climb beyond, not out of, self. To reach the top of the mountain, whole
and free, the spirit must first "marry" the soul.[8]

Madeleine L'Engle's *A Ring of Endless Light* is a straightforward
narrative of the attempt of a sensitive young poet to discover some
meaning for death in a world she loves as ordered and beautiful. Vicki
Austin's grandfather's charge to her "to be a lightbearer. . . . to choose
the light" is a clarion call to her spirit empowered by soul-wisdom to
envision beyond earthly enigmas a calm bright eternity.[9] The novel
embodies the arduous but essential task of achieving union of spirit with
soul in Vicki's ultimate, paradoxical act of "giving the darkness permission." Throughout the novel light and darkness are evident symbols of
Vicki's spirit and soul. Vicki's struggle with mortality undoubtedly
derives from L'Engle's confessed inability to regard death in any way
other than unnatural, a punishment. People, she believes, ought to hate
and fear it, not become resigned to it. L'Engle has explored often in her
journals themes which imbue *A Ring of Endless Light*. Convinced of
story's stunning impact upon the emotions because it speaks to nonra-
tional faculties more powerfully than to the intellect, she asserts that
imagination and intuition, not rationality, affirm the existence of a
benevolent God behind the universe. Literary images take one further in
faith than logic because art can provide experiences of security in an
insecure world, offer glimpses of order in chaos. That intellect and
intuition must, however, work together is a corollary for L'Engle,
whose fiction frequently depicts the fragmentation consequent upon
separation of heart from mind. She would agree with Carl Jung that
"Our intellect has achieved the most tremendous things, but in the
meantime our spiritual dwelling has fallen into disrepair."[10] While her
terminology is different, like Hillman, L'Engle calls for marriage of soul
with spirit.

L'Engle's approach to reality, material and spiritual, embraces paradox. A prevalent theme in her fiction and poetry is the necessity of
coming to terms with paradox, of learning to hold in balance the
antitheses in life, a theme reenforced through her use of oxymoron. A
major motif in *Ring of Endless Light* is the phrase from Henry Vaughan,
"a deep but dazzling darkness," a phrase precursive of a 1952 letter from
Jung to Erich Neumann in which he wrote that an individual in the dark
needs, and is healed by, images not of the light but of the dark, out of
which light will rise."[11]

The preponderance of death in so affirmative a novel as *Ring of Endless
Light* is itself paradox. When the child Binnie dies in Vicki's arms, she
who has staunchly supported others in the face of so many deaths is

overwhelmed. Numbed with grief, crazed by inability to make sense of needless and wasteful death, Vicki screams an anagonized interior scream, burns her clothes as an attempt to annihilate death, then sleeps. She descends into darkness, into the region of "I don't know," of "I can't discern any purpose in these events." Ascent from this soul valley will constitute regeneration, but new birth, too, involves risking, letting go of securities, which are after all only illusions. To seek security, as L'Engle thinks, is to mistake the illusion for reality. When sun streaming across Vicki's face awakens her, she is not yet ready for ascent; she feels heat and discomfort but sees no light: "there was a large, dark blankness in [her] mind, a deep fog of unknowing" (314). Though a part of her does know that Binnie and her dying grandfather are giving her a chance at new life, she is "caught in a black hole in the center, a singularity where no light would ever come, a place of annihilation. Nothingness. Despair" (315).

In an attempt to jolt Vicki, to connect the circuits between soul and spirit, her brother John refuses to acquiesce in her denial of human history: "You're not being asked to bear more than the ordinary burdens of life, the things that come to everybody sooner or later" (316). Neither John's harsh reminder nor Grandfather's gentle exhortation rouses Vicki. Equating Vicki's darkness with her ego, Grandfather repeats a motif sounded early in the novel, in a poem by Thomas Browne painted on the wall of the loft where Vicki sleeps:

If thou could'st empty all thyself of self, . . .

But thou art all replete with very thou
    And hast such shrewd activity,
That when He comes He says, "this is enow
    Unto itself—'twere better let it be,
    It is so small and full, there is no room for Me. (20)

Then Grandfather offers her the gift of his life experience, a two-edged sword: "You have to give the darkness permission" (318). On the one hand, aware "that there are no depths of depravity the human creature cannot sink to" (240), Vicki must allow the darkness its place, its reality; on the other, only if she chooses darkness rather than light can it overcome her. Because Vicki, still in shock, is unable to choose, Grandfather in a gesture evocative of ordination kisses her forehead and chooses for her: "You will bear the light" (318). Not until she has plunged, naked, into the ocean is Vicki herself able to respond. In a poetic passage which pulls together the major motifs and symbols of the novel, Vicki is tossed about by the dolphins, those aquatic mammals noted for their grace, intelligence, and playfulness, and whose friendly presence seamen regard as a sign of a smooth and happy voyage. Vicki again first responds from two levels of her being: on a deeper level she knows the dolphins are trying to bring her out of the darkness and into the light; on a more conscious level, she wills the darkness because the light is too heavy to bear. After a smack from a dolphin's flipper drove her "down into the strange green darkness of sea, shot through with ribbons of gold," Vicki rises "into the blazing blue of sky. . . . And the light no longer bore down on [her] but was light" (323). At last Vicki has both given and refused the darkness permission, has accepted its existence but, like her grandfather and Henry Vaughan, penetrated the vast shadows of Time and seen through and beyond to "A great ring of pure and endless light." The pod sang their alien alleluias and then were gone, "flashing out to sea, their great resilient pewter bodies spraying off dazzles of light, pure and endless light." Vicki, whole and free, swims to shore and with Adam, her soul-mate, is "caught and lifted in the light" (324). The novel ends on this sensation of physical height, a customary component of the triumph of the spirit. The symbolism of Vicki's victory, theologically interpreted, is closer to that of assumption than ascension, of the power of grace rather than human will.

Ouida Sebestyen's first novel *Words by Heart* is less explicit than *Ring of Endless Light*. However, the story of Lena Sills's growing into practical understanding of the Bible verses which as a child she memorized is richer with imagery conventional in the religious literature of East and West that describes the ascent of the spirit. The story opens in the rural community of Bethel Springs (literally the natural flow of water in a hallowed spot), to which Ben Sills has moved his family from the southern, all-black Scattercreek. Lena, "different and comical-looking, oozing like dark dough over the edges of her last year's Sunday dress,"[12] begins, appropriately, the Scripture-verse contest with: "God hath chosen the foolish things of the world to confound the wise; and God hath chosen the weak things of the world to confound the things which are mighty." She wins the victory with verses from Song of Solomon, words she had before this whispered only to herself, words which made her "beautiful, thin as a flower, blooming with the hope of love" (13). As Lena speaks the words slowly, reverently, in front of all those gathered in the hall, she realizes that in revealing her dreams, she is demythologizing them. As the story unfolds, Lena is caught between the timidity of her stepmother Claudie, who yearns to return to the security of Scattercreek, and the faith and courage of her father, who envisions a future in which his children have the freedom to realize their talents and dreams. When Lena borrows Mrs. Chism's book, *Professor Gursell's Illustrated Atlas of the World,* Papa, significantly, pauses at a full-page engraving of mountains:

> "Now that's what I want to see someday," he said softly. There was awe in his voice. "Look at that. The backbone of the whole country. The tallest things in the whole world—a thousand times taller than any building or tree. . . . Those shiny mountains. In the mornings they're all lighted up while it's still dark down where you are. . . . Anyway, if I don't get to see them you all can see them for me. (49–50)

Listening to Papa describe symbolically the high, bright realm of the spirit from the dark soul-valley of tribulation, Lena catches the forlorn longing in his voice and assures him: "You'll see them yourself, Papa, all the wonderful things." Dispirited, Claudie, whose imagination has been fettered by cynicism born of actuality, pricks the fantasy: "And it'll be just the same there as it is everywhere else" (50).

In his mortal life, Ben Sills never climbs his mountains; he gets only to Hawk Hill. Like the eagle a solar bird, the hawk has been variously interpreted as the spirit, as the power and nobility of the heavens, as messenger of the gods. In Egyptian mythology, the hawk is the emblem of the soul longing for solar transformation. Cirlot suggests that, because medieval allegory depicts the hawk tearing hares to pieces, it may also be taken as the symbol of victory over concupiscence.[13] When Ben fails to return from mending Mrs. Chism's fences at Hawk Hill, a job that should have been done by his shiftless and spiteful neighbor Mr. Haney, Lena journeys in quest of her father. She starts before dawn, "flying" in "a wild burst of exhilaration," prototypical of a neophyte in the spiritual way. Before she has gone far, however, cold weeds flap at her legs, farms and trees give way to "rangeland, emptiness, a frozen ocean of curly grass and scrub lifting and falling in rocky waves." She crosses a dry gully; she narrowly escapes flinging herself down upon a mass of rattlesnakes resting on a rock. In the distance, the "medicine hills crouched like giants, daring her to pass between them." Always her eyes are straining to find the "ruts leading toward the river" (134–36). Lena's journey is described in the wasteland imagery common in treatises and poetry of the spiritual quest: imagery of dryness, coldness, rockiness, with evil rattling dangerously close. When Lena has exhausted her own energies, she stops to remember: "Papa used to say a prayer wasn't just a request you shot off to God like an arrow. It was also a standing still and remembering you were a target. . . . They that wait upon the Lord shall renew their strength; they shall mount up with wings as eagles; they shall run, and not be weary—" (137).

For Lena, waiting upon the Lord means encountering Him in tragic reality on Hawk Hill. She discovers her father "down beside the river," mortally wounded by Tater Haney, who lies unconscious but recoverable near by. The Bible verses Lena had thought so beautiful when she learned them now weary her with heavy irony: "Why was it you and not him, Papa? Where was the shield and buckler of the Lord?" Papa's response: "I don't know, Lena. I wrestled all night with that, and you'll have to wrestle too, till you get an answer. There's an answer" (145). Lena indeed grapples, not only with the apparent meaninglessness of her father's death but also with his dying request that she take his murderer back home. Seeing Tater move in the distance ("Ancient, strange shape, a head dabbing down and up again. Prehistoric creature, part of her nightmare") Lena fights off the physically violent temptation to wreak revenge and leave Tater to die alone in the wilderness (145–48). Like an act of grace, she hears Papa's voice echoing in her head, "Love your enemies and do good to those who hate you. Give to him that asketh thee. . . . "The words that had been so beautiful to say, so easy, turned to stone. No one had told her, not Papa, not the preacher, that they could change like that when they had to be lived, and crush her with weight" (148).

Very like Meg at the end of *A Wrinkle in Time,* what Lena cannot do out of love for her enemy, she can do out of love for Papa, who knew how to love him.

Lena's journey home, like her journey out, is enveloped in imagery, this time that of the ascent of the spirit merged with soul. It begins in darkness, her heart at the start an icy core, her body numb: "In the night, the wild geese flew over, hunting the river. A jostle of voices, hoarse, urging. So tired. Exhorting each other: You can do it. Circling. Lost" (150). Neither eagles nor hawks this time, but wild geese, associated in folklore with the descent into hell; with fertility, the Great Mother, the good housewife. And, antithetically, with the sun and the heavens, light, swiftness, and inspiration. Like Lena, the wild geese are for the moment lost, floundering, searching for the river, for life and its meaning, for the promised answers.

When Lena looks up at the stars, realizing that she can no longer look to her father for answers, Sebestyen explicitly allies the girl's plight with the history of her race: "the Big Dipper. The Drinking Gourd that had guided her people running for freedom out of all those Southern nights" (150). Once again she hears her father's voice, this time reading the words of Whitman, his "favorite of all poets. That loving man" (62). The refrain that resonates: "I find letters dropt from God in the street" (63, 139). In order to find Him, Whitman says, you must see Him in yourself, in other human beings, in what transpires on earth, in "perpetual transfers and promotions" between "the stars of heaven" and the "grass of graves" (63, 151). From here on Lena feels in the night "the soft pull of rising road," and "Far away through the crisp dark she [can] see the fragile lights" (152). After she has delivered the battered Tater to his parents, buried her father, and heard the redeemed Claudie's firm resolve to stay *"Here"* in Bethel Springs, Lena has passed through the depths. No longer is she listening for answers. She has learned to trust ambivalence. Like her father and Walt Whitman before her, she is pulsating with the wonders and mysteries of life in and all around her: "She shook her head slowly, the way Papa did when he meant wonders never cease" (162). The words Lena had as a child committed to memory, she has now learned by heart.

Sparer in narrative, in description, and in symbolism than either L'Engle's or Sebestyen's novel, Robert Newton Peck's *A Day No Pigs Would Die* is an autobiographical fiction of a Vermont Shaker family whose fate is tied to the land and the seasons. Peck's flat, frugal, colloquial style suits well the adolescent boy who tells the story and his father Haven Peck, a pig-killer by trade, illiterate but rich in the earthy wisdom he passes on to his son through teaching, example, and, chiefly, by being. Fraught with the violence endemic to impoverished farmers eking out an existence, the Pecks dwell humbly and humorously in the earthy valley of soul. In the initial incident, a ritual of initiation, Rob, who has skipped school to avoid the jibes of his classmates at his odd clothing, is bruised and torn by a neighbor's cow whom he helps in the difficult birthing of twin calves. Rewarded by Mr. Tanner with the gift of Pinky, destined to grow into a first-class brood sow, Rob loves and cares for his pet, who does garner a blue-ribbon at the Rutland fair. At the side of his father during a crude and cruel weaseling of a pet dog, a macabre midnight grave robbing, as well as hunting and routine farm chores, Rob learns to be proud of his Shaker heritage though he doesn't "cotton to all those Shaker laws."[14] At school and on a trip to town—both denied his father—Rob learns reading, arithmetic, geography, and history, and "to be proud of our yesterday just like today" (35). When Pinky proves to be barren, and killing her is the family's only means of survival, Rob helps his father butcher his pet. There are few passages in literature more moving than that in which Peck describes bluntly and honestly the sounds, smells, and textures of that brutal act and of the wrenching but restrained emotions of father and son. When Pinky is dead, while Papa works fast to draw the pork, when "It was all so quiet, like Christmas morning," Rob crosses the threshold to manhood. "That's what being a man is all about, boy," Haven tells his sobbing son from his own broken heart. "It's just doing what's got to be done" (139). Rob, who minutes before had hated his father for killing not only Pinky but the "hundreds and hundreds of butchered hogs" (137), understands and loves the father who "did it because he had to. Hated to and had to." The ineffable beauty of the relationship between father and son echoes the story of Abraham and Isaac:

> And he knew that he'd never have to say to me that he was sorry. His hand against my face, trying to wipe away my tears, said it all. His cruel, pig-sticking fist with its thick fingers so lightly on my cheek.
>
> I couldn't help it. I took his hand to my mouth and held it against my lips and kissed it. Pig blood and all. I kissed his hand again and again, with all its stink and fatty slime of dead pork. So he'd understand that I'd forgive him even if he killed me. (139–40)

Haven Peck, worn out by work, dies before the end of the story. None of the imagery conventionally symbolizing the ascent of the spirit surrounds Haven's burial. He is interred in a "box of raw unpainted wood," "deep in the land he sweated so hard on and longed to own so much. And now it owned him" (147, 150). Yet the Joy and tears evoked by Rob's final "goodnight" to his Papa "down under all that Vermont clay" witness to the triumph of the spirits of Haven and Rob Peck. They have espoused and valued the earth, the hard homespun life of the Vermont farmer, and the rigorous Shaker law. The spirit of Haven Peck has ever abided as one with his soul. *A Day No Pigs Would Die* hints that Rob, when he "turned and walked away from a patch of grassless land" (150), all that marked who his father was and what he had done in his sixty years, may one day forsake the Shaker way of life, but never his Shaker heritage. Regardless of where he goes, what he does, his spirit, indelibly marked by the "thirteen good years" he had with his father, will always be strong.

Reiterating that the self is a unified entity, not a "ghost in a machine," Brian Hill in *Education and the Endangered Individual* designates four "marks of the Spirit," that is, facets of the self's total response indicative of its nonmaterial dimension. These marks are: endurance, that is an "I" outlasting the body's constant chemical renewal with the "capacity for language, which develops symbolic meanings that increase and refine feelings, actions, and the storage capacity of memory"; transcendence, which enables people to stand off from their physical environments, their own bodies with their memories, in order to endow the world with purpose and to influence the course of events; creativity, a power which, while springing from deeper wells, employs reason as a tool in urging the self beyond the requirements of survival and adjustment; and, finally, dialogue, the consciousness of the enduring, transcendent, creative self that it is neither supreme nor alone, but that it must interact with other selves for good or for ill.[15] The marks enumerated by Hill surround like luminescent halos Vicki Austin's grandfather and the fathers of Lena Sills and Rob Peck. These mentors are strong characters, as Hill would say, because they have coordinated the elements of the self toward consistent purposes. The stories of the young protagonists indicate that they too are well on their way toward becoming strong, and also good, because their integrated selves are directed toward good ends: trust, justice, harmony, love even of the unlovable.

In a context which might be construed as auguring the triumph only of the ideal, it may be well to remember that strong characters can direct coordinated selves toward evil purposes too, that evil spirit as well as good can triumph, a fact Robert Cormier's novels persistently and powerfully refuse to let us forget. In *The Chocolate War* the innocent but courageous Jerry tentatively disturbs a universe he gradually realizes is destructive of individuality, of any deviance from an established norm, of the very freedom essential to marriage of soul and spirit. For his Promethean gesture, his refusal to bow to the will of the local gods, his innards are literally torn out. His final words of capitulation along with Archie's gloating prediction of a good year ahead signify that evil predominates—too little challenged and too late. Similarly, the faint hope that Paul Delmonte of *I Am the Cheese* may not only regain his memory but succeed in hiding what he knows from his interrogators offers little consolation. Even should he preserve a tiny core of his integral self from violation by his oppressors, his life, like Sisyphus's, will be continual repetition of actions with precious little, if any, meaning. While the place in literature of books which dramatize the triumph of evil is essential if literary experience is to comprise all of life, to argue that such books educe a joyous response is impossible.

Antithetical to Cormier's fiction is that of Katherine Paterson, whose essays on her art are permeated by faith, like Faulkner's, that the good spirit will not only endure but prevail. In "A Song of Innocence and Experience," for example, she affirms her desire to communicate to young readers her conviction that "maturity is more to be desired than immaturity, knowledge than ignorance, understanding than confusion, perspective than self-absorption. That true innocence is not the absence of experience but the redemption of it."[16] Within the context of Paterson's novels, it seems justifiable to interpret "maturity" and "true innocence" as the effect of the spirit's descent into a variety of hells-on-earth, the displacement there of its illusions by true images of reality forged in the soul, and its resurrection through a willingness to risk being loved and loving. Two motifs from Paterson's first novel, *The Sign of the Chrysanthemum,* epitomize this dimension of the author's vision, consistent throughout her work: the truth Muna learns, that a person, like a mountain, is more beautiful for the scar at the summit which "testifies to the tumult that once raged within"; and the motto on the sword Muna earns, "Through fire is the spirit forged."[17] In each of Paterson's stories the protagonist must come to grips with the weighty realities of cultural and personal history which inhibit the spirit's unencumbered flight. In each story the hero turns potential tragedy to triumph and achieves dignity and happiness by relinquishing egocentric aspirations and accepting the ambivalences attendant upon the human condition. To abandon a reader to despair would violate Paterson's artistic and human standards, as would failing to depict reality as she honestly sees it. Perhaps in none of her novels is fidelity to both tenets maintained in such perilous balance and emotional depth as in *Rebels of the Heavenly Kingdom.*

What L'Engle, Sebestyen, and Peck collectively achieve in their separate novels, Paterson accomplishes in *Rebels.* The meaning not only of death but of the murder of innocent victims in a religious war is agonizingly probed. The story of Wang Lee's and Mei Lin's adventures during the 1850-1853 Taiping Rebellion against the Manchu rulers of China is also the story of their spiritual odysseys. The story is told with a restraint appropriate to the Chinese people and culture and with imagery indigenous to both the story's natural setting and the spirit's quest for soul.

A major theme of *Rebels* is the equality of women with men in the Heavenly Kingdom of Great Peace. Imbedded in this is the more fundamental concept that to be complete, individuals must integrate their feminine and masculine aspects. Frequently in the novel the main characters, the young woman Mei Lin and the boy Wang Lee, are disguised as members of their opposite sex. The novel is certainly too

complex to be read as allegory: roles exchange and interchange; appearances are often discrepant from reality; subtle irony pervades the whole.
Yet there is much in the story to lead one, paradoxically, to associate Mei
Lin with the masculine principle, spirit; Wang Lee with the feminine
principle, soul; and, of course, to interpret their wedding as the union of
the one with the other. Wang Lee's ancestors are farmers; he springs from
the fields, which at the opening of the novel stand "nearly bare, a great
angry wound upon the flesh of the earth," a wound healed finally when
soul and spirit cultivate it together.[18] Wang Lee's captors call him Pigboy,
a name to which he perversely reverts when he must relinquish Wang,
the name reserved among the long-haired rebels only for those whom
"the High God, the Heavenly Father, calls to be king" (35). When Mei
Lin, disguised as a man, buys him from his kidnappers, he reflects: "It
was a miracle. The gods had heard his mother's prayers" (26). His
"savior" leads him out of the "dark narrow streets," through "A massive
wooden gate," into the company of the "God-worshipping society," and
eventually up Thistle Mountain, where the rebels prepare for battle.

     The daughter of a patriarch and a slave, Mei Lin had been taught to
read with her brothers and her feet had never been bound because she
was useless to her father as a woman but had worth as "a beast of
burden" (43). In recounting that part of her history in which she had
been sold for the use of soldiers, Mei Lin discloses a spirit having already
passed through depths:

> What right did this raw boy have to know? How could he begin
> to understand her suffering—her deep shame that even yet, after
> all that had happened, had the power to darken her spirit and
> drag it down? It was like a deserted well into which some poor
> soul in anguish had lept to his death. The well is abandoned, but
> the body remains, putrefying the water. There were still some
> ghosts that even the Heavenly Kingdom had not put to rest (47).

Particularly significant are: the linking of the soul with darkness, depth,
water that is desert-ed, and with the masculine; suffering which can
never be entirely eradicated; and the ascent of the soul with spirit. By the
time Wang Lee meets Mei Lin, she is a captain in the Heavenly Army and
when "the Heavenly Kingdom is established on earth, she will receive
property in accordance with her high position and great valor" (50).

     Much of the action of *Rebels* takes place in the mountains. At first a
reluctant novice, antipathetic to war, Wang Lee gradually becomes a
zealot. Carried forward by mass enthusiasm, almost against his judg-

ment and will he is baptized into the God-worshipping society, that
strange polyglot of Oriental cults and Christianity. Dogmatic propa-
ganda swallows his native arrogance: "He no longer fought just to save
his life. He fought for the Heavenly Kingdom. It was like wrapping his
body in metal armor and filling his heart and liver with the spirit of God"
(104). Three times, he refuses, as Peter does Christ, even to recognize
Mei Lin because she is nothing but a woman. Turning away from her
during a victory celebration, Wang Lee feels his long sword, "cold and
comforting along his thigh. It would not look good for him if he
appeared to be talking to a woman. He had just been promoted to
sergeant and must set a spotless example. His heart must be single"
(104). Though Wang Lee had memorized "one of the earliest declarations
of the Heavenly King: 'You should not kill one innocent person or do
one unrighteous act, even though it be to acquire an empire' " (155), he
betrays his friend Shen who dares remind him that "Under Heaven all
men are brothers. . . . What a pity that men should kill each other" (121).
Already guilt-ridden over Shen's execution as a traitor, Wang Lee is
temporarily deranged when he shoots "a little girl—not more than two.
A streak of black blood ran from her small mouth. The ball had made a
neat round hole in her embroidered jacket. There was no breath in her,
but he could smell her little mouth, mother's milk still sweet upon her
lips" (139). Paterson's lean, stark prose, vividly contrasting sights and
smells of the effect of misguided spirit upon innocents, so horrifies
readers that, with Wang Lee, they retch and taste bile.

It is the act of killing the baby which, literally and figuratively, topples
Wang Lee from the heights once again into the dark, wet regions of the
soul, where he is disabused of his fantasies of glory and realizes the
abomination not merely of war, but of war executed in the name of the
High God of Heaven. Carefully removing his gun and clothing, he walks
deliberately into the river and stoops:

> kneeling neck deep, clouding the water with grime and blood
> from his body, waiting until the current carried the defilement
> away. Then he put his face in. The surface of the water was
> warm from the June sun. He opened his eyes and looked at the
> shimmering stones—like the pavement of some celestial city.
> How easy it would be for him never to raise his face (140).

Because a single impassioned act of repentance is not evidence of
conversion of heart, Wang Lee cannot yet enter the celestial city.
Staggering out of the river, he falls onto the bank "more weary than a
graveless ghost." Once more Mei Lin rescues him from whom she had
been separated for some time both by fortune and decree. She has been

away fighting with the glorious, almost mythical women horse guards. For the duration the kings have decreed the separation of women from men, a spiritual discipline both young people take seriously, Wang Lee sometimes, as we have seen, because it is ego-serving, Mei Lin because she believes she will be spiritually stronger if she is "free from all human entanglements" (107).

Now, when Mei Lin rouses Wang Lee from his stupor, he is conscious of her physical attraction, is seized not by "lewdness" nor the "lust of an animal," but by "a great ache surging through his body" (141). She seems impervious. When in the ensuing battle Mei Lin escapes though she has offered God her life for that of her spiritual father who is killed, Wang Lee admits having prayed God to spare her because she is "more lovely than the Kingdom." On the literal level, Mei Lin draws back in anger and fear, admonishing Wang to "Go and wash and beg mercy." Symbolically, she swings "herself up on the back of the beast, who shuddered as though with pleasure" (151). Thereafter when she thinks of Wang Lee, she has consciously to remind herself that discipline must be maintained, that the spirit must deny the flesh.

The course of war again separates the two. Mei Lin becomes a leopard colonel in the Heavenly Army, believing Wang Lee to have perished "without disgracing her with either his arrogance or his appetites" (180). Recaptured by bandits, forced into various menial services, much of the time disguised as a woman, Wang Lee continues to pray for Mei Lin's safety. Eventually Wang is reunited with her whose fragrance is "like spring on a mountain" in the "Celestial City shimmering in the sun of early summer" (213). That night the two are united, "and it was as though they had plunged into the Son of Ocean and washed away all the shame and suffering and death of the former days" (219).

The epilogue celebrates the union of spirit with soul. The celebration, however, is solemn, even sombre. Wang Lee and Mei Lin have learned with equanimity to live with ambiguity, to go on quietly, with the knowledge of their own, as well as society's, failure to live by the creeds they profess, even betrayal of those principles by transforming meta-phorical truths into literalisms which then become untenable, blasphe-mous. The finale's bleak, realistic view of humankind belies the first sentence in the Chinese primer from which boys learned to read: "At birth men are by nature good" (195). That bleak view is ameliorated by knowledge that people like Mei Lin and Wang Lee will compensate for wrongheaded zealotry by doing what they can to make peace in their immediate environments. They will till and conserve the soil. They will not bind their daughters' feet and will teach them, with their sons, to read.

The realization that although *Rebels of the Heavenly Kingdom* is set in mid-nineteenth-century China, it is still very much about us intensifies its impact. Who among humankind has not known the Heavenly Precepts yet chosen a different path? To know that "the four characters Taiping Tienkuo—Heavenly Kingdom of Great Peace" exist today if "only as a promise sealed in a wall" and that they may one day take root in the earth testifies to the victory of spirit. That victory evokes a poignant joy springing, not from a hope dependent upon finite beings, but from that hope which, in theological terms, is the virtue which relies upon the infinite goodness and mercy of a power beyond the universe, an unfathomable Power who resists all efforts to confine it within human limitations and who continues to reign.

Rebels of the Heavenly Kingdom is a difficult but stunning book in its affirmation of the indwelling of spirit, yearning to transcend the earthly, in soul that forces it to acknowledge terrible reality without despairing. The immature Wang Lee permitted spirit to "pass through on that terrible wave of beauty and power" but "had not known to look for her" (129). When his experience is redeemed, true innocence exults, for Paterson has had "the courage to enter life, for that is where God is to be found, always calling us into tomorrow."[19]

In an address to journalists, Graham Greene once said that the marks of sanctity are: a twinge of conscience accompanying sin; an empathy with both victim and victimizer; and a penchant for disloyalty causing one to question received doctrine.[20] Vicki Austin, Lena Sills, Rob Peck, Wang Lee, and Mei Lin all do wrong they are ashamed of; each proves sensitive to those who inflict as well as those who suffer pain; each refuses to accept pat answers to the enigma of the coexistence of evil with a loving God. A commonplace, if often overlooked, maxim of the spiritual life is that holiness is wholeness. These characters, then—whose spirits have descended into their personal excruciating hells, have there merged with soul, and have risen to see through earthly reality, however darkly, "letters from God dropt in the street" and to believe that "others will punctually come for ever and ever"—are holy because they are whole.

Notes

1. C. S. Lewis, *Surprised by Joy* (New York: Harcourt, 1955), 18.
2. John Shelby Spong, *This Hebrew Lord* (New York: Seabury, 1974), 30–58.

3. Ibid., 34.

4. James Hillman, "Pothos: The Nostalgia of the Puer Eternus," in *Loose Ends: Primary Papers in Archetypal Psychology* (Zurich: Spring, 1975), 54.

5. James Hillman, "Peaks and Vales," in *On the Way to Self Knowledge*, ed. Jacob Needleman and Dennis Lewis (New York: Knopf, 1976), 118.

6. Ibid., 116.

7. Katherine Paterson, Interview, Columbus, Ohio, 22 May 1982.

8. Hillman, "Peaks and Vales," 130.

9. Madeleine L'Engle, *A Ring of Endless Light* (New York: Farrar, 1980), 318. Subsequent quotes from this volume are cited in the text.

10. C. G. Jung, *The Archetypes and the Unconscious,* trans. R. F. C. Hull, 2nd ed. (Princeton: Princeton University Press, 1968), 16.

11. C. G. Jung, *Letters,* ed. Gerhard Adler and Aniela Jaffe, trans. R. F. C. Hull (Princeton: Princeton University Press, 1975), 32–34.

12. Ouida Sebestyen, *Words by Heart* (Boston: Little, 1979), 12. Subsequent quotes from this volume are cited in the text.

13. J. E. Cirlot, *A Dictionary of Symbols,* 2nd ed. (New York: Philosophical Library, 1972), 140.

14. Robert Newton Peck, *A Day No Pigs Would Die* (New York: Knopf, 1976), 32. Subsequent quotes from this volume are cited in the text.

15. Brian Hill, *Education and the Endangered Individual* (New York: Dell, 1973), 257–65.

16. Katherine Paterson, *Gates of Excellence* (New York: Elsevier/Nelson, 1981), 52.

17. Katherine Paterson, *The Sign of the Chrysanthemum* (New York: Crowell, 1973), 125, 132.

18. Katherine Paterson, *Rebels of the Heavenly Kingdom* (New York: Dutton, 1983), 4. Subsequent quotes from this volume are cited in the text.

19. Spong, *This Hebrew Lord,* 34.

20. Alan Jones, "Psychoanalysis and Contemplative Prayer," Friends of Jung, Charlotte, N.C., 3 February 1985.

22.

The Spirit of Faith
in Mormon Children's Literature

JESSE S. CRISLER

Time was when the potential reader of literature written for the children of The Church of Jesus Christ of Latter-day Saints (commonly referred to as the Mormon Church) confronted at best a bleak selection of reading material.[1] Not only was relatively little literature available, but also what was accessible was distinguished by a festival of unrelieved technical mediocrity (or worse): wooden dialogue, pallid characterization, banal style, contrived plots, and tractarian themes are all in evidence in pre-twentieth-century Mormon children's books. For example, two passages from Nephi Anderson's *Added Upon* (1898) illustrate representative literary fare offered to the unsuspecting reader at the turn of the century. In the first, Anderson attempts to describe a needed rain which finally ends a long and ruinous drought:

> How it did rain! For two long months the sky had been one unchangeable color of blue; but now the dark clouds hung low and touched the horizon at every point dropping their long-accumulated water on the thirsty barrens, soaking the dried-up fields and meadows. The earth was thirsty, and the sky had at last taken pity. It rained all day. The water-ditches along the streets of the village ran thick and black. The house-wife's tubs and buckets under the eaves were over-running. The dust was washed from the long rows of trees which lined the streets.[2]

Instead of conjuring up a rich image of a lifegiving torrent, the presence of passive or semiactive verbs in this excerpt coupled with such sluggish phrases as "long-accumulated water on the thirsty barrens" and "the dark clouds . . . touched the horizon at every point" results in an eminently forgettable blur.

The second selection exhibits these same flaws as well as others in both dialogue and style:

"This is the Temple."

"Yes; and what is that for?"

The purposes of temples were explained.

"You say you baptize for the dead?" enquired Henrik, "How is that?"

"Well, as I was telling you when I called on you some time ago—"

"Pardon me, but I must confess that I did not pay enough attention to what you said to remember. I was thinking about those quarreling tenants of mine. Tell me again."

The other smiled good-naturedly, and did as he was asked. Henrik listened this time, and was indeed interested, asking a good many questions.

"Now, about the Temple." continued the missionary—"we believe that every soul that has ever lived on the earth, that is living now, or that will ever live must have the privilege of hearing this gospel of Jesus Christ. There is only one name given under heaven by which men may be saved, and every creature must hear that name. Now, the great majority of the human race has never heard the gospel; in fact, will not hear it in this life."[3]

Suffused with Mormon doctrine, this conversational exchange hardly suggests exciting reading, then or now.

Unfortunately, the current situation in many ways has not improved: Anderson's deficiencies continue to be perpetrated all too often. In the first place, many books for Mormon children in the twentieth century contain improbable, if not inconceivable, plots. Dona Andrews's *To Live with Love* (1982), for instance, recounts the life of Tina Peters whose parents are involved in an automobile accident fatal to her mother; whose family then moves from suburb to city to save money; whose father's continued financial reverses force him to seek work away from home, while his younger children must be separated and placed with various relatives. Tina's high school flame departs for a proselyting mission to Korea. Meanwhile, Tina, refused employment because of a visual handicap, undergoes successful eye surgery; her father meets, courts, and marries another woman; Tina herself withstands the amorous blandishments of a handsome newcomer who is not a member of the Mormon church; her married sister with whom younger siblings reside has her second baby; Tina befriends an unwed mother who eventually gives up her child for adoption; the stranger decides to convert to Mormonism; Tina at length determines to marry her boyfriend just returned from his mission—and all this within a scant two years, told breathlessly in a novel of less than two hundred pages. Equally implausible is *The Secret of the Diamond Fireside* (1981) by Anne Terry. In this Mormon teen mystery à la Nancy Drew, fifteen-year-old Wendy Carpenter is too good to be true except for the social pretensions of her family; she and her soon-to-be boyfriend Jeff Henderson help solve assorted crimes committed by international thieves. Wendy's father, in tracking down the identity of one of the criminals, also contributes his background in law despite his self-admitted meager knowledge of "the cultural entomology [sic] of names."[4]

But unrealistic plot is not the only drawback in currently available Mormon children's books. Some disclose problems with point of view. *Under the Same Stars* (1979), the first volume of a trilogy of historical novels by Dean Hughes covering the experiences of transplanted Eastern Mormons in Missouri in the 1830s, suffers from too great a dependence on strict chronology and actual history. This forces Hughes to cast his protagonist, the boy Joseph Williams, in the unlikely role of nonpartici-pating spectator of mob violence so that certain events in the story can be advanced, events which do eventually affect the fate of Joseph and his family, but to which a young boy would scarcely impute such far-reaching significance as Hughes requires Joseph to apprehend. Another loosely historical story, Howard R. Driggs's *Ben the Wagon Boy* (1944) errs in the opposite extreme by oversentimentalizing the wrenching saga of Mormon westward migration in an effort to capture a boy's view-point. What emerges is a tale devoid of hardship, trials, or tribulation of any kind, and, therefore, devoid of color, passion, and believability, rather than a realistic depiction of a youngster's stirring and maturing adventures during the Mormon exodus to Utah.

Yet cataloguing such blemishes as these in Mormon children's books does not excuse them, nor does it even explain their existence. The would-be critic of the field must wonder how this woeful condition of so much literature for Mormon children came about. Creative investigation reveals three reasons. First, the church is still young, having been founded only in 1830; because of its uncertain status in most parts of the world in its early years, Mormonism had firmly established itself, by 1847, in Utah—at that time little more than a desert wasteland. As members devoted themselves to erecting new communities, forging useful industries, and colonizing fresh locales of the vast intermountain West, they had little time for literary pursuits for several years. When authors such as Anderson and Augusta Joyce Crocheron did begin writing for younger readers, they found no established literary tradition within which to work.[5] Mormonism was different enough from other religions, even other fundamentalist movements, that Mormon writers could not seek models elsewhere. Thus, what began as a minor strain has so remained: Mormon children's literature is still in its infancy. Since few authors claim fame beyond Mormon readership, they consequently do not benefit from the rigorous standards demanded by readers of the best works in children's literature such as *Tuck Everlasting* (1975) or *Bridge to Terabithia* (1977).[6]

Closely allied to infancy as a cause for the poor quality of Mormon children's books is their great diversity. Besides traditional genres such as novels and collections of short stories, the current menu for Mormon children includes *Science Fiction by and for Mormons: LDSF* (1982), a volume of tales of time travel, preexistent speculation, space colonization, Orwellian futurism, controlled procreation, and earth invasion, and Joy Saunders Lundberg's *Book of Mormon Summer* (1983), a quasi-fictional narration of one family's exploits in distributing *The Book of Mormon* to total strangers in compliance with the church's commandment to be a "member missionary"; as well as *Mother Stories from the Book of Mormon* (1911, repr. 1952) by William A. Morton which contains heavily watered down versions of scriptural adventures and *Miracles in Pinafores & Bluejeans* (1977) by Ardeth Greene Kapp which collects gentle polemics designed to promote "an increased awareness and appreciation for the common, precious experiences of each day" ("Preface"). This great variety, like infancy, causes mediocrity in much Mormon children's literature because writers have not yet perfected form. It creates a climate in which almost anybody can write virtually anything, regardless of its worth, with a fair expectation that it will be appealing to a majority of its intended readers—Mormons.

A third cause for what Bauer and Muir term the general "sacrifice" of "literary quality" in Mormon children's literature is the Mormon audience itself.[7] That such works as Anderson's *Added Upon*, with all its obvious faults, is not only still available but considered by many as something of a "classic" clearly suggests a certain lack of discerning literary sophistication and acute critical perception on the part of Mormon readers.[8] Rather than requiring the best from favorite authors, they seem willing to accept any work provided it discusses familiar themes using familiar characters who speak familiar language in familiar situations. Clearly, this lack of wider expectations perpetuates the inferiority of Mormon children's books since writers feel bound to deal only with things Mormon. The resulting works often neither have intrinsic merit for the non-Mormon child, nor do they allow their creators opportunities to explore non-Mormon culture. Therefore, readers must either be Mormon, or they must have extensive knowledge of Mormoniana in order to understand, let alone appreciate, this literature. Without this knowledge, many passages will remain enigmatic or esoteric to the non-Mormon reader. Consider the following excerpt from *Starfire* (1981) by Gordon Allred:

> He remembered Bishop Fielding. Even now Kevin could feel the hands, huge and beefy, yet somehow soft and enveloping, resting on his head. He could feel the combined warmth of their hands, all three men, and although he couldn't recall most of the blessing, he remembered Bishop Fielding's promise that he could be healed according to his faith.[9]

Or consider this exchange from *The Miracle of Miss Willie* (1984), a young adult novel by Alma J. Yates:

> "Bishop," Sister Hollingsworth cut in, "it's almost sacrilegious to let them in the church."
> "But they're not bad," the bishop defended us. "They come to church, they're not Word of Wisdom problems, they haven't started dating before they're supposed to, they—"
> "There isn't a girl that would go with them," Sister Hollingsworth cut in. "That's what the Mia Maids say."[10]

The following, far more prosaic, passage, is from Jack Weyland's *Sam* (1981): "That Thursday a lady who said she was a single adult representative in the ward phoned. She told me that the single adults were having a dance on Saturday and wanted to invite me, especially since I'd never yet been to any of their activities."[11] Terms such as "ward," "Bishop," "single adult representative," "Word of Wisdom," and "Mia Maids" obviously beg for further explanation.

Given these manifold apparent difficulties, one asks if literature by Mormon authors for children is irredeemable. Should it be read? Should it even be written? Is it actually truly worthless? To these questions, one must answer that it should indeed continue to be both written and read; furthermore, it should in time, if not now, be studied by non-Mormon critics, for, despite its manifest defects in plot, point of view, style, and so forth, and regardless of the real reasons which permit the existence of these very lapses, this body of literature, even at its worst, treats significant subjects which illustrate the thorough and inevitable triumph of children's untainted and dauntless faith either in their church, in themselves as members of it, or in the Lord who heads it.

On one level Mormon literature for children fashions a realm out of the fabled "West," a place isolated from pernicious outside influences where good overcomes evil repeatedly through the efforts of individual protagonists. In *Chester, I Love You* (1983) by Blaine M. and Brenton G. Yorgason, for example, Travis Trilby wins a dual battle through his faith in the power of prayer. After pleading with his Heavenly Father, Travis conquers a long-standing personal athletic challenge and simultaneously realizes he must help the lame Canadian goose he has nurtured learn to fly, just as he himself has discovered how to overcome personal defeat. In Anya Bateman's *Big Ben is Back* (1983), egotistical, shallow, insensitive, antifeminist, bigoted Benjamin Van Vleet finally faces the worst aspects in himself because of his desire to make himself appealing to Robin, with whom he has fallen in love. Using first-person narrative, Bateman delineates Ben's plight both humorously and satirically as Ben must discard layer after superficial layer of his personality. Typical is his initial reaction when told he is probably sterile; he asks Robin, "Do you think you can still respect me—as a man, I mean?" When Robin, of course, points out how limited his idea of manhood is, Ben finally understands that just loving Robin as he does will enable him to surmount this problem: "If I could handle this problem, I could handle anything. Yes, problems do make us greater. My problem would make me *more* of a man—a greater, *greater* son of God. . . . I would overcome!"[12] Different as Travis's and Ben's situations are, they yet are linked by the idea of individual conquest. Whether Travis surprises his cruel school coach, or Ben turns to adoption as balm for his pain is immaterial. What does matter is that they, like many characters in Mormon children's books, succeed in defeating personal adversity because of faith in their own God-given abilities as well as in God himself. The examples of triumphant faith which they embody serve as objects of emulation for potential readers who will grasp that they, too, are a part of this place, this "West," where right prevails.

But Mormon children's literature also extends this realm so that it moves beyond individual characters of selected books to encompass an entire theocracy in which characters experience triumph through a kind of ubiquitous collectivity of faith, first "inherited" from Mormonism itself and then fueled by a totally Mormon environment, even when the characters do not actually live in Utah or surrounding states which contain significant Mormon minorities. Elizabeth Petty Bentley's short fantasy "Sybil" affirms this idea convincingly. Set in the Chesapeake Bay area of the Eastern Shore of Maryland, the story depicts an elderly woman, Sybil Powell, who finds her life has no purpose after the Second Coming of Christ because "RP's" (Resurrected Personages) now perform all the real work of living such as cooking, laundry, and household chores, that is, the very tasks Sybil had delighted in taking care of before "The Destruction." After she bemoans her fate for several days, a friend, Brother Swartz, comforts her: "Your work here is important. . . . You needn't feel like you're forbidden to teach just because you haven't been assigned to it formally." Armed with this reassurance, she attempts a teaching venture. When it fails, another friend reminds her that Mormons everywhere traditionally meet problems in a time-honored way: ". . . pray for it . . . but prepare yourself for the answer." Thus, Sybil benefits from the faith of those about her in principles she had momentarily forgotten. Later, after she has prayed, Becky, a three-year-old neighbor girl, brings her a bouquet of wilted flowers accompanied by a simple " 'For Sister Powell. I love you. Becky.' " Sybil finally fathoms that she still possesses skills which need to be imparted to little children. Becky, like Sybil's other friends, nourishes the return of her incipient faith, the seeds of which had been planted long ago as part of Sybil's Mormon heritage.[13]

Naturally, if characters who do not dwell in Utah still manage to undergo an ineffable triumph through their faith, firmly rooted in their church and just as forcefully nurtured by their surroundings, so characters who appear in stories set in Utah itself also encounter an identical phenomenon. Many examples of Mormon children's literature portray the period when converted saints "crossed the plains" to Utah. One of these, Mabel Harmer's *The Youngest Soldier* (1953), while it begins in England where the main characters embrace the church, takes place mainly in Utah, which the protagonist, fifteen-year-old Marty Howe, reaches after enduring the rigors of pulling a handcart over the Rockies from Nebraska in perilous weather. Unlike many books for Mormon youth, Harmer's novel is both readable and credible. She chronicles what history must have been like and peoples her creation with believable characters rather than supplying a flat character who plays spectator to actual history. Her story is perhaps less accurate than Hughes's *Under the Same Stars,* but it is also more rewarding. Much of the reason for its effect on the reader lies in Harmer's apparent awareness that Marty's actions must be plausible. Carefully, Harmer details Marty's experiences as a youthful soldier and scout, showing how each of them builds his character in some significant way. In time, Marty comprehends that he has matured greatly since he left England, not in years perhaps, but in resolve: "He thought back to the time when he had been terribly afraid of the mountains. Now he had conquered that fear. He felt that he could meet almost any challenge of mountain or desert. It gave him a curious feeling of elation."[14] When his family at last joins him in Utah, Marty is able to take them to the house he has laboriously constructed in his spare time, following the good examples of neighbors and friends in Salt Lake City. Like Marty, the reader suddenly apprehends that Marty definitely has become a product of this Utah world where Mormonism surrounds him.

A few other Mormon children's books also manage to make their point without being excessively didactic or painfully ill-written. *The Miracle* (1983) by the Yorgasons is a short novel in which the faith of Myron "Moose" Millett in man's basic goodness as well as his belief in that faith are justified by the changes his own unexpected and largely unmerited kindness works in other characters. Cassi Hancock, a selfish but beautiful girl who not only delights in ridiculing Myron's clumsiness and unpopularity but even initiates some of it, becomes the gracious "queen" Myron initially judges her to be as she perceives the extent of his sacrifice for everyone else, including herself. Her brother Dan already appreciates his best friend Moose, but he is equally amazed at the latter's unselfish acts. Even Ted Gomez, once his contemptuous enemy, becomes Myron's friend, mainly because Myron gives Ted an opportunity to learn the virtue of giving. Last, Myron himself alters from a bungling object of pity to a self-assured, confident young man. Neatly, faith—first Myron's faith in each of his friends but ultimately their faith in themselves and each other—effects all these transformations. Again, a Mormon environment provides an arena where faith can perform, but their beliefs in their Mormon teaching had been the original training ground for these characters' development of faith.

Another novel using modern teenagers in high school is *The Miracle of Miss Willie,* certainly one of the best examples of Mormon young adult fiction. Though not set in Utah, it nonetheless occurs in the small predominantly Mormon community of Snowflake, Arizona. Through the generous and loving patience of their new sophomore English and Spanish teacher, three country clodhoppers metamorphose in a year's time into admirable and respectable young men. Miss Willie develops great faith in the potential for achievement by her young protégés in the course of the novel. When that faith is endangered because of the insensitive boorishness of another teacher, she moves to prevent him from demolishing her work, but she realizes that she must allow her "creations" to act for themselves in order for them to acquire their own faith in themselves. These boys have grown up as regular attenders of the local Mormon church; consequently, they have received certain ideals which lie dormant until the right combination of sympathetic guide and necessary circumstances comes along to unlock them. When that junction occurs, they know "that so many things that had always seemed difficult, if not impossible—school, missions, college, professions—lie within [their] grasp."[15] Miss Willie does perform a miracle, but in doing so she capitalizes on both the Mormon background of her charges and an environment which requires certain behavior of its Mormon youth.

One more well-written young adult novel serves as a final example of the triumph of faith in Mormon children's literature. Gordon Allred, a prolific writer of children's books, published *Starfire,* perhaps his best work, in 1981. In it Kevin Weaver, a victim of rare Perthes disease, which slowly deteriorates his hip, tames a hummingbird whom he names Starfire. Though Kevin, early in the novel, receives a priesthood blessing designed to heal him depending on his faith, he experiences in actuality little relief from his suffering and no increase in his natural abilities. However, his many talks with local legend Elijah H. Marriott, ninety-year-old patriarch of Ogden Canyon, force Kevin to accept the fact that his previous faith has been not only narrow but selfish as well. He wants to be healed, but he does nothing to accomplish his desire. Lije teaches him that true faith results from a life of commitment, fasting, and prayer: "It was an odd sensation—excitement and wanting on the one hand, and on the other, a large economy-sized scared feeling. It had never occurred to Kevin until now that faith, the real, honest, deep-down kind, could take a lot of courage."[16] When Kevin, like Travis in *Chester, I Love You,* frees his pet bird, he knows that his own symbolic freedom is attainable. Lije first awakens Kevin's faith in the reality of God's interest in his children; then Lije systematically leads Kevin to build his own indomitable and complete house of faith.

As in *The Miracle of Miss Willie, The Miracle,* and *The Youngest Soldier, Starfire* succeeds in creating a world in which the faith of protagonists grows collectively both because of the actions of other characters in the same world, and because the theocratic world of Mormonism itself exists. Kevin Weaver, Marty Howe, Moose Millett, and Daniel Johnson, narrator of *Miss Willie,* exhibit this faith in their own particular fashions, but each of them already possesses some degree of faith by just being Mormon boys. This latent faith in turn receives fuel constantly from their Mormon environment, until finally it pushes them into ineluctable triumph at the moment they confront the purposes of their own lives and, therefore, the meaning of faith itself.

Thus, in much of Mormon children's literature faith—a real, lasting, eternal condition—leads characters to both personal conquests of individual difficulties and communal or collective victories over wider problems. Even when the literature is only of average or poor quality, as much of it is, the characters nevertheless merit one's study of and interest in them because they demonstrate their absolute faith in self, church, and God to the reader. And in the best works in the field, their triumph is so nearly tangible that the reader shares it with them, as he does in all the best children's books, regardless of their place, time or philosophic base. Mormon children's literature has not yet come of age, but it has made great strides during the last decade, as references to several works above indicate. Such dedicated efforts by Mormon authors to construct fair pictures of Mormon life probably represent as clearly as their books themselves the triumph of faith they long to project.

Notes

1. This discussion confines itself to Mormon writers writing books about young people who are members of the Mormon Church. Thus, Virginia Sorenson, winner of the 1957 Newbery Medal for *Miracles on Maple Hill* (1956), is excluded because, though she is a Mormon and her adult fiction often concerns Mormon themes or characters, her books for children have neither been about Mormon children nor have they been written for an exclusively Mormon audience, as is the case with the works of authors in this study who have obviously written only for Mormon youth.

2. *Added Upon: A Story* (Salt Lake City: Deseret News Press, 1898), 34.

3. Ibid, 110.

4. (Salt Lake City: RIC Publishing, 1981), 110.

5. Crocheron's *The Children's Book, a Collection of Short Stories and Poems: A Mormon Book for Mormon Children* (1890) opts for conventionally sentimental tales and verse.

6. The one exception to this pronouncement may be the team of Blaine M. and Brenton G. Yorgason, a few of whose works, such as *Windwalker* (1979), have transcended the boundaries of Mormonism in both audience and subject matter.

7. Carolyn J. Bauer and Sharon P. Muir, "Visions, Saints, and Zion: Children's Literature of the Mormon Movement," *Phaedrus* 7 (Spring/Summer 1980), 35.

8. By 1978, *Added Upon* had gone through five editions and forty-five separate printings (Bauer and Muir, 33).

9. (Salt Lake City: Deseret Book Co., 1981), 7.

10. (Salt Lake City: Deseret Book Co., 1984), 18.

11. (Salt Lake City: Deseret Book Co., 1981), 21.

12. (Salt Lake City: Bookcraft, 1983), 136, 139.

13. In Scott Smith and Vickie Smith, eds., *Science Fiction by and for Mormons: LDSF* (Thousand Oaks, Cal.: Millennial Productions, 1982), 70, 76, 77.

14. (Salt Lake City: Deseret Book Co., 1953), 237.

15. Alma Yates. (Salt Lake City: Deseret Book Co., 1984), 183.

16. (Salt Lake City: Deseret Book Co., 1981), 176.

23.

Puritan Triumph:
The Joyful Death Books of
Cotton Mather and James Janeway

HOWARD A. MAYER

A child's death seems unlikely material for children's literature. And a collection of deathbed scenes in which children recount their misspent lives and proclaim their faith in the blood of Jesus seems even less appealing for young readers. Yet the seventeenth century saw the production of several books giving detailed descriptions of the lives and last hours of children intended as religious models for their peers. *A Token for Children, being an Exact Account of the Conversion, Holy and Exemplary Lives and Joyful Deaths of several Young Children* by James Janeway (1636?–1674) was so popular that he soon issued a second part subtitled *A Farther Account of the Conversion, Holy and Exemplary Lives and Joyful Deaths, of several Other Young Children, not Published in the First Part.* Cotton Mather (1663–1728), the famous New England Puritan divine, gathered an American version of deathbed accounts that he published (along with Janeway's) in 1700 as *A Token, for the Children of New-England, Or, Some Examples of Children, In whom the Fear of God was Remarkably Budding, before they Dyed, In Several Parts of New England.*[1] Enormously popular, these accounts of childhood piety were reprinted frequently throughout the eighteenth century. Although the subject matter may seem lugubrious for the modern mind, it appealed both to the reality of the seventeenth- and eighteenth-century world and to the piety and religious sensibilities of the Puritan mind.

Those living in the late twentieth century in developed western countries are fortunate that, compared with previous eras, childhood mortality is remarkably low. The situation was different in the seventeenth and eighteenth centuries. Samuel Sewall, diarist and contemporary of Cotton Mather, gives a painfully vivid picture of family life in the late 1600s when burying a child was an oft-repeated act in a family's life. "Dead children," says a recent critic, "form a grim garland around all the volumes of [Sewall's] diary."[2] Sewall's wife gave birth to a son on December 7, 1685. But the joy soon turned to sorrow as the child sickened within a few days. Beginning on December 20, Sewall's diary records events that were repeated often in seventeenth and eighteenth century families.

> Sabbath-day, Dec. 20. Send notes to Mr. Willard and Mr. Moodey to pray for my Child Henry.
>
> Monday, about four in the Morn the faint and moaning noise of my child forces me up to pray for it.
>
> 21. Monday even Mr. Moodey calls. I get him to go up and Pray for my extream sick Son.
>
> Tuesday Morn, Dec. 22. Child makes no noise save by a kind of snoaring as it breathed, and as it were slept.
>
> Read the 16th of the first Chron. in the family. Having read to my Wife and Nurse out of John: the fourteenth Chapter fell now in course, which I read and went to Prayer: By that time had done, could hear little Breathing, and so about Sun-rise, or a little after, he fell asleep, I hope in Jesus, and that a Mansion was ready for him in the Father's House. Died in Nurse Hill's Lap. Nurse Hill washes and layes him out: because our private Meeting hath a day of Prayer tomorrow, Thorsday Mr. Willard's Lecture, and the Child dying after Sunrise (wether cloudy), have determined to bury on Thorsday after Lecture. The Lord sanctify his Dispensation, and prepare me and mine for the coming of our Lord, in whatsoever way it be.
>
> Thorsday, Dec. 24th 1685. We follow little Henry to his Grave: Governour and Magistrates of the County here, 8 in all, beside my Self, Eight Ministers, and Several Persons of note. Mr. Phillips of Rowley here. I led Sam., then Cous. Savage led Mother, and Cousin Drummer led Cous. Quinsey's wife, he not well. Midwife Weeden and Nurse Hill carried the Corps by turns, and so by Men in its Chestnut Coffin 'twas set into a Grave (The Tomb full of water) between 4 and 5. At Lecture the 21. Psalm was Sun from 8th to the end. The Lord humble me kindly in respect of all my Enmity against Him, and let this breaking my Image in my Son be a means of it.[3]

So on Christmas eve (not, of course, a holiday for a Puritan) Sewall buried his fifteen-day-old son.

Not only was the burial of a single child common, the burial of many children was often part of family life in the eighteenth century. Thomas Mallon, for example, comments on the frequent childhood deaths in Sewall's life.

> The drama of Henry's birth and death is repeated over and over. A year later the baby is named Stephen; he survives for six months. And after that funeral, too, it is easier to list who came rather than what he felt. . . . Sewall's continual fatherings and buryings are eventually benumbing. There are too many to take in. It is only after his wife has delivered her fourteenth child, in January 1702, that Sewall ends an entry of Thanksgiving with the words: "And it may be my dear wife may now leave off bearings."
>
> The terrors of birth rival the terrors of the plague. Measles and smallpox also infect the diary. On January 12, 1690, Sewall tells his eleven-year-old son Samuel that he should be ready to die from the latter, as nine-year-old Richard Dumer just has. Sam eats an apple as he listens, seeming "not much to mind"— until he says the Lord's Prayer his father prescribes and bursts into terrified cries.[4]

Sewall's family was not unusual. Adults and children shared the awareness that life, in particular the life of a child, was precarious. It was to such real situations that the joyful death books, as Janeway's and Mather's volumes came to be called, addressed themselves. At the very least, their popularity stems from the attempt to assess and refine, to portray and understand, the most fundamental and perhaps most terrifying common human experience—death. The popularity and success of Janeway and Mather can be attributed to the way in which their short narratives attempt to shape and give meaning to the phenomenon of death. The joyful death books demonstrate how the human spirit can be noble, compassionate, and courageous—no small feats for anyone, especially remarkable in children—in the face of death. Yearning to understand human finitude, Janeway and Mather view death as the possibility in impossibility.

The joyful death books, however, strike the modern reader first not as lofty attempts to confront the mysteries of life and death but rather as manipulative didactic tracts. And, of course, they are didactic. In our century didacticism has acquired a bad reputation, but almost all great literature is, in some sense, didactic. The nature of the didacticism is the question. On one level, Janeway and Mather are manipulative. Children

ought to behave in certain ways, and literature for children is one way to
encourage such behavior. Although the amoral tenor of the late twentieth century rebels against such manipulation, does not all literature
attempt, in one way or another, to manipulate to move, the audience to a
certain attitude or behavior? Are not Flannery O'Connor's contemporaries who read, say, "Revelation" expected to be offended by Mrs.
Turpin's racism and to change their attitudes? Is not the reader of Kafka's
"A Hunger Artist" expected to be different after encountering the man in
the cage? In the same way, Janeway and Mather hoped to change their
readers. On the simplest level, they wanted better behavior from children. And to the extent that they wanted a healthier, richer life for the
children of their age, they surely were admirable in their endeavors.

Perhaps the clearest example of didacticism is in the last example,
number 7 in the first part of Janeway's *Token for Children*. There we
encounter a "notorious Wicked Child, who was taken up from Begging,
and admirably Converted" (103). This child demonstrates all the traits
that would offend Janeway's Puritanism. Here is Janeway's description
of such an unappealing child:

> A very poor Child, of the Parish of Newington-Butts, came
> begging, to the door of a dear Christian Friend of mine, in a very
> lamentable case, so filfthy and nasty, that he would even have
> turned ones stomach to have looked on him: But it pleased God
> to raise in the heart of my Friend a great pitty & tenderness
> towards this poor Child, so that in Charity he took him out of
> the streets, whose Parents were unknown, who had nothing at
> all in him to commend him to any ones Charity but his misery.
> (103–4)

Janeway's friend, seeing the "Glory of God, and the good of the
Immortal Soul of this wretched creature," befriends him. Such compassion suggests an important theme in the joyful death books: the value of
all human life, even that of a small child, and in this case, the value of a
"notorious Wicked" and "filthy and nasty" child. Janeway goes on to
inform us of the boy's depravity:

> . . . he was a very Monster of wickedness, and a thousand times
> more miserable and vile by his Sin, than by his Poverty. He was
> running to Hell as soon as he could go, and was old in naughti-
> ness when he was young in years; and one shall scarce hear of
> one so like the Devil in his Infancy, as this poor Child was. What

Sin was there (that his age was capable of) that he did not
Commit? What by the Corruption of his Nature, and the
abominable Example of little Beggar-boys, he was arrived to a
strange pitch of Impiety. He would call filfthy Names, take
God's name in vain, Curse and Swear, and do almost all kind of
Mischief; and as to any thing of God, worse than an Heathen.
(104)

Although "Worse than an Heathen" the "worth of his own Soul" (105)
still shines through; "the very Monster of wickedness" is a valued child
of God. Janeway surely wants to discourage the boy's heathen-like
behavior, but more importantly he desires to establish the child as an
eternal soul in the eyes of God, to assert that the boy has a soul deserving
of more than wallowing around in "all kinds of mischief." No doubt
Janeway's narrative sense encourages him to hyperbole in describing the
child's depravity, but only to assert God's largesse. Both Janeway and
Mather hope to influence the behavior of children not merely because
they want to establish social conformity, but more importantly because
they hold that the behavior they desire is an indication of God's presence
in the lives of those who adhere to good behavior. Although social
manipulation is part of the didacticism of the joyful death books, more
significantly they assert that all children are valuable and, consequently,
worthy of behaving in a Godly manner. Because Janeway's acquaintance
befriended the nameless young boy, the boy conducted himself in a way
that society thought appropriate; but, more importantly, because the boy
no longer behaved as "an heathen" and learned that his place was with
God, "the Child died joyfully." In the joy is the triumph.

Children are not the only objects of Janeway's and Mather's didacticism; it extends also to the parents. In fact, the ministry to parents and
adults plays a significant role in the collections made by the two authors.
For in realizing that children have something to teach adults, the joyful
death books attest to the importance of childhood. Children are not
expendable items of mortality; they can be both vessels of God's grace
and the instruments of divine instruction. Giving children such an
important role not only looks back to the New Testament assertion that
unless one becomes a child one cannot enter Heaven (Matt. 18:3) but also
forward to the romantic notion that the child is father to the man, that
the child is in contact with truths that are lost in growing up. To give this
value to children is to elevate the status of childhood higher than many
seventeenth or eighteenth century writers would have done. Consider,
for example, little Mary A. who, "before she was full five years old,

seemed to mind *The one thing needful"* (91) and became a wonder of spiritual maturity. In particular, Mary became an inspiration to her mother who was too much taken with the things of this world. For Mary

> was a Child of a strange tenderness and compassion to all, full of bowels and pity; whom she could not help, she would be ready to weep over; especially if she saw her Mother at any time troubled, she would quickly make her sorrows her own, and would weep for her, and with her.
>
> When her Mother had been somewhat solicitous about any worldy thing, she would, if she could possibly, put off from her care one way or other. One time she told her, O Mother, *Grace is better than that,* (meaning something her Mother wanted,) *I had rather have Grace and thy Love of Christ, than any thing in the world.* (93)

Mary's insight that often times the world, indeed, is too much with us sounds much like the ideas of the romantic imagination.

The modern reader might be suspicious of some qualities attributed to the children. For example, the equanimity attributed to little Mary A. is unusual in a child less than twelve years old. Janeway gives us Mary's dispassionate view of one woman's problems. "One time a woman coming into the House in a great Passion, spoke of her Condition, as if none were like hers, and it would never be otherwise; the Child said, it were a strange thing to say when it is night, it will never be day again" (94). But the importance here is not the insight itself, but that Janeway attributes it to a child. Whether Janeway's portrayal of Mary is, in fact, accurate is irrelevant. That Janeway attributes Mary's insight to a young child makes childhood special and gives a value to childhood that many contemporaries did not share. Thus, the joyful death books are not about the expendability of children but rather about the nobility of childhood.

Such nobility is clearly evident in the way that children become instruments of instruction and, finally, of God's grace. Both Janeway and Mather give several accounts of children who are responsible for the spiritual development of their parents. For the Puritan, of course, the sole end of human existence is to secure eternal salvation. To make a child the means by which such salvation is achieved is to see the child as an important part of God's plan. Janeway, for example, tells of Ann Lane who died in 1640 when she was ten years old. Like many of the children in Janeway's account, she began early to be "Solicitous about her Soul"

(121). But of greater interest is her concern about her father's soul. Janeway suggests that had Ann Lane not acted "as if she were Sanctified from the very Womb" (121) her father probably would not have found salvation. "Having occasion to lie at Colebrook," Janeway says, he

> sent for [Ann Lane's] Father, an old Disciple, an *Israelite* indeed, and desired him to give me some account of his Experiences, and how the Lord first wrought upon him?
>
> He gave me this answer, That he was of a Child somewhat Civil; Honest and as to man Harmless, but he was little acquainted with the Power of Religion, till this sweet Child put him upon a thorow enquiry into the state of his Soul, and would still be begging of him and pleading with him to redeem in Time, and to all with life and vigor in the things of God, which was no small demonstration to him of the reality of the Invisibles, that a very Babe and Suckling should speak so feelingly about the things of God, and be so greatly concerned not only about her own Soul, but about her Fathers too, which was the occasion of his Conversion, and the very thought of it was a quickening to him for Thirty Years, and he hopes never to wear off the Impressions of it from his Spirit.
>
> After this she (as I remember) put her Father upon Family Duties, and if at any time he were for any time out of his shop, she would find him out, with so much sweetness and humility beg of him to come home, and to remember the preciousness of time, for which we must all give an account. (121)

To the late twentieth-century reader there is something distasteful about this Uriah Heepish little girl pursuing her father through the streets whenever he leaves his shop. We find her even less appealing when we learn later that "she could not endure the company of common Children." But such modern responses are not relevant to Janeway's intent. His account of Ann Lane's piety and zeal attributes to a child the means for achieving humanity's highest goal—salvation. She has gained her own and is the means by which her father finds his. Janeway's achievement goes beyond the seventeenth-century religious context; his achievement is testimony to Ann Lane's position as valued part of family, society, and salvation. Janeway discloses a world in which childhood matters.

Cotton Mather also provides an example of the important role that the child plays in God's plan of salvation. The last example in Mather's *A*

Token, for the Children of New-England is "transcribed from the Life of
Mr. John Baily, as it was Related in a Sermon Preached on the Day of his
Funeral, at Boston, N.E. 16.d. 10m. 1697." The short example can be
quoted in its entirety.

> From a Child he did know the Holy Scriptures: Yea, From a
> Child he was wise unto Salvation. In his very Childhood he
> discovered the Fear of God, upon his young Heart, and Prayer
> to God, was one of his Early Exercises.
>
> There was one very Remarkable effect of it. His Father was a
> man of very Licentious Conversation; a Gamester, a Dancer, a
> very Lewd Company-keeper. The Mother of this Elect-Vessel,
> one day took him, while he was yet a Child, and calling the
> Family together, made him to Pray with them. His Father
> coming to understand, at what rate the Child had Pray'd with
> his Family, it smote the Soul of him, with a great Conviction, &
> proved the Beginning of his Conversion unto God. God left not
> off work on his Heart, until he proved One of the most Eminent
> Christians in all that Neighbor-hood. So he Lived, so he Dyed; a
> man of more than Ordinary Piety. And it was his manner
> sometimes to Retire unto those very places of his Lewdnesses,
> where, having that his little Son in his Company, he would pour
> out Floods of Tears, in Repenting Prayers before the Lord. (172)

Although Mather intended his narrative to be largely a tool for encouraging Godly behavior in children and for holding up before them the reality
and proximity of death, Mather also unknowingly emphasized the value
of childhood. John Baily is exemplary in seeing to his own salvation and
in becoming the instrument for his father's. The child in this passage is
not merely a passive participant in the vicissitudes of life and death; he is
an active contributor to the process of salvation. Thus, Mather's narrative is more than encouragement to good behavior; it is a statement of
the lofty role that the child plays in what the seventeenth and eighteenth
centuries considered the grandest drama of all, the drama of salvation.

That drama of salvation makes the narratives of Janeway and Mather
interesting reading. In particular, it is the Calvinist anguish in understanding human salvation that adds the tension to the tales of dying
children who tell of their path to salvation. For the Calvinist, salvation is
never certain in this life. There may be many signs that indicate that one
is of the elect, but those signs are indications, not certainties. All of the

tales in Janeway and Mather end on the optimistic note that the child is indeed on the road to heaven, but the reader's interest is continually excited by the constant doubt about whether the child is truly of the elect. Janeway's account of Sarah Howley, for instance, tells the story of a young girl who was "mightily awakened" when she was eight years old and decided "to make Religion her business." Her life was Godly and devout, and when she was "about fourteen years old, she broke a Vein in her Lungs . . . and oft did spit blood" (81). Sarah Howley's end is clearly near. A saccharine writer might pour out a stream of pious religious sentiments. But, to the very end, the problematic nature of salvation and the tension inherent in the Calvinist's understanding of God's dealings with men and women continue. With the broken vein in her lung, Sarah asks her mother to pray for her and, in phrasing reminiscent of nine-teenth-century melodrama, cries out, "I am undone unto all Eternity." When the mother asks what she should pray for, Sarah responds, "That I may have a saving knowledge of Sin and Christ: and that I may have an assurance of Gods love to my Soul." In the word "assurance" is the guarantee that Sarah's drama of doubt will continue to her end because the Puritan never could have absolute assurance in this life. For the six long pages Sarah lies dying, she yearns for assurance. Janeway the artist skillfully manipulates that yearning into an absorbing narrative. One moment Sarah cries out, "But what shall I do to be Saved? Sweet Lord Jesus" (81). And immediately she realizes that even if she feels she has assurance of her salvation, it might be a false assurance. Consequently, she must be on guard against her presumption. "She was much afraid of persumption [sic], and dreaded a mistake in the matters of her Soul, and would be often putting up ejaculations to God, to deliver her from deceiving her self. To instance in one: Great and Mighty God, give me Faith, Lord, that I may not be a foolish Virgin, having a Lamp and not Oyl" (81–82). The ambiguity of Sarah's spiritual state demands the attention of the reader following Sarah's progress toward death. The child pleads with God to know, yet she cannot be complacent in any feelings that she may have. The promises of scripture are elevating, but the constant doubt remains that they may not be for her:

> Another time her Father bid her be of good cheer, because she was going to a better Father; at which she fell into a great passion, and said, but how do I know that? I am a poor sinner that wants assurance. O, for assurance! It was still her note, O, for assurance! That was her great, earnest, and constant request to all that came to her, to beg assurance for her. (82)

Almost to the very end, Sarah remains doubtful about the future of her soul.

Part of Janeway's success is the realism that he interjects into an account that could dwell wholly on the unrealistic. His deathbed accounts are not sugar-coated depictions of celestial children about to be with God; they are narratives of the sinful natures Janeway saw in all those around him. Sarah, for instance, is herself suspicious of her own motives in seeking assurance of salvation:

> Her Mother ask'd her, if God would spare her life, how she would live? Truly Mother, said she, we have such base hearts that I can't tell, we are apt to promise great things when we are sick, but when we are recovered, we are already to forget ourselves and to turn again unto folly; but I hope I should be more careful of my Time and my Soul, than I have been. (82)

"I hope," she says, but she cannot know. Sarah's lack of certainty, both of her sanctity and her salvation, continues to the conclusion when her soul, "ravished with the love of Christ," finally receives the certainty for which she has yearned: "Upon the Lord's day, she scarce spoke anything, but much desired that Bills of thanksgiving might be sent to those who had formerly been praying for her, that they might help her to praise God for that full assurance that he had given her of His love to her Soul" (86). With that assurance Sarah departs this life, and Janeway's drama of the soul reaches its climax: "She oft commended her Spirit into the Lords hands; and the last words which she was heard to speak, were these, Lord help Lord Jesus help; Dear Jesus, Blessed Jesus.—And thus upon the Lords Day, between Nine and Ten of the Clock in the forenoon, she slept sweetly in Jesus, and began in everlasting Sabbath, February 19, 1670" (86). The power of Janeway's stories also comes from his ability to present his young lives with integrity and honesty as they confront uncertainties in both the physical and spiritual realms. It is one thing to live, as we do, with only the vagaries of the physical world; it is quite another to add to those vageries a concern for the next world. Janeway's dramas are powerful depictions of children whose spirits triumph over forces in both this world and the next.

The Puritan doctrine of total human depravity is the greatest force that Janeway's and Mather's children must confront. This doctrine, most clearly articulated by Calvin, colors almost every aspect of the Puritan world.

> Therefore let us hold this as an undoubted truth which no siege engines can shake: the mind of man has been so completely estranged from God's righteousness that it conceives, desires, undertakes, only that which is impious, perverted, foul, impure, and infamous. The heart is so steeped in the poison of sin, that it can breathe out nothing but a loathsome stench. But if some men occasionally make a show of good, their minds nevertheless ever remain enveloped in hypocrisy and deceitful craft, and their hearts are bound by inner perversity.[5]

The modern mind finds it difficult to imagine that such a world could do anything but create enormous guilt and low self-esteem. But the narratives of Janeway and Mather seldom have the effect of producing overburdening guilt in the children. In only one example do we find a child oppressed by guilt. Janeway's Susanne Bicks "had very low and undervaluing thoughts of her self and her own Righteousness" (137). Susanne continues in phrases that could have been penned by Calvin himself. "But what are we our selves; Not only weakness and nothingness, but wickedness. For all the thoughts and imaginations of mans heart, are only evil, and that continually, we are by Nature Children of wrath, and are Conceived and Born in Sin and Unrighteousness. Oh! this wretched and vile thing SIN!" (137). Such a prolonged meditation on human depravity is unusual in the joyful death books. More often, the children see their sinful states as a condition to be reckoned with, as an enemy, in a sense, that can be conquered. Consequently, human depravity offers the possibility not for guilt, but for victory. The children's corrupt nature is a condition to struggle against, and in that struggle we see the vigor of the Puritan life.

The struggle to triumph over one's sinful nature, rather than to succumb to it, is the Puritan drama. The narratives of Janeway and Mather are poignant depictions of children who are participants in that drama. In their attempts to find grace, they are living out the ancient Pauline doctrine that "where sin abounded, grace did more abound" (Romans 5:20). In the joyful death books, the possibility of victory over one's natural state far outweighs the possiblity of succumbing to guilt.

The narratives of Janeway and Mather seem strange to us. They do, of course, give us a picture of seventeenth-century life and of the literature for children and adults in that period. More important, however, they are great testaments to the potential prominence and heroism of childhood. When childhood becomes a part of the journey to salvation it has a special nobility. The dying children demonstrate a quiet heroism in their triumph over what they thought were the forces of this world and the next. James Janeway and Cotton Mather tell us more than "little children too may die." They show us that little children have a noble and heroic place in the pageant of life.

Notes

1. All references to the texts of Janeway and Mather are found in *Masterworks of Children's Literature: 1550–1739*, ed. Francelia Butler. This is vol. 2 in *Masterworks of Children's Literature*, Jonathan Cott, general editor (New York: Stonehill Publishing Co. in association with Chelsea House, 1983). Page references appear in parentheses after quotations.

2. Thomas Mallon, *A Book of One's Own: People and Their Diaries* (New York: Ticknor and Fields, 1984), 7.

3. Harvey Wish, ed., *The Diary of Samuel Sewall* (New York: G. P. Putnam's Sons, 1967), 40–41.

4. *A Book of One's Own*, 8.

5. John Calvin, *Institutes of the Christian Religion*, ed. John T. McNeill, trans. Ford Lewis Battles, vol. 1 (Philadelphia: The Westminster Press, 1960), 340.

VI.
Historical Approaches

24.

John Foxe's "Book of Martyrs" and Its Value as a Book for Children

BARBARA ROSEN

It is hard for us, as modern parents, to imagine that in 1563 the first books we bought for our children might have been the Bible and *The Acts and Monuments of John Foxe* (most frequently known as Foxe's *Book of Martyrs*);[1] and that we might then have regarded the child's reading needs as filled for several years to come. Many of us would, if pressed, subscribe to Penelope Lively's statement that "We do actually believe now that children's books need to be fun and nothing else";[2] yet even in the Romantic era such a statement would have been regarded as a monumental evasion of responsibility and an extraordinary begging of the question. If we are to understand what prescriptive reading of Foxe or the Bible might have meant to children of the past, it is necessary to divest ourselves of many current notions about children and reading.

The first printed books came out of a monastic tradition of slow and painstaking production, slow mastery, and long-continued use. The educational system associated with them at all levels depended upon authorities accepted for centuries, upon endless repetition of exercises, translation, and retranslation, learning by heart. It was the common understanding that this was what books were for. In England, the first printed book that most ordinary people had wanted to read was the Bible in their own tongue; in 1538 Thomas Cromwell urged bishops to place it in their churches and began the process of licensing cheap editions. The very high value set on literacy by Puritans and Renaissance theorists confirms our sense that reading in the sixteenth and seventeenth centuries meant rereading and reflection on serious material as much as the mere ability to recognize words.

Even for those who were not Puritans, the *Book of Martyrs* stood beside the Bible near the beginning of every path to literacy. After 1571, it was chained next to the Bible in churches and set out in the anterooms to ministers' chambers; abridgments, selections, and at least one tiny "thumb-book" were printed, and we may assume that some version or other was available in most schools or literate homes for a couple of hundred years after its first appearance. It was continually recommended by ministers and godly writers; fondness for it was a key validation of childish virtue in James Janeway's enormously popular *A Token for Children, being An Exact Account of the Conversion, Holy and Exemplary Lives and Joyful Deaths of several Young Children*, which was first printed in 1671 and reprinted for the next 140 years. John Sudlow "was hugely taken with the reading of the Book of *Martyrs*, and would be ready to leave his Dinner to go to his Book."[3] Poor little Charles Bridgman, dying painfully, "called to Mind that Martyr *Thomas Bilney*; who being in Prison, the Night before his burning, put his Finger into the Candle, to know how he could endure the Fire."[4] Even the skeptical William Godwin is said to have remarked of these pious children that, in his own childhood "I felt as if I were willing to die with them if I could with equal success engage the admiration of my friends and mankind."[5]

There is no question that in many families "real reading" of Foxe or the Bible was the medium through which admiration, family affection, and feelings of self-worth were mediated. Adam Martindale records his gleeful discovery of literacy about 1628, when he was five; his mother let him have an "ABC" given by a relative, and he begged lessons from his siblings and his sister's suitor:

> Then of mine owne accord I fell to reading the bible and any other English booke, and such greate delight I tooke in it, and the praises I got by it from my parents, which preferred my reading before any other in the family, that I think I could almost have read a day together without play or meat, if breath and strength would have held out, and thus it continued to the end of the first seven yeares of my life.[6]

Notice that reading for Adam means reading aloud, often in competition with siblings. Thus when Edward Harvey, according to his mother "begins now to delight in reading" and "would not let me be in peace, till I promised him to send for [a Bible]," he is looking forward to a rite of passage into full family membership.[7] When family unity is demonstrated in a religious context (family prayers, family reading, grace before meals) children absorb religious rhetoric as love and security; when one can actively join the magic circle by serious reading, then the content of one's reading becomes material for growth, for play, and for imitation. (Many of Janeway's little saints held services for their siblings, preached sermons, and lectured them on salvation; today we should recognize this as imitative play.) What, particularly, might children have found valuable for their own growth in the content of Foxe's *Book of Martyrs?*

This vast compilation is one of the classics it is easier to be witty about than to read, and much of what is said of it betrays slight acquaintance with its actual contents. Foxe was by temperament and training a scholar as much as a polemicist. In recording the histories of the Marian martyrs and their predecessors he works by overkill; he traveled widely, questioned ceaselessly, consulted mountains of documents. Subsequent discoveries have, as Mozley suggests, tended to make him seem more rather than less reliable.[8] He includes transcripts of Latin and even Anglo-Saxon documents; he gives accounts of lengthy disputes on theological cruces; he prints letters by queens, acts of Parliament, and legal interpretations. In his quest for completeness he prints altogether too much. Yet he is showing us history in the making—the laws, the political pressures which caused them to be made, the people who applied them, the means by which people were entrapped in conversation and brought to trial, the ways in which the courts worked for or against the accused, the reasons for their bias. A child puzzling and skipping his way through must often have been completely bewildered. The complexity of the world and the vast consequences of small actions are on view all at once.

Yet in the midst of this are trenchant, brilliantly dramatic scenes of interrogation or execution, where Foxe's exacerbated sensibilities express their outrage through the selection of telling detail, the contrast between power and helplessness, the pathos of the ignorant caught up in matters beyond their understanding. We think of the death of Cranmer, finally holding steady in the flame the hand that had signed his recantations (8:90) or the farewell of Dr. Rowland Taylor, his wife and son (6:692). Foxe records the ambiguities and unsolved questions which lead the reader away from doctrine to raw experience; when on the same day three Protestants were burned for religion and three Catholics hanged for denying the supremacy of Henry VIII, a foreigner exclaimed, "Deus bone! quomodo hic vivunt gentes?" (colloquial translation: "Good God! what sort of people are these?") and the sight "brought the people into a marvelous admiration and doubt of their religion, which part to follow and take" (5:438). The sheer drama of the set scenes quite often obscures the narrow theological points at issue, and the variety of literary modes presents a reader with changing conventions and genres. The effect is one of multiplicity rather than unity, of a human panorama rather than a sermon. Compared with Janeway's grim single message that children "are not too Little to go to Hell,"[9] Foxe frees rather than constrains the spirit.

Much has been made of the horrifying nature of the illustrations in the larger editions of Foxe, and of the clinical descriptions of torture and elaborated execution. Few of the woodcuts are as graphic as the picture of William Gardiner hung over a slow fire, his hands amputated, or Lambert propped up by pikes in the flames; yet even the formalized cuts of flames and faggots would give some children scope for imagination and nightmares. The descriptions are another matter; the obsessive and pitiless clarity of their physical detail is sometimes hard to bear. It is more understandable when we learn that Foxe pleaded with Elizabeth for the lives of Anabaptists and Catholic priests and, above all, for the abolishment of burning as a form of execution. As he says despairingly "Nor do I favour the lives of *men* alone: would that I could succour the very beasts too. For such is my disposition (I will say this of myself, foolishly perhaps, but yet truly) that I can scarce pass the shambles where beasts are slaughtered but that my mind secretly recoils with a feeling of pain."[10] That pain is reproduced, over and over, in the book, in grief and horror that men could do such things to each other.

Foxe was unusual; the child of the sixteenth or seventeenth century was faced with the sort of direct horror which today is confronted only by the very poor of the Third World. Bodies of felons hung rotting in chains, heads were set over city gates. Traitors were hanged, drawn and quartered in the public streets; children were flogged and animals tormented. Vagrants, sick or crazy, wandered the land or lay dying in ditches outside homes. More than we can easily recognize, the world of Foxe and of the children who read him was a world shaped by expectation of pain; we are separated from it by our own good health. Most of our brothers and sisters survive; we are not used to our mothers and daughters dying in childbirth, without anesthetic (Alice Thornton's autobiographical record of bizarre gynecological disasters is probably not atypical). When children have scarlet fever or pneumonia today, the disease may be cut short by antibiotics. Three hundred years ago such illnesses had to run their prolonged and painful course, with the ensuing complications and relapses. The child of this era had in fact only one all-consuming task, and that was to grow up; the two qualities required for this were obedience and endurance.

Perhaps being a child in the sixteenth or seventeenth century was above all an exercise in felt helplessness, before circumstances and before parents. The poor, struggling grimly for existence, taught children by example that their only real value was that of provider; till they could bring in pay they were liabilities to the family rather than members of it. For the middle-and upper-class child, perhaps the most vivid parental image was that of the Old Testament potter, who could shape the clay to his liking and had the power, without explanation, to deform or destroy it at will. The books of parental advice (mostly Puritan in inspiration, but more widely read than that) show parental love as the norm, but it was a love that operated through discipline. "Whom the Lord loveth, he chasteneth"—and, with the banishment of the Catholic priest, it was the father of the family who held the keys of discipline and salvation, the mother whose constant prayers took the place of the running ground-bass of monastic intercession with God. The psychic weight upon the Puritan child, in addition to ill-health and what we would regard as emotional neglect, was sometimes crushing: particularly for girls, the enjoined silence and control of spontaneous utterance intensified the sense of helplessness and constant religious guilt.

In Foxe's book a child would have read about people who were recognizably fallible, able to be confused in talk or forced into humiliating abjuration by fear of the fire. Foxe's sympathy extends to those who were "molested and vexed and, at last, compelled to abjure" (5:26). The child would have found situations of bondage, imprisonment, and arbitrary pain which, to a few, provided opportunities for heroism. He or she would have seen that a high proportion of those executed were women or young people—even children—who, by bearing what had to be borne, became heroic. The virtues demanded were not those of the Crusades or the warlike saints, but those of Milton's Adam, who performs no active deed—he simply makes moral choices and endures their consequences.

These were virtues peculiarly apt to women and children of the time, for they turned upon the uttering of words, the giving or withholding of oaths, the ability to maintain a sense of self under the threat or reality of pain, the endurance of exhausting conditions and attrition by humiliation. In the stories told by Foxe, children could find models for making inward choices in situations of apparent helplessness; if they must suffer, then they could suffer uncomplainingly, like Charles Bridgman, on the pattern of the great martyrs; if they were treated unjustly or misunderstood then they became part of a silent army of sufferers. Within submission, there could still be an assertion of moral choice; without control of circumstances, there could still be self-control of response. It is easy to see something societally imposed in the picture of a child praying to be good, trying to borrow the courage of the martyrs to endure the pains and trials of his own existence, yet patterning one's life after a model of courageous endurance may be a positive means of self-creation when no other is possible. And some few would perceive the avenue of escape later depicted in Samuel Richardson's *Clarissa:* religious conviction alone offered strength to an adult to defy family or social norms without guilt.

If, finally, we turn back to consider Foxe's book as material for children—as, in our own terms, "fun"—we recall that it was written for adults. Yet it was so long recommended as fare for children that we must consider it at least as part of a background which adults and children shared for two centuries or so. And this brings us to the sharpest distinction of attitude between the shared cultural background then and now.

Death in Foxe is never unimportant; it is not dignified, and he does not show it so, yet he suggests that its grotesqueries do not exist merely in their own right, as sources of curiosity or amusement when skillfully captured on screen, stage, or cartoon. The way in which a man or woman meets death—or even the fact that, however shrinkingly, that person chose to meet it—is seen in the light of eternal destiny. Yet Foxe's eye for character and human foible ensures that we also see the particular nature of a person's death as an extension of a human self, a growth and development. It is shocking to realize how often in films seen by children our only interest in a dying man might be in the pattern his body makes as it falls from a roof, or in the witty verisimilitude with which that body leaks ketchup. Violence and death in Foxe are not transmuted into entertainment or sermon; they are traversed in the service of human courage and ultimate meaning.

What do we suggest about our view of human nature when, for fun on Saturday mornings, we shut up children in an endless loop of cartoons with an obsessively repeated pattern of quarrel-chase-act of violence; or feed them "cop shows" where the good guys endlessly mow down the bad with gunfire, often to cheers and laughter? In Foxe's book, the reader is aligned, not with those who inflict suffering, but with those who bear it; and those who suffer are less guilty than those who execute. Is it necessary to entertain our children with the notion that the hero is always the man with a smoking gun in his hand? Is there finally no room in our concept of children's reading and viewing for stories that show a triumph of the human spirit over violence through endurance? For many victims of racism or colonialism, that is the story of their friends and families.

No one today would see it as feasible to turn back the clock and present six-year-olds with the Bible and the *Book of Martyrs* and nothing else. Yet, by projecting our sympathies backwards, we may see what was positive for the child readers in Foxe, a source of empowerment in a world that was harsh and difficult for them. We may ask whether the reading and viewing we allow our children equally prepares them in strength and compassion for the world that we have made, in which they may feel—and be—equally powerless. And we may be reminded that to find nourishment for growth in unlikely places—to wrench honey from the lion's carcass—as so many children did, is in itself one more proof of the unquenchable vitality and versatility of the human spirit.

Notes

1. Ed. Rev. Josiah Pratt, 8 vols. (London: The Religious Tract Society, 1877). Volume and page numbers follow quotations in the text.

2. "Children and the Art of Memory: Part I," *The Horn Book Magazine* 54 (1978), 18.

3. Janeway, *A Token For Children* (Boston: Z. Fowles, 1771), 49.

4. Janeway, *A Token For Children*, 32.

5. William Sloane, *Children's Books in England and America in the Seventeenth Century* (New York: Columbia University Press, 1955), 45.

6. Quoted Sloane, *Children's Books*, 7–8.

7. Quoted Sloane, *Children's Books*, 48.

8. J. F. Mozley, *John Foxe and His Book* (New York: Octagon Books, 1970), 175–203.

9. Janeway, *A Token for Children*, 4.

10. Mozley, *John Foxe*, 87.

11. For an excellent discussion, see Warren W. Wooden's "John Foxe's *Book of Martyrs* and the Child Reader," *Proceedings of the Ninth Annual Conference of the Children's Literature Association*, March, 1982.

25.

'The Whole of the Story':
Frances Hodgson Burnett's "A Little Princess"

ELIZABETH LENNOX KEYSER

> Between the lines of every story there is another story . . . one
> that is never heard and can only be guessed at by the people
> who are good at guessing. The person who writes the story
> may never know all of it, but sometimes he does and wishes
> he had the chance to begin again.[1]

In her preface to *A Little Princess* (1905), entitled "The Whole of the
Story," Frances Hodgson Burnett explains how, in the process of
adapting *Sara Crewe* (1887) for the stage, she discovered much that she
had failed to hear and thus had left untold. The result of her more careful
listening was an elaborate retelling; in fact, *A Little Princess* is three times
the length of *Sara Crewe*. But Burnett's preface, even as it assures the
child reader that the story is now both fully accessible and complete,
invites the critic to guess at what remains hidden between the lines. For
even if all the secrets of *Sara Crewe* have now been told, the new version
may well possess secrets of its own, secrets that it—like its predecessor—
is keeping even from the author herself.

Sara Crewe is the seemingly straightforward story of twelve-year-old
Sara, a pupil at Miss Minchin's Select Seminary in London. Soon after
the story opens, Sara loses both her father, a British officer in India, and
her supposedly immense fortune. Hardhearted Miss Minchin then employs her as an errand girl in return for a small attic room and what is
often no more than a few scraps of bread. Isolated from her former
schoolmates, Sara's only companion is her doll, Emily, in whom she
attempts to confide. For awhile Sara stoically bears hunger and cold,
loneliness and grief, but one day she loses control and passionately
reproaches Emily for being "nothing but a doll!".[2] Soon after this Sara
makes one friend, a dull student named Ermengarde, who hates to read.
Sara, starved for books as well as for food, reads Ermengarde's, then tells

her the stories in such a way that she cannot forget them. Sara's storytelling gradually leads her to envision herself as the heroine of a story, a princess in exile, and this fantasy enables her to endure her life of drudgery and deprivation. Often it prevents her from retaliating when she is insulted by Miss Minchin or malicious students, but at least once it gives her the courage to rebel. While running errands Sara befriends a beggar girl named Anne, observes a happy family, which she calls the Large Family, and becomes acquainted with the Indian servant of the wealthy invalid next door. The invalid, whom Sara calls "the Indian gentleman," and his servant, Ram Dass, secretly conspire to transform Sara's barren attic into cozy living quarters and to supply her with nourishing food and warm clothes. Before long the Indian gentleman discovers Sara is the child for whom he has been searching, the orphan of his friend Captain Crewe. Upon learning this he not only adopts Sara but restores to her the vast fortune mistakenly believed to have been lost.

In *A Little Princess* Burnett retains the central episodes and characters of *Sara Crewe* but adds others to emphasize the exceptional nature of Sara's imagination. Unlike the earlier version, *A Little Princess* begins with seven-year-old Sara's arrival at Miss Minchin's and her parting with her father. We are shown how her imagination enables her to deal with the separation, adjust to her new environment, and enthrall her classmates, who view her, as she views herself, as a little princess. Burnett also develops Miss Minchin's animosity and that of Lavinia, a jealous classmate, as well as Sara's relationships with Lottie, the baby of the school, and Becky, a servant girl. Through Sara's conversations with Lottie and Ermengarde, who visit her in the attic, and with Becky, "the prisoner in the next cell," Burnett suggests its significance as a kind of enchanted world. One new chapter in particular, "The Magic," anticipates the preoccupation with "magic"—or the power of the imagination to transform reality and thus overcome adversity—in Burnett's masterpiece for children, *The Secret Garden* (1911). In this chapter Sara, having fed the beggar girl instead of herself, returns half-starving to the attic. Ermengarde, hearing for the first time of Sara's hunger, provides a basket of food for her and Becky, and Sara in her delight imaginatively transforms the attic into a banquet hall. Miss Minchin breaks in on the girls before they have even begun to eat, but after Sara has gone to bed hungry, Ram Dass performs in fact the transformation that Sara's fancy had begun. In the later version, then, Burnett encourages us to believe that Sara's power to envision something splendid even under the most miserable conditions somehow helps to bring that splendor into being.

The two versions of Sara's story reflect Burnett's shift from realism to romance during the course of her career. Phyllis Bixler has recently described how Burnett, after the phenomenal success of *Little Lord Fauntleroy* (1885), turned more and more to popular romances for both children and adults, forsaking the working class interest of *That Lass O'Lowries* (1877) and the social realism of *Through One Administration* (1883). The very title of *Sara Crew Or What Happened at Miss Minchin's,* written soon after *Fauntleroy* and before Burnett became a confirmed romance writer, leads us to expect a realistic account of boarding school life. On the other hand, the title of *A Little Princess,* written seventeen years later, emphasizes the way in which Sara's conception of herself as a little princess, her ability to romanticize her exile in the attic, sustains her through the ordeal. As Bixler has observed, "The frequent references to fairy tales and magic make it difficult to mistake *A Little Princess* for a realistic novel of child life."[3] It is as though Burnett, on reconsidering *Sara Crew,* saw how the story could be made to justify her own romantic imagination and the turn that her career, a commercial but no longer a critical success, had taken. Yet the heightened romanticism of *A Little Princess* is accompanied by a subtle psychological realism, a realism also characteristic of *The Secret Garden.*[4] This realistic strain, I would argue, betrays the very ambivalence toward romance that Burnett is attempting to conceal even from herself. Had she had the ear to hear it, she might well have written still another version of Sara's story.

Burnett in the opening chapters of *A Little Princess* emphasizes the benefits conferred by Sara's imagination. Seven-year-old Sara is initially described as "an odd-looking little girl" with a "queer old-fashioned thoughtfulness in her big eyes." We are told that "she felt as if she had lived a long, long time" (3). One reason for Sara's precociousness is her role as "little missus," companion to her widowed father. But another is her love of books. As her father tells Miss Minchin, "she is always starving for new books to gobble, and she wants grown-up books" (10). Not content simply to read, Sara "was, in fact, always inventing stories of beautiful things and telling them to herself" (6). Thus when Sara's father finally leaves her to return to India, she alarms Miss Minchin's sister, Miss Amelia, with her unchildlike behavior: "She has locked herself in, and she is not making the least particle of noise" (15). The next day when an admiring Ermengarde observes that "if she had been like any other little girl, she might have suddenly burst out sobbing and crying," Sara explains the secret of her composure—her ability to pretend things and to share them with others: "If I go on talking and talking . . . telling you things about pretending, I shall bear it better. You don't forget, but you bear it better" (32).

In order to "bear it better," Sara also uses her imagination to create a surrogate family for herself. Before her father leaves, Sara selects a life-size doll to serve as a companion in his absence. Sara, who wants Emily "to look as if she wasn't a doll really," fancies "that there would be a great deal of comfort in even pretending that Emily was alive and really heard and understood" (17). Sara mothers Lottie, who, like Sara, is a motherless child who "had been sent to school by a rather flighty young papa who could not imagine what else to do with her" (38). But whereas Sara is unnaturally controlled, Lottie is completely unrestrained. "When she wanted anything or did not want anything she wept and howled. . . . Her strongest weapon was that in some mysterious way she had found out that a very small girl who had lost her mother was a person who ought to be pitied and made much of" (38). Just as Baby in Burnett's early story "Behind the White Brick" acts out her older sister Jem's grief and rage,[5] so Lottie acts out what Sara has repressed. Sara is the only person who can deal with Lottie's tantrums because she can identify with the other child's misery. When Lottie wails that she has no mama, Sara responds, "Neither have I." She then tells a soothing tale and promises to pretend that Lottie is her child. Like Jem, who finally identifies with her mother rather than with the demanding and unreasonable baby, Sara, in mothering Lottie, mothers herself, the child that Lottie represents.

Sara's imagination endears her to most of her fellow students and enables her to cope with those it does not. Although some, like Lavinia, envy Sara's wealth and position as a "show pupil," most of the girls are fascinated by Sara's "power of telling stories and of making everything she talked about seem like a story, whether it was one or not" (45). When Lavinia, resentful of the attention Sara is getting, ridicules her "new 'pretend' about being a princess," the "pretend" itself makes Sara fore-bearing. "She felt the blood rush up into her face and tingle in her ears. She only just saved herself. If you were a princess, you did not fly into rages." Instead she admits, "I pretend I am a princess, so that I can try and behave like one" (64). Again Burnett shows us how Sara's imagination contributes to her dignity and self-control.

Finally, despite the fact that Sara "saw and lived with the fairy folk or the kings and queens and beautiful ladies" (46), her imagination enables her to discern what others cannot see. For example, Sara immediately sees through Miss Minchin when her father is taken in by her flattery. And Sara's transformation of Becky, the stunted scullery-maid, into an "ill-used heroine" of romance is based less on the desire to gloss over the real hardships of Becky's lot than it is on her perception of Becky's humanity. When Becky is terrified at being discovered in Sara's luxurious room, Sara touches her, saying, "We are just the same—I am only a little girl like you. It's just an accident that I am not you, and you are not me!" (54). Sara's fantasy about Becky is an expression of her belief that all little girls are capable of becoming heroines. Her imagination enables her to perceive what Miss Minchin cannot. To Miss Minchin " 'Scullery-maids—er—are not little girls.' It really had not occurred to her to think of them in that light. Scullery-maids were machines who carried coal-scuttles and made fires" (74). Burnett tells us that Miss Minchin has a "narrow, unimaginative mind" (149), but in this instance it is not so much unimaginative as it is lacking in simple humanity.

Ironically, the dangers of the romantic imagination are first suggested by a parallel between Sara, who represents the virtues of that imagination, and Miss Minchin, who supposedly represents the evils of its lack. In the opening chapter Miss Minchin tries to ingratiate herself with Captain Crewe by praising Sara's looks. Sara, more perspicacious than her father, immediately sees that "She is beginning by telling a story" (8). As Sara continues to herself, "I should be telling a story if I said she was beautiful . . . and I should know I was telling a story" (9). Sara's repeated use of the phrase "telling a story" for telling a lie reminds us of how closely related the two acts are. Further, Sara implies that one can lie, or falsify the truth, without being aware of it. For Miss Minchin, lying has become second nature; for Sara, who values the truth, lying would have to be a conscious, deliberate act. At this point Sara is unaware that her own kind of storytelling, while capable of revealing and preserving truth, can also become a way of unconsciously obscuring it. But if Sara is unaware, her creator is not, and this awareness, I believe, is a source of her ambivalence.

Burnett seems ambivalent about other benefits of the romantic imagination such as Sara's self-control and charisma. For example, Sara's stoic response to her father's departure further associates her with Miss Minchin. Miss Amelia, as we recall, is alarmed at Sara's unchildlike behavior, but the hardened Miss Minchin grudgingly approves: "It is much better than if she kicked and screamed as some of them do" (15). Miss Minchin's approval should cause us to question our own, especially if we see a resemblance between Sara and Paulina Mary, whose unnatural self-control in the opening chapters of Charlotte Brontë's *Villette* so disturbs the narrator, Lucy Snowe. Moreover, when Lavinia exposes Sara's princess fantasy, it is immediately appropriated by her friends and exploited by Miss Minchin: "her adorers were much pleased with the picturesqueness and grandeur of the title, and Miss Minchin, hearing of it, mentioned it more than once to visiting parents, feeling that it rather suggested a sort of royal boarding-school" (65).

Burnett presents her strongest arguments for the romantic imagination and expresses the greatest ambivalence toward it during Sara's exile in the attic. There, as upon her arrival at Miss Minchin's, Sara resorts to her imagination in order to maintain her self-control. As she tells herself, "Soldiers don't complain. . . . I will pretend this is part of a war" (102). And, as before, in comforting Lottie, Sara succeeds in comforting herself. At first Lottie is "aghast because the attic was so bare and ugly and seemed so far away from all the world" (111), but when Sara lifts her up so that she can see the view, Lottie becomes "enchanted. From the attic window . . . the things which were happening in the world below seemed almost unreal." In her excitement Lottie cries, "I like this attic. . . . It's nicer than downstairs" (113). Warmed by the enthusiasm that she herself has kindled, Sara "was able to point out to her many beauties in the room which she herself would not have suspected the existence of" (115). Ermengarde too is enchanted by the attic, especially when Sara, who has begun to pretend that she is a prisoner in the Bastille, communicates with Becky, the "prisoner in the next cell" or attic room. At this point Ermengarde cries out in glee, "Oh, Sara! . . . It is like a story." Sara then tells Ermengarde that " 'Everything's a story. You are a story—I am a story. Miss Minchin is a story.' And she sat down again and talked until Ermengarde forgot that she was a sort of escaped prisoner herself" (123).

As Sara's conversations with Lottie and Ermengarde indicate, the attic itself serves as emblem for Sara's state of mind. She tells Lottie, "You can see all sorts of things you can't see downstairs. . . . it all feels as high up— as if it was another world" (112). Sara, by being forced to live so much in her imagination, is more than ever learning to see what others are blind to. When she does enter the downstairs or everyday world, she unsettles people like Lavinia by looking at them "without speaking—just as if she was finding them out." Sara admits, "That's what I look at people for. I like to know about them. I think them over afterward" (101). Thus Sara's exile has its advantages: she can see more for being above the "world," and she can do so safely because she is removed from it. As the narrator's remark about Ermengarde as an escaped prisoner suggests, the downstairs or real world is itself a prison from which the attic or imaginative world is a refuge, an escape. And so rich is Sara's imaginative world that to Lottie it seems preferable to the real one. Yet the attic, cut off as it is from contact with the outside world, is nonetheless a prison. Sara's ability to look through people, to find out about them, and to find stories in them, is no substitute for communicating with them. Sara, after Lottie goes, confesses that the attic is "a lonely place. . . . Sometimes it's the loneliest place in the world" (116).

Sara is desperately lonely in her attic room, despite the loyal friendship of Becky, Lottie, and Ermengarde, in part because her imagination erects a barrier as well as forges a bond. Sara is determined to prevent her friends from pitying her. And in addition to her pride, her generous spirit wants to save them from anxiety on her behalf. The narrator explains that if "Nature has made you for a giver . . . though there may be times when your hands are empty, your heart is always full, and you can give things out of that" (67). But Sara, in her effort to give to her friends even while in distress, so convinces them of the attic's glamor that they actually come to believe that to live there is privilege, not privation. What is for Sara real misery becomes for them still better entertainment than she provided as a little princess, the heiress of diamond mines. Thus when Ermengarde comes to visit, it never occurs to her that Sara might be hungry. "The truth was that Ermengarde did not know anything of the sometimes almost unbearable side of life in the attic, and she had not a sufficiently vivid imagination to depict it herself. On the rare occasions that she could reach Sara's room she only saw that side of it which was made exciting by things which were 'pretended'. . . . Her visits partook of the character of adventures" (189). All unwittingly, Sara's romantic imagination invites Lottie and Ermengarde to feed off it and to offer little sustenance in return.

The vicarious nature of Sara's attic life and the way in which she provides food for the imaginations of others is pointed up in her relationship with what she calls the Large Family, a family whose home she passes when doing errands for Miss Minchin. "Sara was quite fond of them, and had given them names out of books—quite romantic names" (126). But "the Large Family had been hearing many stories about children who were poor. . . . In the stories, kind people . . . invariably saw the poor children and gave them money or rich gifts. . . . Guy Clarence had been affected to tears . . . by the reading of such a story" (127). That day he sees a shabbily dressed Sara passing by and, taking her for a beggar child, offers her a sixpence. At this Sara's cheeks burn, for "she had known that she looked odd and shabby, but until now she had not known that she might be taken for a beggar" (129). Guy Clarence's mistake suggests how absorption in stories can lead one to misread reality. Further it shows how Sara's habit of viewing herself and others as fictional characters has begun to trap her in the roles that others would have her play—such roles as princess, prisoner, pauper, and, especially, storyteller.

Echoes of *Jane Eyre* also serve to call Sara's use of the imagination into question. Helen Burns, Jane's friend at Lowood Academy, lives much of the time in books and fantasies. The evening Miss Temple invites Jane and Helen to her room, Helen holds her audience spellbound much as Sara does: "something in her own unique mind, had roused her powers within her. They woke, they kindled. . . . Then her soul sat on her lips and language flowed, from what source I cannot tell"[6]. When Jane is unjustly punished, Helen sustains her much as Sara sustains Becky: "It was as if a martyr, a hero, had passed a slave or victim, and imparted strength in the transit" (58). When Helen herself suffers unjust punishment, she loses herself in a daydream while Jane marvels: "She is looking at what she can remember, I believe; not at what is really present" (45). Helen's calm acceptance of unjust treatment, while it incites her oppressors to still greater cruelty, gives her a moral victory. Her philosophy seems to anticipate that of Sara, who says to herself: "I never answer when I can help it. When people are insulting you, there is nothing so good for them as not to say a word—just to look at them and *think*. . . . When you will not fly into a passion people know you are stronger than they are, because you are strong enough to hold in your rage, and they are not. . . . There's nothing so strong as rage, except what makes you hold it in—that's stronger" (131). Yet there is a bitterness in Sara's reflection that seems more typical of Jane than of Helen. It is as though Sara, who is described as having "a fine, hot little temper of her own" (26), would impose Helen's self-control upon Jane's passion, unaware that Helen's self-repression resigned her to death whereas Jane's self-expression enabled her to live.

Thus a crucial scene, central also to *Sara Crewe,* is the one in which Sara loses her temper with her doll, Emily. As we have seen, Sara's imagination transforms the doll into a companion when her father leaves her. And in this too Burnett seems to have borrowed from Brontë, for at the Reeds, Jane "in the dearth of worthier objects of affection . . . contrived to find a pleasure in loving and cherishing a faded graven image . . . half fancying it alive and capable of sensation" (24). When searching for a doll to buy, Sara complains to her father that "the trouble with dolls is that they never seem to *hear*" (12). Upon moving to the attic, Sara begins to pretend that "Emily was a kind of good witch who could protect her" (131), but she is bothered more than ever by her lack of responsiveness, a lack that she tries hard to excuse: "Perhaps Emily is more like me than I am like myself. Perhaps she would rather not answer her friends, even. She keeps it all in her heart" (132). One night, however, "Emily's stare seemed so vacant, her sawdust legs and arms so inexpressive, that Sara lost all control of herself" (132). "She looked at the staring glass eyes and complacent face, and suddenly a sort of heartbroken rage seized her. She lifted her little savage hand and knocked Emily off the chair, bursting into a passion of sobbing,—Sara who never cried. 'You are nothing but a *doll*,' she cried; 'nothing but a doll—doll—doll. You care for nothing. You are stuffed with sawdust. You never had a heart. Nothing could ever make you feel. You are a *doll!*' " (133).

This scene, as extraordinary as the one in *The Secret Garden* in which Mary loses her temper with Colin, is important in a number of ways. For one thing, just as Colin is forced to recognize the truth about himself, so Sara is forced to acknowledge the limits of her imagination and confront reality: Emily is neither a caring companion nor a good witch who can protect her. Sara at one time had only pretended to believe these things, but pretending, like lying for Miss Minchin, had become so habitual that she had begun to lose her consciousness of doing so. Moreover, as Sara gives up her pretense about Emily, she gives up the unnatural self-control that pretending had enabled her to maintain. Finally, Sara sees in Emily an image of her usually controlled self. The doll's enigmatic silence in the face of her passion is infuriating, and Sara feels for the first time the frustration Lavinia and Miss Minchin must feel when Sara refuses to answer them. But in raging "you are nothing but a doll," Sara is not only reproaching herself; she is confronting the threat of her own dehumanization. By keeping it "all in her heart," by concealing so much of herself from others, Sara has allowed them to project whatever they wished on to her, so that she has been in danger of losing her own identity. After the storm of passion has subsided, Emily "seemed to be gazing at her . . . with a kind of glass-eyed sympathy," and Sara smiles. Although Sara appears to be pretending once more by attributing human feelings to Emily, she is actually beginning to accept them in herself.

This experience with Emily enables Sara to express her emotions in such a way as to stimulate the imagination of others rather than make them dependent upon hers. When Miss Minchin boxes her ears, Sara tells her exactly what she is thinking and succeeds in frightening her: "It almost seemed for the moment to her narrow, unimaginative mind that there must be some real power hidden behind this candid daring" (149). Sara reveals her thoughts a second time when Miss Minchin breaks in upon the attic banquet. "It was very like the scene in the schoolroom.

There was no pertness in Sara's manner. It was only sad and quiet. 'I was wondering,' she said in a low voice, 'what *my* papa would say if he knew where I am tonight' " (206). Sara does revert to passivity once Ram Dass and the Indian gentleman befriend her, but she is passive out of genuine indifference to Miss Minchin, not out of repressed rage. And Sara does speak up one last time, leaving a legacy of rebellion to Miss Amelia. On learning that Sara has refused to return to Miss Minchin's, Miss Amelia finds the courage to call her sister "a hard, selfish, worldly woman." "And from that time forward . . . the elder Miss Minchin actually began to stand a little in awe of a sister who, while she looked so foolish, was evidently not quite so foolish as she looked, and might, consequently, break out and speak truths people did not want to hear" (254).

In the "magic" chapter, Sara, by enabling Ermengarde to share something of her inner life, kindles the imagination of even that dull child. In this episode Sara bravely conceals her hunger from Ermengarde "and dispensed generously the one hospitality she could offer . . . the imaginings which were her joy and comfort" (190). But on overhearing Miss Minchin accuse Becky of stealing, Sara suddenly gives vent to her grief and rage. "Ermengarde, hearing this unusual thing, was overawed by it. Sara was crying! The unconquerable Sara! It seemed to denote something new—some mood she had never known. Suppose! Suppose—!" (193). Ermengarde, instead of letting Sara do her supposing for her, guesses for the first time that Sara is hungry and runs to fetch the hamper of food she has just received from home. Sara, elated at the prospect of a decent meal, uses a few relics from her trunk together with her imagination to transform the attic into a banquet hall. But it is not Sara's transformation of the attic that is magical any more than the ensuing transformation performed by Ram Dass. The real magic is the way in which Sara's revelation of her misery transforms the selfish, parasitic Ermengarde into someone who is also capable of supposing— supposing in the sense of empathizing with another human being. "Here in the attic . . . this simple, cheerful thing had happened like a thing of magic" (197).

During her ordeal in the attic Sara finds it harder and harder to imagine herself a little princess, a soldier, or a prisoner in the Bastille, but, like Ermengarde's, her own imagination begins to take the form of empathy. On learning of the invalid gentleman from India, Sara adopts him for a friend. As she thinks to herself, "You can do that with people you never speak to at all. You can just watch them, and think about them and be sorry for them, until they seem almost like relations" (151). At the same time, without her knowledge, Sara becomes a source of interest to Ram Dass, who tells the gentleman's secretary, "All her life each day I know. . . . Her going out I know, and her coming in; her sadness and her poor joys; her coldness and her hunger. . . . If she were ill I should know, and I would come to her and serve her if it might be done" (177). The biblical echoes in Ram Dass's speech suggest the power of imaginative sympathy. Sara's story, not the story she tells to console herself but her true story, is more absorbing to Ram Dass and his master than any fantasy.

Sara, however, is still in danger of having her story misinterpreted. After her adoption by the Indian gentleman, "the mere fact of her sufferings and adventures made her a priceless possession. Everybody wanted to be told over and over again the things which had happened to her. When one was sitting by a warm fire in a big, glowing room, it was quite delightful to hear how cold it could be in an attic. It must be admitted that the attic was rather delighted in, and that its coldness and bareness quite sank into insignificance" (258). Although Burnett here mocks the tendency to glamorize mental and physical anguish, she herself, as she may have feared, seems liable to the same charge in *A Little Princess*. As we recall, Guy Clarence earlier embarrassed Sara by mistaking her for a beggar after having read stories in which "kind people . . . invariably saw the poor children and gave them money or rich gifts or took them home to beautiful dinners" (127). This seems almost to describe the kind of story Burnett has written and Sara has told to an admiring audience.

But Sara, after telling the story of her attic adventures, "of the little princess in rags and tatters," tells another story to her guardian alone. As she sits gazing into the fire, he asks her what she is "supposing." "Then she told him the story of the bun-shop, and the four pence she picked up out of the sloppy mud, and the child who was hungrier than herself. She told it quite simply, and in as few words as possible; but somehow the Indian gentleman found it necessary to shade his eyes with his hand and look down at the carpet" (262). This story, a very different sort from any Sara has told before, prompts her guardian to action, and together he and Sara seek out "the child who was hungrier than herself." The end of the book, with its meeting between Sara, "the little-girl-who-was-not-a-beggar," and Anne, the little girl who *was*, can be read as still another idealization of poverty—an idealization Sara shared when she first viewed befriending Becky as "scattering largess to the populace" (57). As the outcome of Sara's simple, unadorned, and realistic story, however, it can also be read as the triumph of her imagination—an imagination that no longer idealizes suffering so as to deny it but that can empathize with its victims. The last sentence of the book begins "And, somehow, Sara felt as if she understood her. ..." Even the ambiguity of the pronouns (does Sara feel that she understands Anne or that Anne understands her?) suggests a sympathetic identification that goes beyond Sara's earlier success in "finding everybody out." It is *this* use of the imagination that constitutes Sara's triumph as well as the whole of her story.

Sara's story, if one reads "between the lines," recounts the triumph of emotional honesty over self-deception, active opposition over passive aggression, and acceptance of reality over romantic compensation. Although it has been read as a Cinderella story, in which patient merit is finally recognized and rewarded,[7] it is actually a story of maturation and self-discovery. That is Sara's story, but is it the author's—either the story she retold in order to give us all she eventually came to see in it or the story of her own life? Phyllis Bixler and Burnett's biographer Ann Thwaite agree that Sara Crewe is an imaginative projection of Frances Hodgson Burnett just as "a little princess" is an imaginative projection of Sara Crewe. According to Bixler, Sara's reliance on her imagination makes her "a fictional sister to the child Burnett portrayed herself to be in her memoir."[8] Thwaite goes even further: "Sara was undoubtedly Frances herself. She imagined herself as she would have liked to have behaved if she had ever been in Sara's position."[9] Yet Sara differs in significant ways from the heroine of Burnett's memoir, *The One I Knew the Best of All,* for "the Small Person" is relentlessly sunny: "She was an extremely healthy and joyous Small Person, and took life with ease and good cheer."[10] Like Sara, the Small Person can captivate an audience with her stories, but she tells them not out of need or as compensation but from sheer innocent delight. In fact, the Small Person seems less the one Burnett "knew the best of all" than Burnett as she "would have liked to have behaved." Sara, on the other hand, seems more like the mature writer for whom fantasy—both private and public—has become both a psychic and economic necessity, and who occasionally resents the way in which her fantasies are consumed or appropriated by others. Even in her memoir Burnett describes how the Small Person "told many stories . . . to the Listeners whose property she seemed to become" (203), and we have noticed how the Large Family finds Sara's "sufferings and adventures . . . a priceless possession" (258). A Little Princess, then, far more than the memoir, tells Burnett's own story of being trapped within the attic of the imagination—of having elected to become an entertainer and of being forced to dispense a kind of hospitality even when the attic cupboards are bare.

Sara, by time and again transforming her bare, cold attic into a place of enchantment, resembles the aging author, but she differs from her no less than from the innocent Small Person. According to Thwaite and Bixler, Burnett was both disappointed as a woman and compromised as an author: in life she was always "waiting for the party"; in both life and art she came to rely on stock romantic formulas.[11] In *The One I Knew the Best of All* she attempts to rationalize her choice of romantic over realistic fiction:

> I have never been quite able to decide whether she [the Small Person] was a very weak or a very determined creature—weak, because she could not endure to see Covent Garden merely as the costermongers saw it—or determined, because she had the courage to persist in ignoring the flavour of the raw turnip and bestowing on it a flavour of her own. . . . In life itself, agreeable situations are so often flavoured by the raw turnip, and to close one's eyes steadily to the fact that it is not a sun-warmed peach, not infrequently calls upon one's steadiness and resource. (204–5)

The memoir is unconvincing because it is itself an attempt to close one's eyes to the turnip and see only the sun-warmed peach. The emphasis on Sara's "magic," her ability to transform the attic with the power of her imagination, seems an effort to justify such attempts. When Sara tells Becky that the attic has become a banquet hall, Becky innocently repeats, "a blanket-'all!" (201). And it seems as though this is what Sara's imagination, like her creator's, tries at first to do—to blanket all the unpleasant facts of existence. Sara, though, does not go on living in a fairy tale—she cannot blanket the fact that Emily is not a good witch but is "nothing but a doll," and her last work of the imagination, her straightforward tale of Anne, the beggar girl, acknowledges both the sordid facts of Anne's existence and Sara's kinship with and responsibility for her.

Burnett, by making Sara a more imaginative child in *A Little Princess* while retaining the realistic episodes of *Sara Crewe*, does not succeed in justifying her own and the Small Person's determined preference for sun-warmed peach but rather Sara's conversion from sun-warmed peach to raw turnip. But the later version, by dramatizing Sara's conflict between her romantic imagination and the facts of reality, constitutes a far more complex and truthful story than the memoir and thus a successful argument for works of the imagination. As Burnett suggests in her preface, "the whole of the story" never can be told: "Between the lines of *every* story there is another story" (my emphasis). For as the connection

Burnett makes between lying and storytelling indicates, every story, by falling short of complete disclosure, is a kind of untruth. *A Little Princess,* in that its author tries to get us to believe in "magic," is a story in this pejorative sense; it is at best a partial truth. But if every story is less candid than it purports to be, it is also more revealing. *A Little Princess,* in that it allows us to read between the lines and discern the ordinary human traits that enable us to bear reality without denying its existence, is a triumph of the imagination. Burnett did not really want to give us the whole of the story, but she did give it in spite of herself. This, as she recognized, is what storytellers do.

Notes

1. Francis Hodgson Burnett, *A Little Princess* (New York: Scribner's, 1905), v. Page numbers for subsequent quotations from this volume are given in the text.

2. (New York: Scribner's, 1924), 24.

3. Phyllis Bixler Koppes, "Tradition and the Individual Talent of Frances Hodgson Burnett: A Generic Analysis of *Little Lord Fauntleroy, A Little Princess,* and *The Secret Garden,*" *Children's Literature* 7 (1979), 195.

4. As I have tried to show in " 'Quite Contrary': Frances Hodgson Burnett's *The Secret Garden,*" the realistic portrayal of Mary Lennox at the beginning of the book makes the "magic" surrounding Colin's recovery anticlimactic (*Children's Literature* 11 [1983], 1–13.).

5. U. C. Knoepflmacher, "Little Girls without Their Curls: Female Aggression in Victorian Children's Literature," *Children's Literature* 11 (1983), 29.

6. Charlotte Brontë. *Jane Eyre.* (New York: Norton, 1971), 63.

7. Phyllis Bixler Koppes, in "Tradition and the Individual Talent," argues that "Like the Cinderella tales, Burnett's stories do not emphasize a change within the main character but rather in the recognition of that character's true nature" (193). She also sees Sara's challenge as that of maintaining "the charitable nature and even temper of a princess" (194), whereas I see her challenge as that of acknowledging her emotions even when it means a temporary loss of self-control.

8. Phyllis Bixler, *Frances Hodgson Burnett* (Boston: Twayne, 1984), 89.

9. Ann Thwaite, *Waiting for the Party: The Life of Frances Hodgson Burnett* (New York: Scribner's, 1974), 105.

10. (London: Frederick Warne, 1893), 185.

11. As Bixler says in her book, *Frances Hodgson Burnett,* "fictional formula often became a lens through which Burnett perceived herself" (54). According to Bixler, "Thwaite suggests that Burnett's excessively romantic temperament urged her to escape unpleasant realities by trying to make her life a fairy tale" (122–23.)

Index

Title Index